The Landscape Approach

PENN STUDIES IN LANDSCAPE ARCHITECTURE

John Dixon Hunt, Series Editor

This series is dedicated to the study and promotion of a wide variety of approaches to landscape architecture, with emphasis on connections between theory and practice. It includes monographs on key topics in history and theory, descriptions of projects by both established and rising designers, translations of major foreign-language texts, anthologies of theoretical and historical writings on classic issues, and critical writing by members of the profession of landscape architecture.

Bernard Lassus

The Landscape Approach

Introductions by Peter Jacobs and Robert B. Riley

Afterword by Stephen Bann

 PENN

UNIVERSITY OF PENNSYLVANIA PRESS

PHILADELPHIA

Publication of this volume was assisted by grants from
the Getty Grant Program and the Graham Foundation for
Advanced Studies in the Fine Arts. Support for preparation of
the translations came from the Ministry of Foreign Affairs of
the French Cultural Service.

Translated by Stephen Bann, Paul Buck, and Catherine Petit

10 9 8 7 6 5 4 3 2 1

Published by
University of Pennsylvania Press
Philadelphia, Pennsylvania 19104-4011

Library of Congress Cataloging-in-Publication Data

Lassus, Bernard.
The landscape approach / Bernard Lassus ; introductions by
Peter Jacobs and Robert B. Riley ; afterword by Stephen Bann.
        p.   cm. — (Penn studies in landscape architecture)
    Includes bibliographical references and index.
    ISBN 0-8122-3450-2 (alk. paper)
1. Landscape architecture.   2. Landscape architecture—
Europe.   3. Visual perception.   I. Title.   II. Series.
SB472.L375   1998
712.6—dc21   98-26259
                                    CIP

Frontispiece: "Un air rosé," 1965

Contents

Illustrations

Author's Note

The writings gathered here, at the invitation of the editor of the new Penn Studies in Landscape Architecture, consist almost entirely of points of departure for the laying out of gardens or designed landscapes; hence the importance of the illustrations.

In a few cases, where I had written nothing, I rely upon the acute critiques of Stephen Bann.

The writings are therefore linked rather to the tangible results they have brought about, of which they constitute a verbal beginning.

This means that the reader may occasionally encounter the repetition of some ideas, though slightly different on each occasion where they function as part of the particular or local case.

The reader will also perhaps find certain phrases invented in the course of this work that it did not seem possible to explain at that precise moment; to have done so seemed an undue interruption of the process of their elaboration. Those who wish may track such terms now through the Index of this collection.

translated by John Dixon Hunt

Les textes ici rassemblés, à l'invitation chaleureuse de John Dixon Hunt, sont presque tous les points de départ d'aménagements de jardins ou de créations de paysages; d'où l'importance des illustrations.

Pour les quelqu'uns que je n'avais pas écrit, j'ai repris les fines critiques de Stephen Bann.

Ces textes sont donc plus liés à ce qu'ils ont rendu tangible et en constituent les émergences verbales.

Ce qui implique que le lecteur peut parfois rencontrer des répétitions, mais chaque fois différentes puisque fractions de ces "cas particuliers."

Peut-être rencontreront-ils aussi quelques unes des locutions construites au cours de cette démarche, mais il ne m'a pas paru possible de les expliquer au même moment. Ce qui me semble-t-il aurait cassé le rythme du processus d'élaboration, mais, ceux qui le souhaiteraient pourront les consulter dans l'Index.

Bernard Lassus

The Sensual Landscapes of Bernard Lassus

Peter Jacobs

Bernard Lassus reverses the process Monet developed in constructing his gardens at Giverny. Whereas Monet used the garden to invent his art, Lassus uses his art to invent the landscape.

Notwithstanding the scope and quality of his work, Lassus is largely unknown in North America, in part because his work lies somewhat outside the functional, ecological, and formal schools of landscape design. His is a world of imaginative perspectives, of novel insight, and of carefully developed tales. He has revived the world of landscape narratives, of stories both fanciful and serious; rendering the improbable in terms of the reasonable and feasible, suggesting the immeasurable through the apt manipulation of the tangible and finite.

His thoughts and actions substantially enrich our perception of landscape practice, challenging conventional wisdom that informs current discourse in North America. He is preoccupied as much with the nature of culture as with the culture of nature, suggesting that "a sensory approach that involves making visible both Nature and our own nature is an indispensable way of reconciling science and the sensory world." Lassus seeks to return the sensual to its rightful place as a means of knowing landscape, arguing with Ruskin that "the flower is a living creature, with histories written on its leaves, and passions breathing in its motion."[1] He asks in "The Garden of the Planets," "What of yesterday and today will be maintained in the sensory approach to tomorrow?"

The path chosen by Lassus thirty years ago was a bold gamble, "un beau risque" undertaken at a time when the landscape was

[1] Robert L. Herbert, ed., *The Art and Criticism of John Ruskin* (St. Louis: Da Capo Press, 1964).

Bernard Lassus has derived considerable stimulus from his extensive observation of "popular" gardens such as those of Mr. Charles Pecqueur, gardens whose programmatic content and formal organization support the personal narratives of the anonymous gardener while lending themselves to collective interpretations.

seen almost exclusively as a utilitarian commodity. Lassus has never adhered to a utilitarian dogma, nor does he compromise his firm commitment to the need for new landscapes of poetic interest. He challenges the primacy of functional criteria in landscape design, not as a set of requirements that do not warrant attention, but as the set from which all else is determined. The price paid for this choice was a significant period spent in an intellectual and professional wilderness where his ideas matured, his methodology was honed, and his convictions were clarified. That many of the landscape projects are now built and embraced by their users speaks eloquently of the force and utility of his narrative approach to landscape design.

The same can be said with respect to the ecological approach to landscape design. Here, too, Lassus has no objection to carefully thought out requirements related to the maintenance and enhancement of natural processes, only to the idea that these criteria must necessarily serve as the genesis of landscape design. As a generator of programmatic intention, however, Lassus is constantly attuned to the ambiance and conditions of nature and the landscapes that surround him.

In the project for the Park of Duisburg-Nord,[2] he seizes on the heavily polluted Emscher River as a symbol of the need for the metamorphosis of the Ruhr Valley as a whole. Rather than hiding this problem behind landscape screens, he proposes experimental gardens with a variety of systems that address the decontamination of soils resulting from nearby laboratories. These gardens would be made visible and accessible to the public as a means of illustrating the process of landscape metamorphosis. A preoccupation with natural process is neither minimized nor shunned, it is simply placed in the context of the larger cultural problem of which it is a part.

And so it is with a formal approach to the generation of landscape. Lassus's career has been built upon a series of carefully constructed stages in his pursuit of an art of landscape in opposition to a landscape of art. Here, too, he distinguishes himself from the experiments of land art in his search for strategies of rendering visual the cultural forces at work in shaping the landscape. While inspired by some aspects of the "concrete poetry" of Ian Hamilton Finlay,[3] Lassus is less concerned with social comment than with the structural underpinnings of the cultural landscape. His attitude toward the formal approach to landscape design is best captured by one of his collaborators: "Form is not primary, it is induced from the articulation of intention."[4]

Form is never imposed on the substance of a project or place. Lassus approaches the opportunities and the challenges of landscape from the programmatic point of view. He develops a story built around and deriving from the site and the project brief. It is with reference to this narrative that activities can be planned and the economical, ecological, and social processes of the site integrated into an overall scenario of landscape development. Significant expansion in the field of landscape practice and experimentation results from this narrative approach to landscape design, substantially contributing to programmatic and formal innovations in the field.

[2] Lassus, "The Park of Duisburg-Nord," in "The Landscape Approach of Bernard Lassus, II," *Journal of Garden History* 15, 2 (April–June 1995); see "The Park of Duisburg-Nord," this volume.

[3] Stephen Bann, "The Gardens of Ian Hamilton Finlay" and "The Garden and Visual Arts in the Contemporary Period: Arcadians, Post-Classicists, and Land Artists," in *The Architecture of Western Gardens: A Design History from the Renaissance to the Present Day*, ed. Monique Mosser and Georges Teyssot (Cambridge, Mass.: MIT Press, 1991).

[4] Pierre Donadieu, cited in Lassus, "The Inventive Analysis": "La forme n'est première, elle est induite par l'articulation des intentions."

Landscape Ambiance

Bernard Lassus arrived at the practice of landscape architecture from the bias of a painter and a practitioner of the fine arts.[5] His early experiments lean heavily on the inquiring and experimental background of the artist, an ability to redefine and invent new perspectives that inform his search for meaning and structure in the landscape. His unusually poetic sense of the syntax of ideas and of forms enable him to express his views in ways that are provocative and challenging. Visual images inform the verbal, and in their turn his reflections and deep commitment to the intellectual and cultural history of the landscape generate a rich array of images. It is this somewhat unique ability to manipulate both the literary and the visual worlds, and an intimate understanding of both, that furnish the rich background against which Lassus's practice can be judged and understood.

Lassus's practice is built upon a feeling for landscape, a theoretical structuring of the idea of landscape, and a passion for intervening in the landscape in ways that give meaning to places and to the activities of people who dwell in these places. His compassionate commitment to the senses as a vital instrument in the organization and understanding of landscape is central to our understanding of his work.

Lassus starts from a reading of the sensual nature of land-scape, its sounds, sights, and smells, developed through a continuing set of experiments with people and their relationships to landscape. Perhaps the best known and certainly the most elaborate such experiment consists of a landscape built from a single *red dot* on a white field, used to stimulate the imagination of an unspecified public.[6] As the walls of numerous public sites where the experiment was conducted filled with individual contributions—imagining the red dot as a sun, an eye, a ball, etc.—a wealth of material on the behavior and structuring of collective art emerges. Covered with a field of red dot drawings, two scales emerge: a visual scale that consists of the pattern of red dots forming a grid, and the more tactile scale built of individual sheets that have been "touched" by each participant. Lassus distinguishes the tactile and visual scales of the landscape as a means of distinguishing between the immediate sensory knowledge of place derived by touch and smell and the more integrative vision derived from an overall view.

A number of these exercises turn the landscape experience inside out to better understand the syntax of the landscape experience. The patient exploration of *pine bark*, the insertion of a white piece of paper into the bowl of a *red tulip* in order to borrow the red of the flower without in any way transforming its physical properties,[7] or the elegant description of a walk on the stones of a stream at the bottom of a *gorge* represent personal attempts to understand and appreciate the complexity of the basic

[5] Lassus studied in the studio of Fernand Léger and was appointed Professor at l'Ecole des Beaux Arts by the Minister of Culture, André Malvaux, at approximately the same time as the students were protesting the state of education in France in 1968. He was the youngest professor ever appointed to the position, in an attempt to renew and revitalize the venerable but increasingly rigid curriculum.

[6] Peter Jacobs and Philippe Poullaouec-Gonidec, "Red Dots and Other Tales," *Landscape Architecture* (January 1989); see "The Game of Red Dots," this volume.

[7] See "The Tulip," "The Gorges of the Aradin," and "The Pines," this volume. See also Louis Grodecki, "The Rationale for the Change from

Conversely, the use of "red dots returns the compliment by providing a congenial springboard for individual expressions **within a simple collective and repetitive framework.**

components of the landscape. They are the finger exercises of the pianist, or the stretching exercises of the athlete designed to loosen and to render supple the organs required to perform, to act, and thus to create.

Not surprisingly, one experiment leads to another, and the preoccupation with light and its transfer from one material to another in the case of a tulip or the perceived depth of a running stream is further explored in the three-dimensional space defined by a cube within a cube ("Ambiances 13"). The inner cube is made to appear larger than the outer one through the manipulation of light sources and of our learned perception of materials that are solid and those that are not, in this case brick and glass. The experiment suggests that the sense of scale and volume is not produced by light alone but depends as well on our learned sense of materials. The combination of the two contributes to our sense that the larger cube is the smaller and the smaller larger.

Clear to Stained Glass Windows in the Cathedral of Saint-Denis, Paris," in *Les Vitraux de Saint-Denis: Etude sur le vitrail au XIIe siècle* (Paris: Centre National de la Recherche Scientifique, 1976).

Lassus is full of these counter-intuitive insights, derived from his ability constantly to redefine the terms of reference of what we consider conventional wisdom. A pebble thrown into a *well* makes no noise as it falls to an infinite depth. Lassus revels in the anticipation and anxiety that would be produced by such an artifact, knowing full well that a sense of silence exposes the possibility that the dimensions of the landscape may be both measurable and immeasurable and that the tension between the two may be the ultimate reward of the landscape architect.

Given this search for the surface and underlying strata of a landscape dynamic that Lassus refers to as the landscape of *mille feuilles*, it cannot be treated from the perspective of concrete space or surface volume alone. The complimentary perspective of the landscape of imagination implies a discovery of and a weaving together of both the physical and the sensual, the real and the imaginary, the external and the internal. The task of translating this into a viable practice of landscape design depends on innovative landscape methodologies.

Landscape Inventions

The need to articulate the counter-intuitive, the paradoxical or the initially incongruous aspects of landscape as an integral part of a landscape narrative cannot be developed in the absence of a theoretical framework. The desire to search for—and articulate the invention of—new landscapes within this theoretical framework is a second but equally complex task. The structure of this discourse, based as it is on a broad knowledge of the history and practice of landscape architecture and the art of gardening, is in part methodological and in part dialectic.

Lassus refers to his methodological approach as *Inventive Analysis.* It consists of totally immersing oneself in the site and seeking to understand its structure—those aspects that are present in force, absent, or simply uncoordinated. Frequent visits at different times of day and in different conditions render the observer a sponge, soaking up the earth and the sky almost to the point of boredom. Coupled with the views, stories, and memories of the site, its specificity and singular characteristics emerge. New hypotheses as to the past, present, and future potential of the site are selected, refined and tested against studies that anticipate the way the project will be used and man-aged—leading to scenarios for the formal organization of the project.

Minimal intervention in a park in the new town of Marne-la-Vallée illustrates some aspects of the method used by Lassus.[8] Observation and discussions with park users revealed that the invasion of sound from automobiles, planes, and a thermal heating plant adjacent to the park was unheard and totally ignored by the park visitors. Lassus hypothesizes that the acknowledgment of the sound would have destroyed their discovery of a wilderness in the New Town, a place for family and friends, and forced them to see the eroding river banks, automobile carcasses, and litter. In response, he proposes to locate an earth mound capped by a fortress wall with a partially destroyed tower next to the thermal station but within the park boundaries, recalling the destruction of the walls of Jerusalem that tumbled from the sound of trumpets. In the same manner that Lassus avoids the obvious approach to perceived problems, he seeks to highlight opportunities. The park is also located close to a major chocolate plant in the town. Lassus proposed that a sign be placed in the wildest part of the park: "Chocolate mousse courtesy of the westerly wind."

There is a refreshing rigor in the nature of the observations and the conclusions drawn from Lassus's approach to *inventive analysis.* He attacks, articulates, confronts the imponderable pleasures and mysteries of the landscape. He refuses to reduce the landscape to its component parts and embraces the incongruous and the critical. The body of his poetic insight defies

[8] Lassus, "Minimal Intervention," conference, Gibellina-Nuova, Sicily, 1981; see "Minimal Intervention," this volume.

rigid structure, although his writings tend to focus on transitions between one physical or imaginary state and another. The structural form of his argument is designed to establish a bridgehead in an otherwise hostile territory of conventional wisdom and practice. The frontier that exists between two conditions that form and reform our understanding of the landscape animates his projects both suggested and built.

The frontier fascinates Lassus; it inspires some of his most provocative thinking and generates a number of useful insights that lend themselves to the invention of new landscape conditions. His exploration of frontiers, including those between the tactile and the visual; those between the past, present, and future; and those that define the physical and the imaginary, is at the core of his practice. On the subject of landscape conservation and our attempts to integrate development into the landscape, Lassus suggests the irony and ambivalence in our official policies and informal actions. He observes that as a matter of policy we seek to absorb development and to make it disappear as quickly as is possible into the landscape setting, yet equally we seek to distinguish our homes and artifacts as distinct and special places—adding dwarfs and naval ships to our front lawns.[9] The first presents a modest face of quiet and calm, the second a revolt against the official leveling of taste and standardization of lifestyle.

These oppositions and transitions across landscape frontiers define the conditions that nurture paradoxes such as the conservation of past heritage and the invention of new traditions, the fragility of the permanent and the power of the ephemeral.

Everywhere there is poetic imagery: "The fundamental difference between the mineral and the vegetable, the town and the country, is that grass bends in the wind, while stone does not."

These images leave little doubt as to the position of the author or his mission in the invention of landscape. Nor does his observation that having conquered the frontiers of wilderness and the horizontal plane, the next frontier lies within the vertical extension of landscape (monument, depth), a premise that informs many of his competition projects.

Landscapes of Movement

The marriage of theory and practice is the essence of garden art. Much of Lassus's theory can be deduced from his work rather than from his written arguments. In fact, many of his writings, while both stimulating and imaginative, do not address the principal themes of his built work.

One of these is his ability to create landscape scenarios that operate creatively and comfortably through both space and time. In his search for the muli-variant nature of landscape, his viewpoints vary in the belief that landscape is a virtually inexhaustible source of inspiration. While the idea of landscape precedes and informs each scenario, all are based in one way or another on developing a landscape story.[10] Lassus is a master of inventing landscapes of movement. These are built on narrative scenarios that are the programmatic basis of his design propos-

[9] See John Dixon Hunt, "Bernard Lassus in Eden," *Eden: Rivista dell'architettura nel paesaggio* 3 (1996).

[10] See also Lassus, "The Landscape Approach of Bernard Lassus, I, II," trans. and intro. Stephen Bann, *Journal of Garden History* 15, 2 (April–June 1995), reprinted as the Afterword to this volume.

als. Movement through various spatial scales in the landscape is illustrated by the project for a pedestrian Butterfly Bridge and the vehicular rest area of Nîmes-Caissargues.

In the town of Istres, at precisely the same time that the Parc des Salles was designed for the community, another arm of government decided to split the park with a highway. Notwithstanding the absurdity of the context, the landscape challenge was to link the two halves of the park with an elevated pathway that would be sufficiently compelling to discourage children from taking the more obvious path across the highway. The solution proposed extends well beyond the merely functional. The narrative proposed was built of rock and lightweight metal. Rather than passing beside the rock, the highway is aligned to tunnel through it, as if it had always been there and was incontrovertible. The second half of the path is light and airy, with metal butterflies animating the guard rails on either side of the bridge. The overpass invites the community to participate in this newly imagined "historical" landscape. This they have done, insofar as the site is a favored location for newly married couples to pose for their wedding albums.

Similar narrative strategies are developed for the rest area of Nîmes-Caissargues, where the Colonnade of the old theater of Nîmes appears at the end of a "green carpet of Versailles," instantly establishing a historic landscape with the express purpose of anchoring the new rest stop in the context of the city.

Movement through time in a number of schemes captures the essential core of the past and present while inventing the potential of the future. Lassus conceives the landscape as an accumulation of various actions over time, as a series of deposits or strata on a landscape of "mille-feuilles." An important contribution to the issue of landscape conservation eschews any attempt to anchor a landscape in one particular period and advocates a visible rendering of the diversity of landscape change over time.

This proactive approach to landscape conservation, including the archaeology of future landscapes, is illustrated in the narrative of the Garden of Returns, built around the need to reestablish the historic relationship of the town of Rochefort to the Charente River. It seeks to rekindle the importance of the naval staging area in the military policies of seventeenth-century France and in the settlement of the New World, when ships' empty hulls were filled with plants, including the begonia and the large flowered magnolia, for the return voyage to France. Decrying the current monocultures of begonia grown in Dutch and German fields, Lassus seeks to reestablish a more diverse culture in Rochefort. Biodiversity in this case is seen as an economic and cultural act that builds on an historical tradition as a means of planning a future landscape.

The competition entry for the Jardin des Tuileries[11] adopts an uncompromising position in favor of a layered landscape that suggests the unfolding of successive periods of garden history through the vertical articulation of the garden designs of the Medici, Mollet, Le Nôtre, and a new contribution from the twentieth century. Diversity is celebrated and no attempt is made to avoid the "incongruous mixture of styles" that so concerned Frederick Olmsted and his colleagues in the nineteenth century.[12]

[11] Lassus, *Le Jardin des Tuileries* (London: Coracle Press, 1991); see "The Tuileries: A Reinvented Garden," this volume.
[12] For Olmsted's purism, see Charles E. Beveridge, "Towards a Definition of Olmstedian Principles of Design: The Seven S's" (manuscript), to which I am indebted.

In the proposal for the Park of Duisburg-Nord, a temporal "pen," composed of alternating rows of deciduous and coniferous trees, is used to distinguish yet unite yesterday's landscape of the blast furnaces and the landscapes of the day before yesterday, when they were essentially rural and agricultural. The sinuous curves of the Emscher riverbed are reestablished and contrasted with the hard lines of the industrial canal to express this transition in time. The landscapes of tomorrow consist of gardens of soils, sounds, and smells.

Landscapes in Time

Lassus believes that landscape is by its very nature cultural, "a construction of spirit born of the senses." He suggests that the scope of landscape is more non-visual than visual, a play of seen and hidden, directly perceived, remembered, and imagined. He asks "Is not the landscape that fragile moment where the visual, auditory, olfactive fragments are linked to my feelings at a moment in time to form a view?" and regrets that in fracturing the landscape into its component parts we destroy it.

In his work, Lassus attempts to characterize the landscape in a number of different ways. In each he seeks to reveal a different dimension, a different way of articulating what is so profoundly intriguing a concept: "Is not landscape that which is beyond our imagination, the horizon always beyond our reach, unattainable? I certainly can't touch it, and at the very moment that I grasp the landscape, as with a magic wand, it is transformed into a tangible place where my senses take over and guide me through it" (tactile/visual). In the tactile acts of moving from the car to the curb or across the stones in a riverbed, our general view of the landscape, the large view of the physical objects in the visual field, is rendered infinitely more precise.

Lassus reminds us that it is not always necessary to modify an existing landscape, to plant trees, modify the topography, enlarge or change the course of a riverbed to effect landscape change. It is more than sufficient to offer other ways of seeing, reading, or hearing an existing one. Introducing a small red tractor into a bucolic rural scene might suffice to modify the meaning and hence the perception of the physical scene, as might the placement of a statue of Snow White in a garden.

In all of Bernard Lassus's work a landscape is built upon the need to sustain the potential of the site: to affirm its present potential and to invent its future. It is a hypothesis of what from yesterday and today will be perpetuated in the sensual approach of tomorrow, an argument for imagining new ways of touching and evoking the singularity of the landscape. Above all, Lassus celebrates the diversity of landscape experience (the heterogeneous). These and other insights provide a key to decoding the projects that follow, a frame from which they can be viewed, an ambiance within which they can be felt.

Experience and Time in the Work of Bernard Lassus

Robert B. Riley

Coming to grips with the work of Bernard Lassus is not easy, even given the lucid, occasional explications by Stephen Bann (see the Afterword to this volume). It is an obligation, however, for anyone seriously interested in landscape experience and design. Not since the Eckbo-Rose-Kiley writings of the early 1940s, or Ian McHarg's in the 1970s has any body of work offered more potential for broadening, deepening, and enriching the discourse of landscape design.

Lassus's prime distinction, the characteristic that sets him apart from other landscape designers and writers, is the speculative base of his work and thought. He offers no rules, no easy credit, certainly no stylistic conventions, but rather explorations, journeys of uncertain destination, into the nature of the landscape experience. Moreover, practically alone among contemporary landscape designers (Ian Hamilton Finlay perhaps excepted), Lassus's philosophical concerns precede and determine his design work. They seem truly the *source* of particular solutions: neither rationale nor explanation. Indeed his reputation, even among those who have followed his work for three decades, has been as a speculative philosopher of the landscape who someday *might* get a chance to build in fulfillment of that philosophy . . . as he now has. Equally significant and important is the fact that each of his major conceptual explorations has its corresponding project and vice versa; each expands the other. If more designers of intellectual bent were to follow this dual mode, in elaboration of a core of consistent concerns, our designs would be better informed and our theory better grounded.

Lassus's explorations are not easy to summarize, reduce, or categorize, but they do have a consistent core. There may be as many different articulations of that core as there are people who follow his work, and most may be valid, if not always valuable. Let me offer this gloss: Lassus has a concern for how *intervention* produces *transformation* in the *landscape experience.* This concern holds whether the prospect is a piece of cardboard inserted in a tulip, a tractor moving into a field, or a design for the Tuileries.

To pursue this postulated core, not as a summary but as one entry point into the Lassus oeuvre, one must begin where he does, with *experience.* Experience in this sense is the *gestalt* of a person's reaction to, involvement with, a landscape, and involves all the psychologically standard steps or states: perception, recognition, affect, evaluation, . . . on to fantasy and behavior. This explicit concept of the participant's experience as the entry point to thought and the destination of design sets Lassus apart from virtually all his contemporaries. Design, to be sure, is primarily intended to structure, serve, and enhance experience. Then is it not strange that to begin there should be so unusual, if not unique? Yes, strange, and sad, and true. It is not that other designers ignore experience, but rather that for them it is a postulated by-product, an expected result of formal or didactic exercises. For Lassus, it is start, essence, and end.

The reader can explore the importance of experience in a variety of manifestations in the writings and projects that follow; it is always a most reliable touchstone for understanding Lassus's journeys. So, too, with *intervention* and *transformation.* These terms are constantly of explicit concern in Lassus's writing. They are as well, through a variety of specifics and contexts, the instruments not only for shaping experience, but also for expressing Lassus's other overriding obsession, *time.* This term *time*, abstractly and as the history of a given site, has also recently reentered landscape discourse, at least in North American academe, after an absence of a few decades. Some landscape architects have trivialized it to an entry on their check list of a site's "cultural resources." Others (e.g., Brenda Brown, James Corner, Margaret McAvin, Elizabeth Meyer) have seen it as a major concern, integral to, or determinant of, design. Site as palimpsest is now a cliché. Few, however, have given time so heavy a role (and burden?) as has Lassus, who seems to conceive the site as a time-lapse film, a cinematic history of interventions and transformations past, present, and future.

This view of a landscape as dynamic, coupled with the primacy of participatory experience, makes Lassus critically important to any theoretical discussion of landscape. To "design" and to "intervene, producing transformations" are not equivalent. The distinction is more than semantic Jesuitry. The phrases imply different concepts about the role and responsibility of the agent of change (consider *designer* vis à vis *intervener*) and about the nature of landscape and the landscape experience.

Lassus often phrases, indeed develops, his intellectual explorations by posing dualities: visual/tactile, environment/ landscape, homogeneous/heterogeneous, vertical/horizontal, measurable/immeasurable, natural/artificial, with examples as concrete as geranium/refrigerator and drawings as explicit as iceberg/palm tree. In current landscape debate dualities are out of fashion, in fact deemed incorrect, on the grounds that they inherently privilege one of a pair and imply an "other." Lassus uses such dualities as they should be used, as artificial and useful tools to develop clarity and understanding, a step taken and passed on an intellectual journey. This fact needs to be kept in mind, given his often difficult prose, lest those easy dualities be taken as end points instead of tools.

Lassus's emphasis on experiencing landscape offers a firmer, more developable approach to landscape exploration than does the barren ecological versus formal debate that persists in schools and journals. It raises its own problems as well. How predictable is the landscape experience? And, a related but separate question, how diverse is that experience? Visual assessment literature to the contrary, life is not a photograph: expectations count—and change. Lassus makes some sensible, believable contentions about landscape stimulus and human response. If they are not proven, they are at least testable. He is, in fact, the only landscape writer or designer I know who openly confronts the imponderables of familiarity and psychological accommodation/adaptation vis à vis the landscape, down to such specifics as his discussion of sounds at Champs-sur-Marne. His observation of the difference of experience of a place between a person who knows a place well and one who is seeing it the first time is acknowledgment of an obvious fact totally ignored in contemporary landscape design. It is, of course, another manifestation of all-pervasive time, one I think Lassus recognizes in his evolution from the powerful but perhaps transient impact of the Well and the Uckange murals to the subtlety and sophistication of the Tuileries project.

Lassus's concern with time and experience raises new issues even as it adds to our understanding and our conceptual repertoire. Perhaps even more significant is the working model he offers us, a way of bonding theory and practice.

Part 1   From Ambiance Research to Landscape

The Tulip / 1965

The tulip, from the genus *Tulipa*, whose name derives from *tuliband*, a vulgar Turkish pronunciation of the Persian *dulband* (turban), has a flower that resembles that form of head-dress. Belonging to the family *Liliaceae*, whose flowers are hermaphroditic and regular, it has a caducous perianth shaped like a bell and divided in six parts. These oblong, or obovate, petaloid divisions appear devoid of nectariferous cavities. Inside the bell can be seen six stamens, much shorter than the perianth, whose filaments, enlarged at the base, are inserted into the receptacle. The anthers are erect and attached to the filaments by their hollow bases. The style does not exist, but three short and thick sessile stigmas can still be seen. The capsule, oblong or obovate, has three sides. The leaves, lanceolate or linear, sometimes oblong, are often undulating and always alternate. The flower blooms alone at the top of its erect stalk. It is red.

But is there anything else to notice?

By "anything else," I am saying that I am going to try to enlarge on what I know about this tulip. I take a pair of scissors and a sheet of white card, and cut out a narrow strip whose width is less than the internal volume of the flower. This shape allows me to insert it right to the bottom of the bell while still retaining a part of the card outside.

I hold the strip delicately, in such a way that it neither brushes against the walls, the petals, nor touches the bottom of the bell. This action allows me to ascertain that the white surface plunged deepest into the volume of the flower has become rose, a rose color that, as it approaches the upper part of the perianth, becomes a lighter tone.

That reflection of light inside the tulip reveals to me, quite suddenly, that the rose hue is only the sign (the mark), and that it is the totality of the volume into which I have plunged that strip of card that is rose. The reason is simple: the light reflecting on the divisions of the perianth in a play of multiple reflections, each time coloring with a little more red, has formed a volume filled with color.

Thus the tulip has walls that isolate "un air rosé" from a blue or pale green "air." In other words, from other "airs" in which this volume, a balloon of "air rosé," is isolated.

Then I withdraw the card from the tulip as delicately as I had introduced it. If the flower appears to be the same, it is not and no longer will ever be. Indeed, could I ever look at a tulip again without considering that it can be a volume of "air rosé"?

My knowledge of the tulip's external appearance is thus transformed, even though I have not transformed it physically!

Is not the landscape another knowledge? Other than what the concrete, a certain apprehension of the concrete, offers me? And if, in some cases, I must leave the card in so that the "air rosé" interpretation of the tulip continues to exist, it is also possible for me to remove it. Thus, for there to be a landscape, there does not need to be a physical transformation, as the landscapers seem determined. It is perfectly clear that what is required is a red tulip, along with the participation of the sun, a sheet of card, a pair of scissors, fingers, but also . . .

The Gorges of the Aradin / 1967

Turning sharply on the narrow, tortuous road, I glimpse, through the lattice of dark branches, a sparkling brilliance: water whose roarings heralded it no sooner had the road left the plateau and hurtled down toward the depths of the gorge.

This bend, at which the descending road starts rising, is a bridge buried in the foliage . . . to clear a thicket, to tumble down a meadow, to leave brightness for shadow, to part branches and discover a waterfall several meters high, impassable. Here is where the walk will start: stepping into the bed of the torrent, there where the water, pierced by light, glides on a bed of clearly visible pebbles. Now I move forward in the direction of the current, evaluating at each step the spot on which to place my next one.

At certain moments diverse choices are posed. Here I prefer a more linear progress, chopped by vertical ruptures, there a more horizontal, though extremely sinuous, course. Compared to those of a walk through town, these movements have length and depth at the same time. Each step combines the two dimensions in varying proportions, and can even be interchanged.

The question is rarely posed so clearly, since the nature of that on which I walk is not given, but is there to discover. Reflections, dark depths of water . . . luminous bottoms . . . At what depth will I strike the bottom? Will it support my weight? Preference is most often conceded to what appears the hardest: rock. And yet, will this rock be slippery in spite of my striated rubber soles?

The shadows of the leaves and branches criss-cross on the bumpy surface, more or less concave or convex, on which the

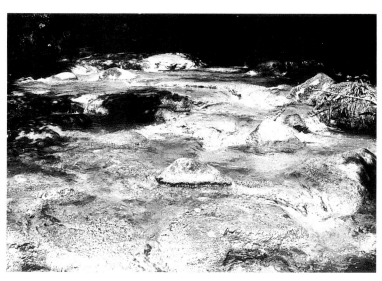

**2a–d. During the
walk, in the bed of the
torrent.**

water flows . . . A clear bottom that appears near but where one
finds oneself up to the waist in water, then a mirror where the
sole collides abruptly with ground that one supposed, through
the total impossibility of where one believed it was situated, was
obviously lower. The stake of this walk is not to find oneself im-
mersed, as will occur through an irretrievable imbalance or an
error of appreciation of the depth.

After some trials, each time it is the foot . . . in, then under
the water, before a finer approximation of distances can be
effected. From time to time, when the change of slope is very
sharp, and involves a small drop, the steps change into leaps.
From the top of the cascade, because of the force of the water,
in order to advance, one can only jump into the hollowed out
basin. There, by contrast, a certain depth is desired to deaden
the shock of the arrival. There, too, depth is difficult to perceive
through the frenzy of white froth encircling the innumerable
fractions of sprays rebounding on the rocks.

From the obscure depths of the water of the basin steadily
emerge, from all sides, rock, sand, and gravel, and then the flow
and its fine surface, sliding across these accumulations, recopy-
ing their forms.

The Game of Red Dots / 1967

Munich, September 1971. The weather is beautiful, even a little warm. People crowd on the Jakobsplatz, one of the places in town transformed for a few days into Kunstzone: "erste freie Produzentenmesse," as many yellow and black posters proclaim. Beneath the immense tents, orchestras, beer (of course), and artists from all over have come to dialogue, in their own ways, with the public (tens of thousands of visitors will pour through from the 7th to the 12th). As for myself, I have a stand consisting of three walls painted white and, between the closest and perpendicular to one of the walkways, a long table stacked with two piles of paper: one of photocopies of a text describing the game, and the other of sheets of beautiful drawing paper (21×27), in the center of which an orange circle is printed. Between the piles are black felt tip pens and open boxes of drawing pins with white heads. All those who pass can use them at will and, if they so desire, draw with, on, from, against, around this dot, and then, if they so desire, fix their drawing on one of the walls of the stand beside the drawings that have preceded it.

Some years earlier Stephen Bann described this game in the magazine *Art and Artists* in these terms:

> As the walls are gradually covered, it becomes possible to appreciate the development of a "double scale," which corresponds to Lassus' division between the "visual" and "tactile" scales. From a distance, the surfaces are unified by the framework of orange spots appearing in the centre of each sheet. But as the visitor comes closer, this overall structure yields to the heterogeneity of the individual drawings, which deflect attention from the regular patterning. It is worth mentioning that the orange dots are not simply used to establish the visual scale

from a distance where tactile relations are impossible. They also to some extent determine the character of the individual drawings themselves, since the transformation of this central dot into a sun or eye is often the keynote of the design. This must surely be seen less as an infringement of the participant's liberty than as an inducement to participation. The hostility of the white page is relieved by the presence of the colour-forms, which can be seen as initiating a dialogue with the participant. It is hardly necessary to point out the relevance of this form of interaction to the wider problem of conciliating individual freedom of expression with overall planning.

In Munich, beneath the tent, and behind the table, I am constantly feeding the two piles of texts and paper with red dots, replacing the worn felt tip pens, opening fresh boxes of drawing pins, and sometimes helping to fix a drawing to one of the walls. A minimal presence, but indispensable to the pursuit of the game. It is simply a matter of facilitating the actions of those who desire to draw, whether it be in Warsaw, London, Paris, Hamburg, or Oxford, since that first attempt in 1967. But, through its very vacuity, that presence is transformed by slow degrees, and involuntarily, into a forced observation. And, after all its manifestations, evidence has emerged, though the places and public are very different each time, that this game unfolds according to an identical process. The visitors only start drawing at the point when around sixty drawings are already pinned up. Then the drawings executed become more and more numerous. Thus, from a slow start, this movement accelerates progressively.

Coming to the edge of the table, hesitating, the visitor watches out of the corner of an eye, gently inquiring, waiting for

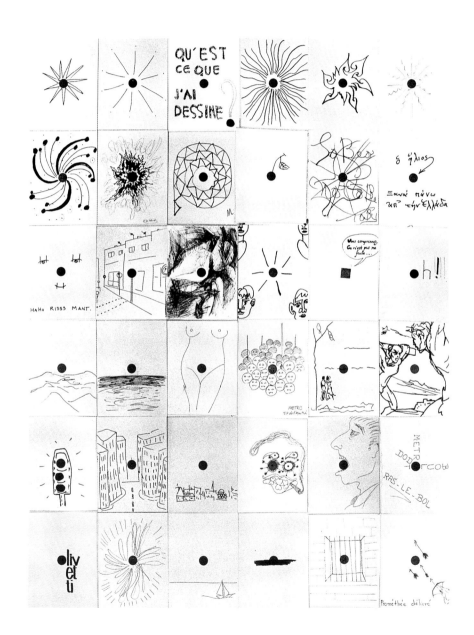

the slightest sign of assent on my part; then takes one of the examples of the text, and, encouraged by the action, glances at it,
reads it, steps back to embrace with a single scan the whole of
the surface systematically dotted with red spots; then returns,
approaches, and discovers a sun among the palms of an oasis, a
cherry in a glass of water, then the pompom on a sailor's beret.
The frame of geometric order is eaten away little by little, like
a persistent image, transforming into a succession of heterogeneous spaces, each including a red dot: *the Japanese flag next to a
clown's nose . . . the O of joint, a soap bubble, an ear-ring . . . the monocle
of an aristocrat, a cut finger . . . the sun behind the bars of a prison, the
cheek of a little girl who has a toothache, the O of love, the glowing tip of
a cigar, the eye of an octopus, of a rabbit, of a cat . . . the O of no, the ball
attached to the foot of a convict, the O of rouge, a pill on the tongue, the
knot in a plank of wood, a drop of blood . . .*

It is only after this lengthy investigation that our visitor, after
some moments of wavering, takes a felt pen and sheet with a red
dot, leans forward, and draws. It is unusual for the visitor, ado-
lescent or adult, to draw without having attentively looked one
by one at all the exhibited drawings beforehand. It is clearly
not the same for the young children, whose parents make or
help them to draw. Finally, smiling, the visitor makes a gesture
to hand me the drawing, decides against it, grabs some drawing
pins, lifts his or her arms and fixes it beside the others.

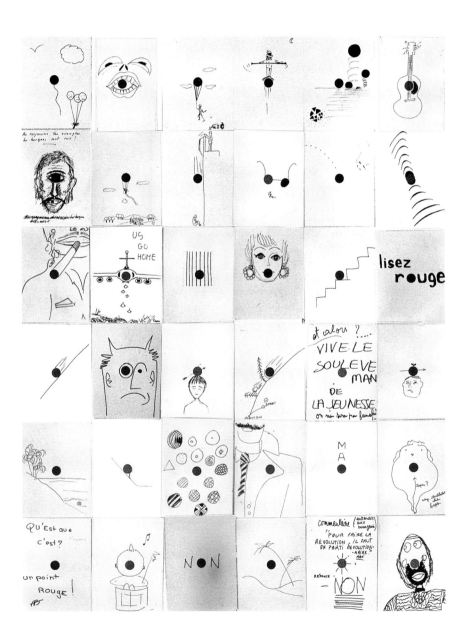

If the game is continued for several days, which is the most usual case, it is not uncommon to see the same visitors return once, twice, sometimes three times, to resume their dialogue with the collective work they had nourished the previous day, or the day before that, with their drawings. They return to complete it, deny it, or open out their fantasies. What has become of that work of which they felt themselves partly the authors? What have their successors made of it? How have they responded to the same ensemble of drawings, augmented by their propositions? What new themes have emerged? And, eventually, what role have their propositions been able to have in that evolution? For them, the development of that work must no longer be entirely unpredictable, for they desire both to acknowledge and to discover it. Still others return because a new idea has come to them and they desire to assure themselves, before preparing it for one of the walls, that it has not been expressed in the meantime: *the nose of a dog, a ladybird, the stone of Sisyphus, H_2O, the button on a coat, an egg on the plate, the O of bof, a car's headlight, the head of a butterfly, the wheel of a wheelbarrow, the sun above the sea, a hedge, behind a mountain, in the clouds . . . the O of way out, a red fire, an apple, a navel, between the hammer and the anvil, the world, a varnished nail, a ball on the horn of a rhinoceros, the neck of one guillotined, and you are amused by that?*

During that interval the drawings have grown to 2,500, or 3,000, perhaps more . . . At that moment, simultaneously, several phenomena come to light. Though the number of visitors is close to those of the preceding days, the number of drawings executed diminishes rapidly, holes begin to appear in the frame because drawings disappear, and the sheets with red dots on the

table are stolen. Once this threshold is reached, the repetition of these phenomena at each manifestation leads me to the following hypotheses: the creators of the drawings act only through a dialogue with the existing, in this case the growing mass of executed drawings. That step implies that each intervener has sufficient time at his disposal to take stock of the totality of drawings before drawing. So long as the drawings fixed to the walls do not exceed several hundred, one can presuppose the visitors scarcely pay attention to the question of time they will consecrate to this game, even if, by participating, they cut short their visits to other rooms in the exhibition.

Once what I am really obliged to consider as a threshold is reached, say 3,500 drawings, overflowing the walls and invading the neighboring space, the behavior of the visitors is transformed: the snow becomes water once again. Certainly they still peck with their eyes at the drawings, here and there, but draw almost nothing. The collective work is no longer apprehended with all its ramifications and seems to change into a mass that they cruise through without really stopping . . . Would the visitor, hesitating, not question the amount of time necessary to examine it in its totality, then to reflect a little, before finally drawing? The very questioning, and the rough assessment of the awareness of indispensable time, will that not be dissuasive of recognition? As the whole exploration of the drawings is no longer under consideration, why draw? To risk making a "useless repetition"? Another consequence of the effect of the mass . . . , a hand that would discover itself once again as clumsy. The confrontation, then, is no longer situating itself in relation to the sole criterion of ability to draw. For a brief moment, potential authors, new visitors rediscover themselves as "amateurs" . . . Finally the word is out. Until this stage of the evolution of the collective work, any distinction like "artist" has been revealed inappropriate, indeed obsolete, as much for the initiator of the game (it was, besides, one of my avowed objectives) as for the thousands who have intervened, for the game reveals that they are indiscriminately "amateurs" or "artists." Through their drawings they have become, among other things, something else: the authors of a collective work of which no one person would alone have been able to be the author, the "artist," on account of the complex diversity which it presents at that moment and which results in the multiplicity of its interveners.

Departing from the red dot, to my great pleasure, a common implicit attitude appears at the outset, and reverberates from drawing to drawing, in the course of each manifestation, invading all the work: that all can play, no matter to what sociocultural group or age group they belong, and, through that intervention, become the co-authors of the collective work. Thus, the majority of the participants are situated in the dominant plan of the "idea" that they will be initially "amateurs" or "artists." The latter give their knowledge to make their proposition more evident and funnier, hence perhaps the slightly low number of abstract drawings. For some others, because there had already been a purposeful drawing on the paper, the circular surface covered with vermillion, one does not spoil it by simply affixing a caption. The fundamental structure of the work appears thus to be the finely woven web of interconnections that bind all these drawings, with my admitted affiliation, to rhyme, diversion, derision . . . from almost nothing, a red dot.

The collective work has reached its maximum scale and can no longer be stretched. No longer being able to be approached in all its complexity, the work starts to lose its foundation. Aside from some drawings that have disappeared, almost nothing else moves. The collective work, like a house of cards, starts to collapse into as many drawings. The absence of one or another will no longer alter the work. Henceforth visitors can take those which please them the most, and that is what happens, naturally. The diminution of the number of people to draw, and the disappearance of drawings, are thus consequences of the same phenomenon: from being collective, the work has become an exhibition of "drawings."

A twenty-centime coin, the earth is blue like an orange (Eluard), the head of one hanged, the porthole of a liner, the O of OK, a squirrel curled on itself, a lustful eye, William Tell's apple, the ball of mercury in a thermometer, Atlas carrying it on his shoulders, the ball of an ice cream cone, have you seen my planet? She is right above us said the Little Prince, she

is beautiful! said the snake (Saint-Exupéry), the mouth of a jet engine, a hole in gruyère, the O of oh, eureka, a ball on a Christmas tree, I'm fed up with being round, I'm fed up with being red, Mickey's nose, little girls playing ball, the tip of your breast that I love, The end . . . go dark: an eclipse . . .

Places where the red spots were put on
Plan and projects as art, Kunsthalle, Bern, 1969
Salon de Mai, Musée d'Art Moderne de la Ville de Paris, 1969
Salon Confrontation, Dijon, 1969
Kunstler machen plane: andere auch, Kunsthaus, Hamburg, 1970
Art Cinétique, Maison de la Culture de La Rochelle, 1970
Art Cinétique, Théâtre Gérard Philippe de Saint-Denis, 1970
Klub Miedzynardowej Prasy I Ksiazki, Warsaw, 1970
Foire aux Architectes, Liège, 1971
Maison Française, Oxford, 1971
Royal College of Art, London, 1971
Kunstzone, Munich, 1971
Design Français, Musée des Arts Décoratifs, Paris, 1971
Art cinétique, Galérie d'Art Expérimentale "Formes et Muraux," Lyons, 1971
Paysages Quotidiens, Musée des Arts Décoratifs, Centre Beaubourg, Paris, 1975
New 57 Gallery, Edinburgh, 1977
The Landscape Approach, Dublin, 1979
Institut Français des Pays-Bas, Amsterdam, 1979
Scottish National Gallery of Modern Art, Edinburgh, 1978/79
Centre d'Action Culturelle Pablo Neruda, Corbeil-Essonnes, 1981

Successive Ambiances 13 / 1968

This experience is a visual game that systematically takes up various texts, sometimes old ones, on the study of differences between appearance and physical presence, between redundancy and miniaturization.

Ambiance was shown for the first time on the occasion of the exhibition Cinétisme, Spectacle, Environnement, which took placc at the Maison de la Culture in Grenoble in 1968.

In that version, the visitor proceeds down a long, narrow, brightly colored passageway, emerging into a cubic volume, the walls comprised entirely of plate glass surfaces, where the visitor's image is reflected to infinity, beyond the geometry of the volume, which remains perceptible through the recognition of the joins between walls and between walls and ceiling.

When the intensity of the source of light, situated in the center of the volume, diminishes, the image of the spectator fades by degrees and the brick walls appear, provoking an unexpected narrowing of the space. These brick walls constitute the walls of the cubic volume (B), bigger than the mirror volume (A) it contains.

The plate glass walls are separated from the brick walls by a space 30 cm thick creating a void between the exterior walls of volume A and the interior walls of volume B. Here are concealed powerful banks of lighting that illuminate the brick walls when the source of light situated in the middle of volume A dims.

When the source of light is between the spectator and the plate glass, the spectator perceives his or her image reflected as in a mirror. If, on the contrary, the source of light is situated behind the plate glass, the latter plays the role of a simple glass and allows the appearance of what that source of light illuminates, in this case the brick walls.

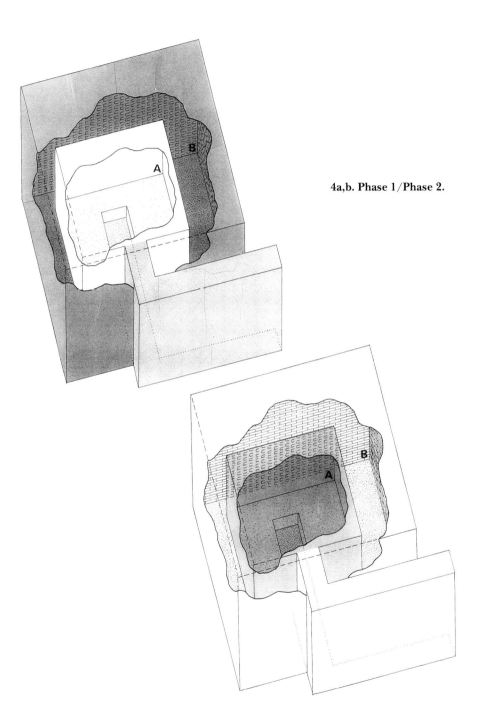

4a,b. Phase 1/Phase 2.

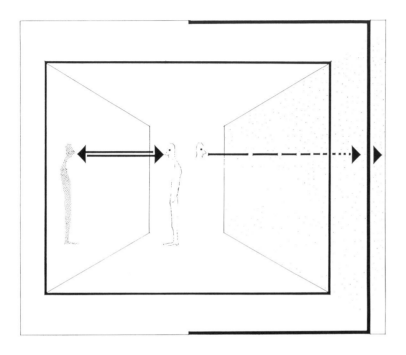

The alternating lighting between volume A and the walls of the surrounding wall B offers the spectator a passage between reflection and transparence. The surrounding wall B, which is larger, then appears smaller than the surrounding wall A. The alternation between transparence and reflection, that is, between the materialization of the approaching brick surface and the dematerialization of the mirror surface, through the multiplication of the image, leads to a fluxing of space and movements of volumes that we would like to know better.

That experience reveals that a volume can appear smaller than the volume it contains.

4c,d. The alternating lighting between volume A and the walls of the surrounding wall B offers the spectator a passage between reflection and transparence. The surrounding wall B, which is larger, then appears smaller than the surrounding wall A.

Stockholm, the Landscape / 1969

Beneath the sun in June 1969, traveling along a quay in Stockholm, I was suddenly pulled up short. Emerging from the vegetable mass of building sections I thought I saw in the distance, on the port's horizon, there materialized before me the shape of a long and powerful warship. It had remained hidden thanks to its camouflage. Until then I had thought that camouflage was reserved for the land army. But here the pattern of a paratrooper's battledress, mainly green but also strewn with maroon and streaked with some black, represented a design that had grown to envelop the whole of the boat.

Then I experienced what a landscape is: the sudden grasp of all those sections of various colors—houses, factories, or trees—in an assemblage, making possible the insertion of new objects all the time without the assemblage itself being modified, and without the objects being able to be recognized. In one single move, not held up by the specific identification of any particular object, a reading of the vast horizon, in its total sweep, had been made possible by the gathering of multiple, dissociated, and momentary sections, of objects which from another view were integrated parts. Was not this "the landscape"? In that specific case, the one of camouflage in the dominant vegetation of the Swedish marine-front, the horizon of the port of Stockholm. The displacement of that battledress from the paratrooper to the warship is explained through the structure of the fjords along the Swedish coast. At anchor, the warships must be more ground than sea. But if, in this northern country, land can be identified as summer vegetation, is not winter a vast whiteness? In Alaska, the dominant vegetation of armored vehicles is augmented with stains of snow whatever the season. Further to the south, the play of desert ochers excludes all others. But, along with the blue gray of the ocean, all that only constitutes a limited number of landscapes: sea, sky, vegetation, desert, snow.

One to two millimeters of paint subdivided the warship into complete multiple surfaces without discontinuity involving other sections, trees, or constructions, and with it constituted the horizon of the port and outlined the limit where ground meets sky. What a contrast between that minutely thin skin, which visually effaces the boat by enlarging it horizontally "in landscape," and the thickness of the plate of the hull, the turrets, and their guns, radar, machines—a few millimeters opposed to two or three tens of thousands of tons.

5. The port in June.

24

1. Stockholm, the
landscape, 1969.

2. The Pines installation, Coracle Gallery, London, January 1981.

3. The garden game,
Château de Barbirey-
sur-Ouche, 1996.

4. Traffic circle at the Champs Elysées, Paris, 1981. (a) Elevation of a circular bank to make perceptible to motorists the external form of the circle, especially because the internal slope is covered with a solid mass of flowers that vary according to the seasons. (b) The presence of the bank allows the space to be divided into two: one for motorists and one for pedestrians, between the external slope of the bank, also covered with flowers, and the façades of the building.

5. The snake and the butterflies, 1981. Because children were getting hurt crossing the highway, it was necessary to build a footbridge. But because nobody climbs up a footbridge, this one had not to appear as one. Here we have the separation of what is usually seen as a footbridge into two parts: one in imitation rock (not as an excuse for the mistakes of those who built the highway), the other in metal. And, to effect a better contrast with the "rock" part, butterflies flying over real lavender plants.

6. The slope, the meadow, the vertical garden: proposal for the Parc de la Villette, 1982. This park is part of the slope of the Seine Valley; hence, on the plan, a metaphorical slope between the Belleville Heights and the Seine River. A response to the measureless dimension of space and depth: a vertical garden.

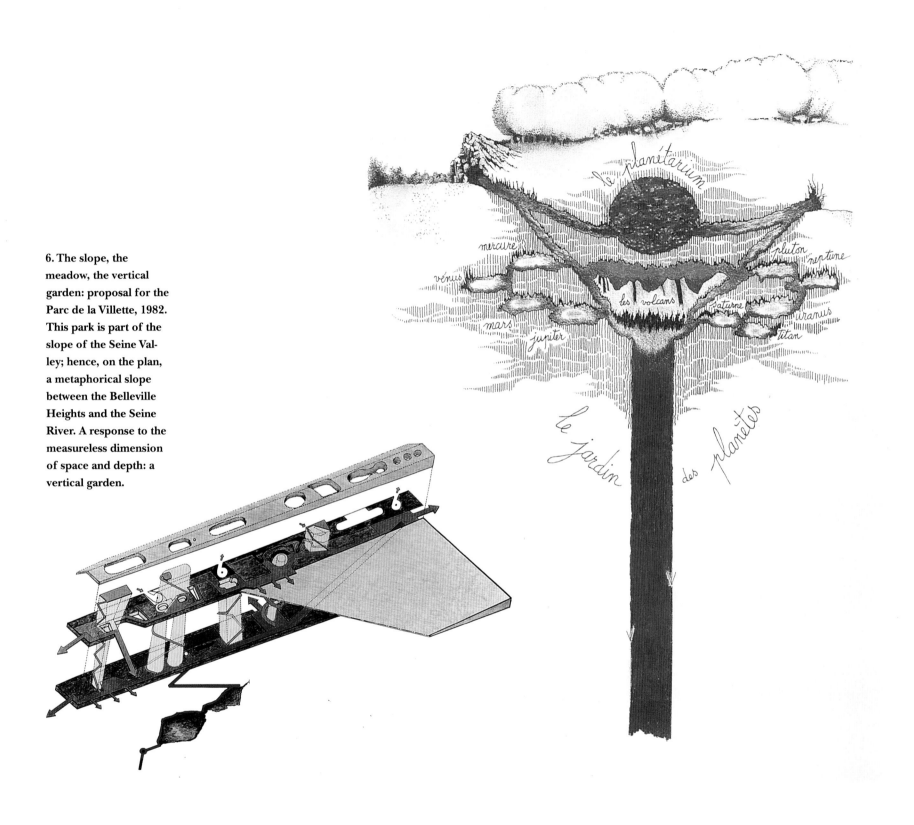

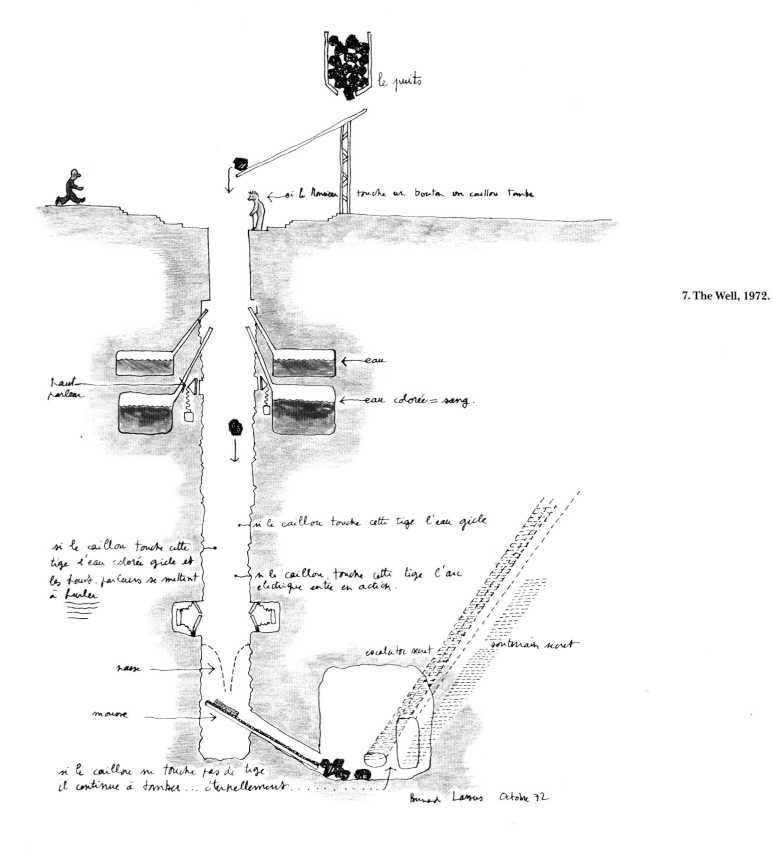

le puits

si le Monsieur touche un bouton un caillou tombe

eau

eau colorée = sang.

haut parleur

si le caillou touche cette tige l'eau gicle

si le caillou touche cette tige l'eau colorée gicle et les hauts parleurs se mettent à hurler

si le caillou touche cette tige l'arc électrique entre en action.

escalator secret   souterrain secret

nasse

mousse

si le caillou ne touche pas de tige il continue à tomber ... éternellement ....

Bernard Lassus   Octobre 72

7. The Well, 1972.

8. Uckange, Batigère, 1981–87. Of 1400 apartments, 700 had to be destroyed due to the economic recession (Lorraine was an iron and steel producing area). Thus the task was to create a new city from a half-destroyed place. A new construction was not possible, so all the soil surfaces had to be moved to construct a new landscape, a real place instead of the suburbs. Across the façades a puzzle of landscapes and houses for the inhabitants of the various nations and cultures, landscapes that played, too, with real trees and new lawns.

The Well / 1972

Unrealized Project for the Garden of the University of Montpellier

Is there anyone who has not, once in a while, thrown a pebble into a well and then waited, expectantly, for the moment when the pebble hits the water or the pebbles at the bottom, so as to be able to gauge the depth which the darkness prevents from being estimated visually?

Let us imagine for a moment that we do not hear the pebble; in other words it keeps on falling . . .

The pebble can then wound the Loch Ness Monster, or pass through the Earth and rejoin the thousands of pebbles which rain in Eternity, or make Truth erupt, naked and angry, from the well.

The camouflage and the relationship "thrown pebble/well" have each to stretch their own dimension. Thus the camouflaged surface spreads it way beyond its object support, as far as the limits of all that surrounds it between sky and water, and the absence, always delayed, of the noise of the pebble on the bottom of the well postpones its depth until . . . infinity.

With other studies like the landscape at Stockholm, it opens the field of hypotheses to explore from the indispensable re-evaluation of the basic structure of the classic scheme of the art of gardens and landscape that I had considered as essential: the relationship measurable/immeasurable. Or, as I have stated:

measurable/measurable
measurable/surroundable
measurable/demeasurable
measurable/immeasurably vertical.

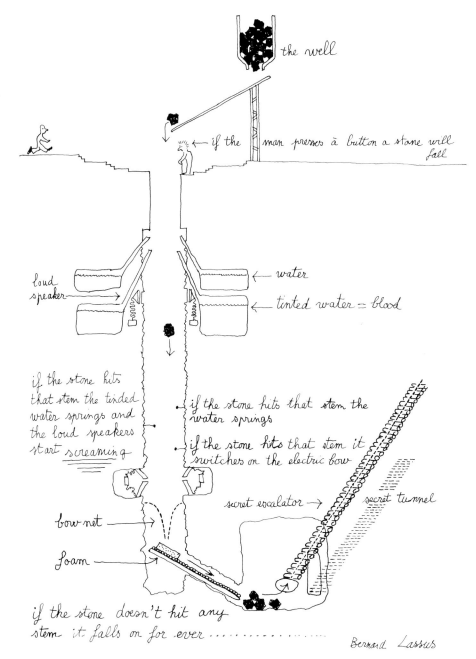

the well

if the man presses à button a stone will fall

loud speaker

water

tinted water = blood

if the stone hits that stem the tinted water springs and the loud speakers start screaming

if the stone hits that stem the water springs

if the stone hits that stem it switches on the electric bow

secret escalator →

secret tunnel

bow net →

foam →

if the stone doesn't hit any stem it falls on for ever . . . .

Bernard Lassus

Games of Displacement / 1975

The natural seems to me bound to a determined visual field. Unless the visual field is homogeneous, there is always one element that can be considered more natural than another, and it is through its opposition to another element, which by this fact is qualified as artificial, that it is situated.

It is very probable that if you have a potted plant in your kitchen, you will consider it more natural than the white enameled refrigerator on which it is placed.

If you introduce a new element into your visual field, either it will be inserted between the natural and the artificial, or it will become the most natural or the most artificial element: hence there is a displacement of one or more former elements. More or less natural, more or less artificial, is an identification which involves a classification.

We invite you to proceed with classifications from the most artificial to the most natural.

7. Games of displacement, Centre Georges Pompidou, Marsan Pavilion, Musée des Arts Décoratifs, Paris, 1975.

Glasses and Bottles I / 1975

Game of Similarities and Differences

The new landscape depends on relationships set up and identified between the elements that appear in the visual field.

What can be the absorption of the constructed from a landscape substratum where not only relief and the color count, but also the quality of the light, the transparence of the tree, the sound of the stream?

That attempt to substitute for the landscape in order to choose its new contributions leads to other criteria and makes perceivable how the labored insertion of the old ways of "bringing on" risks producing boredom and monotony.

Before any establishment of a construction, an analysis and a list of the characteristics of the elements of the site are needed.

Everyday objects, more manipulable, also permit reflections on landscape relationships.

This text was presented to visitors, but this game having not entailed as much manipulation as the red spots and the visual prolongings, I revised and extended it . . . today it is a visual piece.

8a–f. From small to minute differences, Centre Georges Pompidou, Marsan Pavilion, Musée des Arts Décoratifs, Paris, 1975.

Glasses and Bottles II / 1976

Substratum + Contribution = New Landscape

When one speaks of building a new house in a landscape, on the most general level of the relationship construction/site, whether urban or rural, one intends that the new contribution be integrated properly into the site where it will be built. But what does the use of that term "integration" imply? First, a willingness to receive, supposing that the new contribution is different in part from the elements that constitute the existing landscape, and that it is suitable for it to blend into the landscape context in the best possible way through formal similarity. Consequently, one often uses the term integration to anticipate a difference that will emerge, rejecting it in advance, since it must be abandoned, and thus one avoids having to consider the implications that would be introduced by a new presence. Because each time there is a contribution there is new landscape, one could wish that the contribution might not solely augment one of the elements of the existing landscape, but facilitate the presence of new contributions (always the most important) and open possibilities to the evolution of the site. The contribution can thus reduce or increase the receptivity of the site. Thus, it is not through a homogeneous landscape, reinforced each time with contributions whose characteristics are similar to those of the constituent elements of the site, that the most favorable reception can occur, but through its differences. It appears that only a sufficiently heterogeneous landscape substratum will permit the reception of original contributions. The relationship contribution/support seems to imply that it concerns a priori a relationship object/landscape, yet one cannot ignore the current case where the substratum is constituted by a landscape fraction and an object, for example, a building erected in a suburban habitat zone.

According to this hypothesis, contrasts between an object of this kind and the elements of the landscape fraction affect the conditions under which a new contribution becomes a landscape element. To the extent that the new contribution exhibits fewer contrasts with the elements of the substratum than it does with the object, which remains an intruder, it will be driven back by this object toward the landscape elements, whereas with the same degree of contrast and the object being absent, it would itself have continued to function as an object. But the object can formally be redundant or miniaturized through its signification. Thus, a church tower discovered in a visual field will appear as normal, not because of its form, but through what it signifies, whereas a water tower of the same height will be felt as infinitely more voluminous, and as aggressive. Among the numerous reasons could be because the nature of water is to flow downward and not be fixed at the height of a cement pillar.

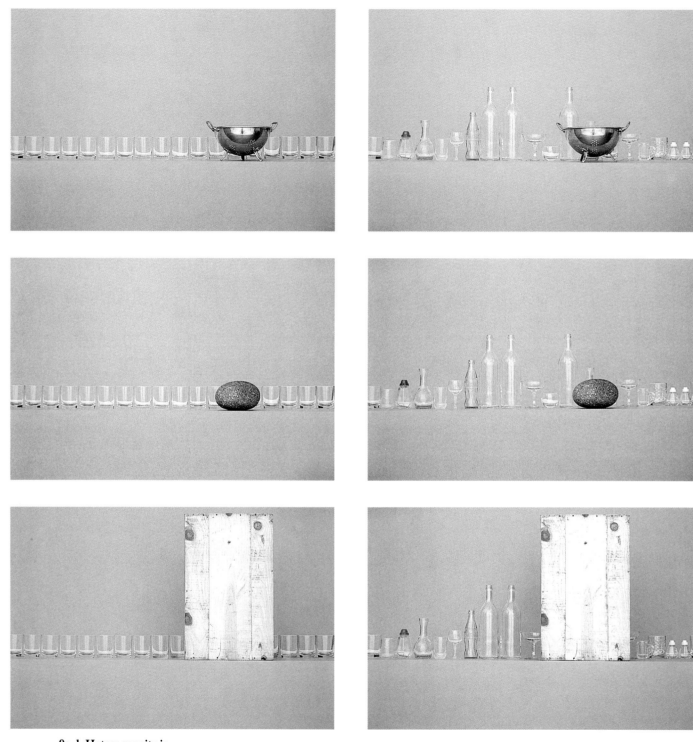

9a–l. Heterogeneity is more receptive than homogeneity.

31   Glasses and Bottles II

The Pines / 1980

Stephen Bann

For a number of years, Bernard Lassus has been in the habit of photographing the barks of the pines in the Forêt de la Courbre, on the French Atlantic coast. Following a precise method of working, and paying little attention to the wider landscape around him, he makes a record of this series of barks, photographing each from different angles and in different light conditions.

This study can be directly related to the work which Lassus was engaged upon in the 1960s: for example, his "Ambiance 10" (1965–66), which aimed to recreate through artificial light the play of reflections in the forest, or indeed his series of "Brise-lumières," which he compared at the time to the "effect" of leaves multiplying and light being reflected among the different levels of leaves, which are thus colored and take on nuanced tints of green. The "genuine color/light material" he conceived then as forming a "genuine continuity between the individual forms of the leaves" is evoked once again in the successive appearances of these pines.

What then does the forest represent for Lassus? In the first place, no doubt, it is a question of dematerializing this concrete environment, of sacrificing the relation of each individual element to the other elements, and to an overall context, in favor of the image of continuity—a continuity that is itself inflected, as with a musical phrase or the rhythmic syntax of a poem. At a second level, however, we can see that it is a question of a game of substitution, perhaps even of metaphor. The new "material" Lassus has obtained lends itself to new interpretations, even very daring ones—like those of the French poet Francis Ponge, who described his own "pine wood" as "the bathroom of a wild but noble creature." Should we not pose ourselves the kind of question Ponge has posed, in relation to the metamorphosed wood?

10. The Pines installation, Coracle Gallery, London, January 1981.

"Why has she chosen brushes with green hair and violet wooden handles all chiseled with verdigris lichen? Perhaps because this noble savage is brown-skinned, who will later take her dip in the bathtub of lake or sea nearby. Here we have the dressing room of Venus, with Phoebus' light-bulb placed in the wall of mirrors."

The Monument / 1980

The two men have been walking on slowly for hours, perhaps even days, along a slope that bristles with rocks and compels them to take a meandering path.

Each of them imprints the heavy and ocher-colored soil, between the masses of stone, with the weight of his toiling footsteps. Then the first in line stops, lifts up his head, and tries to glimpse the summit. Without altering his pace, his companion catches him up and passes him.

Buniak now takes up his position again behind Qyzil, who has just seen appearing in front of him, on the ground that has been so monotonously the same at every step, a dull gray pebble—smooth and with bluish highlights, not really standing out from the ground, roughly the same size and shape as an avocado kernel.

Hanging rocks, dark caverns and impetuous cataracts which pour on all sides from the heights of the mountains; the trees are misshapen and seem to have been broken by the violence of the tempests. Here we can see some of them upturned and impeding the course of the torrents, seeming as if they have been caught up in the fury of the waters. There they seem to have been struck by lightning, to have been burnt and cloven in pieces. Some of the buildings are in ruins, others of them half consumed by fire: a few puny huts, scattered here and there over the mountains, seem to indicate at once the existence and the misery of the inhabitants.[1]

Bats, vultures and all the birds of prey flutter in the thickets. Wolves, tigers and jackals howl in the forests; hungry animals are wandering in the plains. From the middle of the roads, you see gibbets, crosses, wheels and the whole apparatus of torture; and in the most aweful recesses of the woods, where the pathways are crooked and covered with poisonous plants, where every object bears the signs of depopulation, you will find temples dedicated to vengeance and death; caverns which, by way of brushwood and brambles, lead on to subterranean habitations. Near to them are placed stone pillars, with sad descriptions of tragic events, and the horrible story of the innumerable cruelties committed in these very places by the outlaws and brigands of ancient times. And to add to the sublime horror of these pictures, there are cavities hollowed out in the summits of the highest mountains which sometimes conceal foundries, lime-kilns and glass factories, whence there spring immense gusts of flame and continuous flows of thick smoke, which give these mountains the appearance of volcanoes.[2]

Three of them, then five . . . nine . . . as they become more and more numerous, the pebbles form a surface and then a thick layer. The soles of their shoes jar against this strangely consistent ground covering. At each step they take, slowed up considerably, a metallic crunch echoes off the closest of the rocky wall surfaces.

With all their attention taken by the changes in this granular layer, whose elements are becoming larger and larger in volume, Buniak and Qyzil have only just realized that the slope has become steeper, the rocks have disappeared, and the line of the ridge is close by. The ground finally falls away before them, and our travelers discover in the distance, on an immense plateau whose boundaries are indistinct, an enormous dark-colored sphere with green highlights that floats above the ground, trembling slightly. Fascinated, the two advance toward it, and the globe, measuring 200 or perhaps 300 meters in diameter, turns

[1] William Chambers, *Du Traité des édifices, meubles, habits, machines, et ustensiles des chinois* (Paris, 1776), p. 25.

[2] Pierre Boitard, *L'Art de composer et décorer les jardins* (Paris, 1834), p. 17.

softly on its axis and slides in their direction. In between the black and sticky rocks, which are shaken by continuous currents of wind, the sparse vegetation bends in every direction.

All of a sudden, a gust of wind invades the calm patch of air around Buniak and Oyzil. It shouts in their ears:

"REMEMBER THAT ON 16 JULY 1969 ARMSTRONG, ALDRICH AND COLLINS LEFT THE EARTH ON BOARD APOLLO XI FOR THE MOON."

Scarcely have these words been pronounced when the wind increases in vigor and an icy shadow comes over them. Crudely, the light returns and brings into view a second sphere that is already close by, a smaller one with a diameter of roughly 100 meters.

> Betwixt them
> lawns, or level downs, and
> flocks / Grazing the tender herb,
> were interposed, / Or palmy hillock, or
> the flow'ry lap / Of some irriguous valley
> spread her store, / Flow'rs of all hue, and without
> thorn the rose: / Another side, unbrageous grots
> and caves / Of cool recess, o'er which the mantling
> vine / Lays forth her purple grape, and gently
> creeps / Luxuriant: meanwhile murmuring waters
> fall / Down the slope hills, dispersed, or in a
> lake, / That to the fringed bank with myrtle
> crowned / Her crystal mirror holds, unite
> their streams. / The birds their choir
> apply; airs, vernal airs, / Breathing
> the smell of field and grove,
> attune / The trembling
> leaves . . .[3]

A group of birds, leaving the chorus, surrounds them in spiral flight, singing:

"REMEMBER THAT ON 21 JULY 1969 NEIL ARMSTRONG WALKED ON THE MOON AND SAW THE EARTH."

Rising abruptly, a new sphere blots out the second—is it the first yet again? No, it is similar to it in every respect, but smaller. And the wind thunders again:

"REMEMBER 23 JULY 1969, APOLLO XI RETURNED TO EARTH."

Then it softens to a whisper:

"THIS MONUMENT WAS RELEASED ON THE OCCASION OF THE BI-CENTENARY OF MAN'S FIRST STEP ON THE MOON."

As the Earth has grown smaller, losing the immeasurable dimension of its landscapes that have submitted to the measurement of machines, techniques, and apparatuses, it should have been transformed into a Garden of Eden or a Garden of Delights. But has it been?

Blemished, over-exploited, resisting interpretation—this is our landscape today. But can it be rediscovered and/or invented anew?

[3] John Milton, *Paradise Lost*, quoted in L'Abbé de Lille, *Les Jardins, ou l'art d'embellir les paysages* (Paris, 1776), p. 133.

The Garden Game / 1996

Stephen Bann

Let us begin with an old story. Here is what the great English critic, John Ruskin, advises in the very first lines of his work, *The Elements of Perspective*:

> When you begin to read this book, sit down very near the window, and shut the window. I hope the view out of it is pretty; but, whatever the view may be, we shall find enough in it for an illustration of the first principles of perspective (or, literally, of "looking through").
>
> Every pane of your window may be considered, if you choose, as a glass picture; and what you see through it, as painted on its surface.
>
> And if, holding your head still, you extend your hand to the glass, you may, with a brush full of any thick colour, trace, roughly, the lines of the landscape on the glass.[1]

Thus begins, under the aegis of Ruskin as drawing master, the education of the young artist who wishes to learn the laws of perspective. Yet everyone knows that this empirical means of proving that we can represent depth of space on a flat and transparent surface goes back far beyond the nineteenth century. As we take it back, we come across another kind of demonstration, similar in kind but with metaphysical rather than practical consequences.

Listen to George Herbert, the English seventeenth-century poet, who is himself echoing the celebrated passage in the Apostle Paul's Epistle to the Corinthians:

> A man that looks on glasse,
>   On it may stay his eye;
> Or if he pleaseth, through it passe,
>   And then the heav'n espie.[2]

The drawing master and the poet are describing two quite different practices. For Ruskin, the act of "roughly" tracing the lines of the landscape (we might well ask what these lines may be) is simply a brief preliminary exercise in preparation for the study of geometry in the tradition that leads back to Alberti's *De Pictura*. Ruskin, for his part, takes his view of the landscape in the open air. Still, it is reputed that every evening when he was in his study at Brantwood, in the beautiful area of the Lake District, his butler used to announce at the appropriate time: "The sunset, Mr Ruskin!" For Herbert, on the other hand, glass serves merely as a metaphorical support for what can be seen *beyond*, that is to say with the eyes of faith. The glass is an aspect of a universe made up entirely of signs that offer themselves to interpretation. Seeing "the heav'n" is seeing beyond the visible world, to what only makes its appearance as a result of meditation and prayer.

I have been very summarily describing two ways of reading what can be seen on glass and what can be glimpsed beyond. In a certain sense, however, these two traditions are brought together in the type of mildly ironic painting practiced by the Surrealist painter René Magritte. In a number of paintings, he seeks to establish an equivalence between the canvas, placed right in front of us as spectators, and the view through a window painted in exactly the same fashion as the plane surface worked by the fictional artist. Could there be, in the place of the canvas,

---

[1] John Ruskin, *The Elements of Perspective* (London: George Allen, 1910), pp. 1–2.

[2] George Herbert, *The Temple: Sacred Poems and Private Ejaculations* (London: Elliot Stock, 1885), p. 179.

nothing but a hole? Certainly not, since Magritte takes care to show us the detail of the tacks on the edge of the support so that the canvas appears in perspective. Everything leads us to think that this is no more than an ironic game that puts the apparatus of perspectival representation on display. But there is at least a trace of metaphysics, and of the kind of stimulus that the imagination can receive from the world of signs. Did not Magritte choose as his title for a work in this series *The Human Condition?*

These few remarks can serve as a Preface to "The Garden Game." Bernard Lassus is a painter, poet, and professor. He is also a landscape gardener. Formerly a student in Léger's studio, and author of a range of texts that present his work in an original and striking fashion, as well as Professor at the Ecole d'Architecture of La Villette, he expresses himself in a practice that has always had as its object the landscape on the scale of real life. But it has been precisely the furtherance of this practice which has led him to do experimental work at other levels. Over twenty years ago, he compiled a set of documents relating to his "games with the public" in a delightful book.[3] At the Château of Barbirey-sur-Ouche in Burgundy, with the cooperation of its owner and the Grand Public association, the game has begun again.

Michel Conan underlined in his introduction to the 1977 collection that by "game" Lassus wished to stress the element of participation by the public. This principle no doubt takes its origin in the statements made by the kinetic artists of the 1960s: artists who invited the spectator to intervene in rearranging the content of their works. Bernard Lassus was himself identified

[3] Bernard Lassus, *Jeux*, preface by Michel Conan (Paris: Galilée, 1977).

with this movement of younger artists, while at the same time he was setting up a Center for Research in Ambiance that looked to more permanent achievements. What distinguished him from the kinetic movement, however, was the close and persistent relationship he established between game situations and the development of new landscapes. In Michel Conan's words, it was a question of emphasizing the productive character of work in landscape, rather than creating definite art objects. "Showing a new landscape would be offering only one piece of work. These games provide in a schematic form a number of examples of mechanisms for transformation; just a few among the myriads to be created."[4]

At Barbirey-sur-Ouche, the approach is completely new, even though Bernard Lassus has learned the lesson of his earlier experiments. In his "Study for a Framework or Ambiance Support," also called "The Red Dots," he invited the public to make their interventions on sheets of paper that carried large red dots: replaced in an overall framework, these sheets bore witness at the same time to structure (signaled by the repetition of red dots) and to freedom of expression (people could all make the drawings they liked). In the Salon of the Château, the glass panes on the side of the garden already form a framework. Lassus has retained symmetry by taking sixteen from among them, and printing a range of drawings on them, in the form of a permutation. At first sight, it seems that the spectators are no longer being allowed to give form to their own ideas with the means at their disposal. But in fact the game involving the imagination has just moved one stage further. I will explain why.

The question "What is the time of a garden?" runs the risk of seeming rather simplistic. Obviously the time of a garden is the rhythm of the seasons, as we can follow it in the park of Barbirey, and the rhythm of each day, which casts different lights on the landscape scene that appears from the windows of the Salon. But gardens also have a history that belongs to a more extensive measure of duration. In the case of Barbirey, it has required an almost archaeological process to disengage the large kitchen garden beside the old farm buildings. In front of the Château, as the little guide published by Grand Public makes clear, the existing park brings to mind the archetype of the turn-of-the-century garden,[5] which is to say that it relates to a specifically historical model. But were there other gardens at an earlier period? And what will happen when, in the years to come, the trees that are today at the height of their strength die off one by one? The garden has its past. No doubt it will also have a future. But how can we imagine, in the face of the present, the changes that may take

[4] Ibid., p. 10.

[5] "Le jeu du jardin, mode d'emploi": text distributed to visitors to the garden in connection with Lassus's intervention.

place, or indeed a past existence that might have come to pass? This is why the garden game has been invented.

In a sense, Humphry Repton, the English landscape gardener of the late eighteenth and early nineteenth centuries, was the author of a game of this type when he composed for his potential clients "Red Books," where the proprietor of an estate could view his domain from different angles. In the first place, Repton showed the existing landscape. But this landscape was painted in part on paper flaps that could be raised and turned back to reveal the landscape park Repton planned to design. Obviously he wanted to prove that his new arrangements were superior to the previous ones. That was his sole purpose. But for us, as we are not necessarily convinced by his solutions, the "Red Books" become something quite different: "games" that offer two readings, two landscapes, for comparison.

Bernard Lassus has already made a study in depth of a French garden which counts among the most prestigious of all, but has had a specially difficult historical evolution. In *Le Jardin des Tuileries* (1991), he proposed a revolutionary approach to the restoration of a historic garden, which consisted in superimposing different levels corresponding to the different historical stages traversed by the garden. He wrote: "A good way to show the history of this garden would be to construct it in successive steps, from the oldest to the most elevated and recent."[6] This is an approach that can also bear fruit in a project of quite a different character, as Lassus has underlined in a different context.

In his project for the Park of Duisburg-Nord in Germany, he envisages rehabilitating a landscape that has been blighted by industrial installations. Behind the river, which has become a canal between factories, it should be possible to recreate the river within its original context: "the fields in the zones not liable to flooding will be available for forage, and wind and watermills." This is not just nostalgic reminiscence. It is a matter of reinstating a more diverse chronology: "We must have the day before yesterday in order to understand yesterday, but that involves not simply restoring a river; it is also a matter of context."[7]

At Barbirey, the "garden game" is not designed to transform the landscape. It aspires to catch the visitor's imagination and facilitate the emergence of many possible landscapes from a terrain that is simply the park of the Château. The visitor can experiment with the perspectival effects that are available, re-

[6] Bernard Lassus, *Le Jardin des Tuileries* (London: Coracle Press, 1991), p. 37.
[7] See "The Park of Duisburg-Nord," this volume.

turning to his place on the terrace the little white cock who was straying in the distance, and precipitating onto the lawn, like a flying saucer, the kiosk from the Belle Epoque that might well be contemporary with the origins of the existing garden. Other drawings inspire reverie about the development over time of a former quarry which is not visible from the Salon, but is within easy walking distance.

Going backwards and forwards, between the drawing on the windowpane and the real space of the garden, can amuse us for a time. But there are other ways of playing. We can use the game as a way of seeing the garden better. But it can also help us confront the shock effect of a new element. By placing at the side of an old sequoia (visibly inspired by the one we see in front of us) this monstrous head that seems to transgress the laws of the natural world, Bernard Lassus impels us to think about the almost brutal aspect of creation. It is heresy to imagine that the landscape can be no more than Nature in her primitive state, when it is a knowing form of composition! Looking at the goggle eyes of this great head, or Folly, we see that it is just a ball game. But surely the point is that we are inventing the landscape when we play the game?

In the end, that is the *Human Condition*.

Part 2   Essays in Landscape Theory

Tactile Scale—Visual Scale / 1961

For the pedestrian, the basement, window, and front door, located at eye level, are part of his immediate scene, and are only partly associated with the façade.

The tactile scale is the one in which we move, in which it is required to acknowledge ourselves with precision: to park our car, locate the stairs, and open the door. This scale is not restricted to ourselves, but also includes the dimensions of our instruments' activities (buses, cranes, marker lights for planes, harbor movements along the quay . . .).

This tactile scale is the zone within which the confrontation of imprecise information, transmitted by the eye, must correspond to images registered in our memory to allow ourselves to move easily. The space may not be faked, but at least it may be animated, with the proviso that what is there remains subject to everyday requirements of judgment on distances.

Beyond the tactile scale is the visual scale, a zone in which phenomena, even if they provide us with various sensations, are only visual. In that scale, we do not, as a rule, have utilitarian reasons to encumber ourselves with considerations in regard to the volumes that exist.

Apropos of the Landscape Process / 1978

Trivial, perhaps, but it still needs to be repeated: since the nineteenth century, in the name of pseudo-rationalities professing to be serious, we have put aside sensory knowledge in the course of our schooling, from primary school to university. We have been concerned to forget that man maintained sensory connections with his milieu: sounds, colors, surfaces, volumes, smells, touch, taste. Instead of being the foundation of our education, sensory knowledge is considered as an addition.

Let us take an actual example: integration with landscape. What does the use of that term imply? A willingness for a new construction to disappear as much as possible, through formal similarity, into the landscape context. On the other hand, some inhabitants do not want a pastiche, they prefer to look for a fundamental connection by giving life to a habitat which, as it is, as it is "given" to them, is experienced by them as lacking all links with the individual and with a world of primordial elements. They react to that "given" by an exuberant and rich presence that mingles, in complicated play, bright colors, various types of grain, colored lights, sounds of running water, garden dwarfs on a lawn suggesting a forest, or boats on the edge of a roof recreating the ocean.

Let us not be mistaken: it is a true example of rebellion on the part of the inhabitant against that mutilation of the tangible which materializes as a "frame of life." Others desert everything to discover how to walk barefoot in the water of a stream or run through the forest at night.

If the inhabitant must be able to intervene, he must also be able to dispose of elaborated places. The analysis of that contradiction therefore leads the artist to new ways of intervening. He then has to abide by some conditions. First, it is not possible to extrapolate onto these new scales, the *plastic* practices, sculpture or painting, gained by the study of the "object," taking into account the multiplicity of levels of information to be encountered. Second, the "object" here is a presence open to many other interventions: the landscape. In the end, another condition: the *plastic artist* intervenes either in a group including the representatives of various disciplines, or in a succession of various studies, the materialization of his intervention only being exceptionally identified in a precise way.

The *plastic artists*, who intervene in that field, are concerned about the respective contributions of the new social sciences and thus are confronted with complex processing of information. They try to discover new methods for the approach and elaboration of landscape, to conceive of the only works which can be called social as being those which result from this exchange, because they wish to substitute the restrictive notion of the "frame of life" for the notion of the more open "landscape substratum," because the substratum serves as a support for other existences.

Indeed, plastic artists can propose their direct interventions to the inhabitants, but also, inversely, because they are specialists, put others in situations of creativity, in that way resulting in self-effacement. The artist's role can be to collaborate on the elaboration of a "sensory substratum" (from the presence of the tree to that of the water . . .); to propose methods of intervention on different scales or to attempt new readings of urban reality, allowing in particular the emergence of new *plastic* activities; or, equally, to become a mediator between various sociocultural groups.

13. Part of a vegetable façade among those forming the pyramid-shaped buildings overlooking the nearby urban park. Some panels are references for the optical touch (visual material); those with palms are for viewing at a distance. The panels are cast concrete, with the molds struck off twelve hours after onsite pouring. The first plantings, in pots distributed across the façades, were undertaken at the same time as the construction of the buildings.

In the new town of Evry A, near Paris, with reference to the framework of building 2, I was able to show an articulation between material façade and vegetable façade that illustrated furthermore a possible application for the stimulating scheme at Marne-la-Vallée.

Material Fraction

The scheme of ambiance of phase 1 provided for the narrowest intervals between the buildings, which correspond to the streets, to be treated in the dominant material in order to appeal to the optical touch. That tactile reference would bring the pedestrian still closer to the façades of those places, and the façades to each other, because the material was carried down to the ground, in other words, to the tactile scale itself.

The decision, taken with the architects, to use the dominant material as the main structure for the appearance of the streets of the first phase, led to the proposal to use bricks for the façades facing the road of buildings 1, 2, and 3, and for the treatment of the ground.

If it was possible to consider using part brick for the façades of the envisaged buildings 1 and 3, for economic reasons it was not so for the façades of building 2. That is what induced a treatment of those façades in "false brick," in concrete cast and colored in bulk.

Vegetable Fraction

Before the areas in which vegetation dominates can be experienced as such, three or four years are required, since the vegetation needs time to develop and overgrow the various containers and façades.

In order that this element might already be present for the arrival of the inhabitants in their homes, it seemed necessary not only to effect the planting as quickly as possible, but to signify, on the formal level, the façades as vegetable, using motifs in cast concrete suggesting vegetation.

Depth—A Vertical Beyond Measurement / 1980

The landscape—that which is furthest from us, the final spectacle before the horizon—is, as we know, an assemblage. But we do not necessarily perceive it as such—we see it as a whole whose component elements are hard to separate from one another. The best way of representing this concept is indeed to show how an element can form part of it without being noticed, as in camouflage: so we have military camouflage, or the partridge in a field of corn, or the tiger in the Savannah . . . the "picture" changes, and becomes transformed by the interplay of appearances, by the way in which surfaces are modified in relation to the observer's entry into the "picture," as the stimuli of sight and sound are supplemented by the olfactory and finally the tactile.

The Marquis de Girardin, planning the gardens at Ermenonville, had paintings made of the different horizons that could be seen from the house, and these paintings were later filled in with a range of different foreground elements. He wrote:

> Keep the Painter in your company. If you find that the view from the salon is interrupted by obstacles, climb up to the top of the house. From there, single out within the countryside the backgrounds and distant prospects which afford most interest, and take care to retain whatever there is in the way of constructions or established plantations that can be utilised in the composition of your picture. Then let the Painter make a sketch in which he composes the foreground in relation to the background which the countryside offers you.

In the words of the poet Malcolm de Chazal, "it is the look which is the largest rake." But a look can only retrieve for perception one part of a concrete space. A patch of sky . . . a reflection gathered by the water's side . . . the verges of a forest . . . part of a roof. These are fractions of objects, but they are also representative of the basic elements of landscape—the sky, the forest, and the ocean. The visible offers itself a little at a time, and is itself a mere fraction of what is "hidden," either by the shade of mighty trees, or by the mist rising from the river, or by the line of the hills. Tiny fragments are indeed all we see, even if we are not travelers but familiars of the place.

Strangely enough, the breadth suggested by the term "landscape" extends over a great deal more of the nonvisible than of the visible. We have what is largely an interplay between the "seen" and the "hidden"—between what is directly perceived and what belongs to memory and imagination.

Thus, in certain of Poussin's paintings, which represent landscapes that are unknown to me, I discover personnages illustrating a moment of a scene drawn from the Old or the New Testament, or from Greek mythology: if I recognize the instant shown in the picture, I am also able to recollect its "before" and "after," in other words the whole story.

If I had been familiar with the place that forms the backdrop to this scene, I would have had relatively little difficulty in remembering its hidden places. But if I were a traveler confronted with an unknown place, I would not be able to advance into it and explore it, but would be confined to imagining it—perhaps by analogy with other more or less similar places I have met elsewhere.

The story the personnages suggest to me is a substitute at once for the recollection of the place by someone who knows it well and for the traveler's discovery, which is impossible in the circumstances: it is "before" and "after" working together indissolubly.

Let us look at the classification Francis Ponge proposes in his poem "Landscape":

- The horizon, overscored with accents of mist, seems to be written in small letters with an ink whose degree of paleness varies with the play of light
- As for what is closer to me, I enjoy it no more than if it were a picture
- As for what is even closer, I enjoy it as if it were sculpture or architecture
- Next is the reality of the things that come up to my knees, as if they were my food, which I experience with a feeling of genuine indigestion
- So that finally everything is engulfed in my body and flies out by way of the head, as if it were a chimney issuing forth in the middle of the sky.

The garden and the far-away landscape are in a relation of propinquity to us that corresponds to the distinction between the tactile and the visual scales. In the case of the garden, hands and feet can verify the visual, or even gain prior knowledge of it, "make it grow"; in the case of the landscape, the information remains exclusively visual, not capable of verification and always pushed back toward the horizon. By walking, we turn concrete space into a garden, and the garden into a "landscape" that has been explored.

For a number of years, my interest in different forms of gardens has been particularly captivated by the type that seems to belong entirely outside the world of the specialized gardening magazines, or the aesthetic standards of judging committees.

I have looked at people who had no desire to rise in the social scale by providing their plot of land with the regulation lawn and clipped hedge—the badge of the "group" they thought of themselves as belonging to, or hoped to form part of—but had a concern primarily with "making" something. These people, once they "started speaking," demonstrated their creativity and its consequences in concrete, existential terms.

The enormous number of gardens that are set up around small, modern detached houses demonstrate to us that the art of the garden is without doubt the popular art of today. But, compared with the eighteenth-century garden, what is there for it to open on to? A landscape that is blemished, over-exploited, and not easy to interpret?

What countryside, what horizons can be drawn into the garden? There are some who dare to give an answer. Like Charles Pecqueur, a modern alchemist who places a life-size statue of Snow White, in painted concrete, at the end of his garden. From this point she can contemplate orchards, a railway line, and a rubbish dump, all of which are changed into a deep forest peopled with birds and fawns . . .

Most frequently, it is through miniaturization that these landscapes are created in the midst of the garden, since the miniature is a means of warding off direct exploration by touch. A few sailboats, a lighthouse, a cement boat, or a siren seated on the edge of a pond "are the ocean," just as the stag and deer "are the forest" that also no longer exists. Is this not the same kind of nostalgia that impels others in increasing numbers to take to the ocean with a few square meters of sail, made of plastic admittedly, but without the support of a motor, which is the important thing?

The landscapes that took their basis of articulation from the great forest and the ocean, considered as limitless, exist no longer except in occasional moments. The airplane may have transformed the sea into a lake, but the storm reminds us that it remains a domain beyond measurement.

It is the classical attitude to measurement—measurement that presumes a variable distance from an ultimate degree of wildness—which is now open for debate. Can we keep on making oppositions between measurement by touch (the cottage whose every corner I know with my eyes shut) or by sight (the château with its gallery of mirrors), and the standard of immeasurability offered by the forest? Can we any longer attempt the traditional ways of progressively conquering wildness with constructed forms in the horizontal dimension, such as the topiary hedge, or in a more ironic vein, the "artificial bush" formed from hundreds of balls of enameled metal, in various colors, which is placed between an orthogonal, metal-framed building and a wood?

Is it not worthy of note that the Abbé de Lille's poem *Les Jardins, ou l'art d'embellir les paysages* concludes its defense of the natural garden with a eulogy of the navigator James Cook, who had been massacred two years earlier in the Sandwich Islands?

Numerous figures, from Columbus to Charcot, have carried out this progressive exploration of the horizontal dimension, man's basic sphere of activity. It is no longer possible to have the same ambition as James Cook—to go not only further on Earth than any man had yet been, but as far as it was even possible to go.

Nearly thirty years ago, on 23 July 1969, Neil Armstrong walked on the Moon and saw the Earth.

As the Earth has grown smaller, losing the immeasurable dimension of its landscapes that have submitted to the measurement of machines, techniques, and apparatuses, it should have been transformed into a Garden of Eden or a Garden of Delights. But has it been?

The horizontal dimension is experienced at present as a continuum of man-made installations within which we must live. It is no longer possible to escape—no longer possible to leave everything and set out for the West, like the hero of a Western.

Exploration of the immeasurable in the horizontal dimension is succeeded by the approach to immeasurable verticals: the conquest of space, of the depths of the sea and the earth. The surface we tread upon is also a depth—immeasurable, vertical, and obscure.

Minimal Intervention / 1981

Conference at Gibellina-Nuova, Sicily, September

Pushed aside since the beginning of the century by pseudo-rationalities or rationalities too linear, the debate on the art of the garden and landscape is now being renewed.

Minimal intervention: what is the meaning of those words?

Is it impossible today to rediscover and/or invent a landscape from the one that is blemished, over-exploited, and not easy to interpret?

The cultural renewal of the symmetrical or hierarchical garden, as seductive as it is, must not make us forget that the garden has almost always anticipated the connections between humanity and nature and between society and nature. Therefore the garden, the hypothesis on what, from yesterday and today, will be perpetuated in the sensory approach of tomorrow and its new ways to touch and be moved, is not such a garden before all else philosophical?

To make landscape possible again, that still almost impossible landscape, the first necessity is to speak of it, to speak of it again, and to make it manifest. To suggest a landscape, it is not therefore always necessary to modify, a relief, even slightly, to plant a number of trees, or to widen a river. To say, to show, to make understood, is to propose other readings without changing the constitution of the concrete space. At that point, to develop a place is, by an often important change in the physical space, to try to substitute a planned landscape for landscapes we did not know how to conceive or guess.

Often, we do not know sufficiently what those substitutes take away from us, perhaps for ever, or what they bring to us. An intervention, even a very slight, minute, minimal one, can create landscapes for what was only a heterogeneous succession of objects, or can question again the usual reading of a place. The landscape is nature interpreted.

To reinvent the existing is to rediscover in the use of places what has been obscured from view by habit, perhaps still present but in the process of disappearing. Is it not advisable to rediscover it before it has disappeared, as later generations usually do once they have got beyond the stage of what is called purgatory?

It is required just as much to bring to the visible traces of new practices, the not-yet-identified, to contrast what is considered as heterogeneous (contrast, we know, is a mode of passage), to reduce the effect of time. The landscape is nature aroused.

As an example, let us invoke the use of "plastic mechanisms."

One can introduce into the visual field a heterogeneous blip in the form of a small artificial object. Remember the first appearance of a small red and very noisy tractor in that far-off field down there. Instantly, the old contrasts changed and certain objects considered as heterogeneous, that house with a red roof, became, entirely, elements of landscape hypothesis.

Through the introduction of that artificial object we witnessed a slide toward the natural of all the present elements: a displacement and, at the same time, perhaps an enlargement of the existing field.

At a further stage, the transformation of elements that constitute an existing place leads to the proposal, at the same time as we observe them directly, of hypotheses on their possible evolutions.

In following those proposals through, is it not suitable to use the de-realization of the poetic and the relational approaches of the picturesque so that suddenly a "luminous simultaneity" ap-

14a. "Pruned trees," 1982.

14b. "Un air rosé."

pears through the tangling of the different times of the cloud, the stone, or the tree: a landscape?

To quote Bernardin de Saint-Pierre on his journey to Mauritius: "The art of expressing that nature is so new that the terms have not yet been invented."

Is it not true that any contribution which alters this evolving totality makes it imperative to respond to the implicit constraints—and to what could indeed be called the constraints on freedom, that is to say, the entire field of possibilities which the explicit constraints (those with which urban and landscape functionalism is exclusively concerned) succeed in bringing to light or, alternatively, covering up? In both cases, frustration occurs. The choice of hypotheses and the solutions they enable already permit the imagining of some of those possible whose emergence we will try to bring about. The simple fact of foreseeing an opening—an explicit constraint—brings along many possibilities whose "actual experiences" generate other possibilities: implicit constraints.

The attention to the existing in its movements, and to beyond, in other words, the answers envisaged in the implicit, requires maintaining the potentialities of the place.

The emergence is prepared in the dark just as the seed germinates only in a favorable environment and only grows in interrelation with the ground, water, and air. The insistence in that preliminary phase on the "visible" leads to another notion: the notion of substratum, that is, what makes other existences possible. Not only fundamental elements in their polydynamism are concerned; the matter is also to envisage, still in terms of substratum, the possible connections between inhabitant and substratum and, if necessary, between professional and inhabitant.

However, the point today is no longer to provide one single answer for an elitist culture, but rather several answers for the different socio-cultural groups concerned.

Here we have a new difficulty as formulated by Merleau-Ponty: "There is a way in which culture is informed by perception that allows us to speak of culture being perceived."

That concern for feeling and understanding the interactions of various systems of what surrounds us does not have for its purpose to accept any existing situation, to guarantee such or such a development; on the contrary, the minimal process makes easier, if only a priori by its lightness of physical effect, the insertion into the visible, through a visible or any other sensory approach, of a landscape critique.

The minimal intervention leads thus to the critical landscape, either by showing the absurdity of such concrete space or illustrating its future, or else by suggesting that it could have been different . . .

Analysis can be creative.

Let us be "showmen" and "speakers" of landscapes.

The Heterodite / 1985

Let us consider that we have identified the different entities of a place, from the most intimate and precious retreats to the largest expanses. Thus the moment has come to appreciate heterogeneity and to choose to foreground those entities which present among them the greatest differences, and that in every dimension mentioned.

A plan of the contradictions of landscape entities present on the terrain facilitates the disarticulation of the entities/fractions and then the choice of layers to organize on the places. The term "to organize" indicates that to bring forward a new object, the surface to develop, is not the point here; the point is to constitute an influx, from rediscovered to invented, in a process, a movement, the movement of the place in which it is inscribed.

Then, from the concrete fractions of the landscape entities and the faults parting and opening their oppositions, there will spring, through tiny sensory suggestions, the entirely imaginary entities and all their spaces, from the closest to the most remote.

The deliberate absence of transitions and the importance of the dissociations introduced, facilitates for each visitor who wishes it, the presentation of simultaneity or the successions of presences concrete and/or imaginary, in the order he wishes.

"Is not heterogeneity more welcoming than homogeneity?"

But, despite all these precautions, does heterogeneity still exist? Does not the simple fact of organizing it already make a breach in it? Without speaking of the eventual constant frequentation of the terrain, of its entities?

And also, by the progressive smoothing of some dissimilarities, through familiarity, do we not attend concurrently to the discovery of other differences?

I call that organization of a different type the *heterodite*: the mirror of a particular space.

The Landscape Entity / 1987

From the Parc de la Villette to the Parc du Roi Baudouin in Brussels

Let us consider the attitude, so often adopted, which can be characterized in this way: I cannot, for that development from a "given surface," foresee what will happen on adjacent sites, even if some seem fixed or oriented for a few years. But I can create that "surface" as being able to serve as a referent for the subsequent neighboring interventions or, more simply, to protect it for the sake of its own internal life, from the eventual intrusions of sound, smell, or sight, as from the wind, the cold . . . This can also take the form of a preemptive strike in response to possible threats of intervention. According to this hypothesis, the surface would be treated more or less as a transmitting object, even to the extent of encroaching on neighboring surfaces like a transistor radio on a beach.

Instead, let us go back to the style of approach that tends in multiple ways to go from the interior to the exterior of a place, then from the exterior to its interior.

15a–c. Yesterday to today, the Brabant pasture.

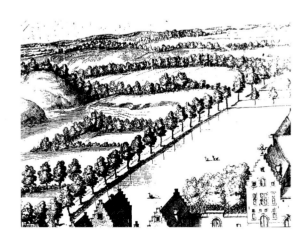

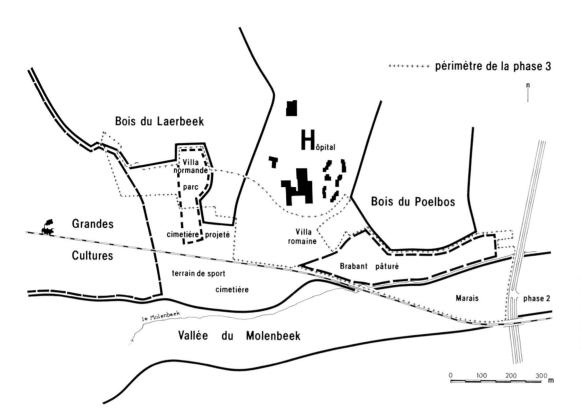

++++++++++ périmètre de la phase 3

n

Bois du Laerbeek

Hôpital

Villa
normande

parc

Bois du Poelbos

Grandes

cimetière projeté

Villa
romaine

Cultures

Brabant pâturé

terrain de sport

cimetière

Marais

phase 2

le Molenbeek

Vallée du Molenbeek

0   100   200   300 m

**15d. Valley of the
Mollenbeek, compe-
tition for the Parc du
Roi Baudouin, Brussels,
1984.**

Before stating what has been mentioned in the magazine *Urbanismes* (215, August–September 1986) under the title "The Choice of a Landscape Entity," it is necessary to say what that term is related to, that is, in the first place, the moment at the beginning of a method of approach, of the development of a place. The place presents itself as a surface at the limits of a fundamental chance, often a bearer, at the time of its supposed freedom, of the dreams and needs of the population, considered as such by the community's representatives. Thus what is involved is a "surface to develop," whether it be the Parc de la Villette or the Garden of Returns at the Corderie Royale in Rochefort. We establish immediately what is going on in those places, the numerous images that haunt them, and those of the person who is asked everything at the same time: what to do, how eventually to do it, and what to put together in that locality.

A first, temporary situation could make an alliance with the geomorphology, as, for instance, the site of La Villette inscribed on the slope of the valley of the Seine going up to Belleville Heights. But we could also retain, as for the Parc du Roi Baudouin in Brussels, a factor like the trees on the edge of a large

wood. The entity becomes at that point the place of several fractions: an island taking the place of a particular rural area, the landscape of the Brabant or the missing place of a Roman villa and its outbuildings. Then we understand that we could develop it not only from the basis of its concrete and visible space alone (the encircling entity like the Bois du Molenbeek), but also from that of its imaginary spaces, by establishing, from the start, that all the fractions and their internal and/or external entities are equal.

So we have to organize from common denominators, fewer rather than more numerous, a weaving of consistencies: for example, by the meaning between the physical discontinuities, between the discontinuities of meaning: the heterodite. In that way, the depth of the surface is introduced, a depth which, through the choices that are made, can become the stratification of different temporalities and thus different landscapes. That depth changes consequently in successive crusts with different thicknesses: a possible awareness for the walker, at the same time or otherwise, of several chosen moments of those places, tied to the hypotheses for the crusts to come, and therefore, a walk

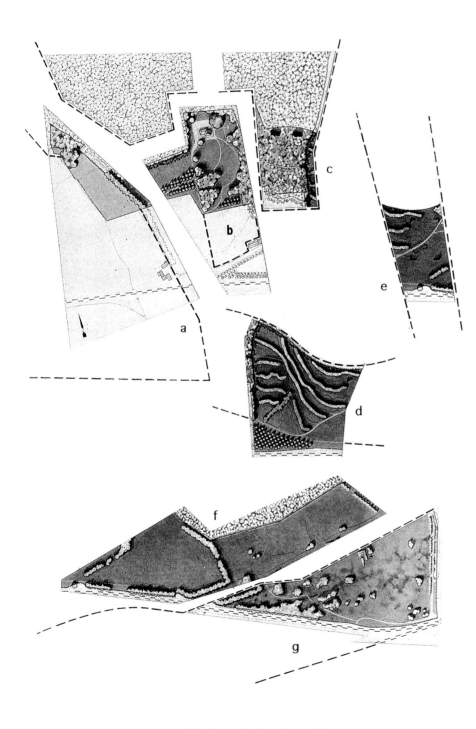

15e. Each area of the park (a–g) has been selected and marked off, either for its resemblance to the nearest external area ("a" becomes part of a large cultivated area; "c" becomes part of the Laerbeek Wood), or so that it rediscovers its most appropriate meaning (for "e," the Roman villa, which like the park of the Norman villa in "b" has disappeared; for "f" the Brabant pasture, which in previous times covered the whole countryside).

no longer at a particular depth but in the past and future thicknesses, a *mille-feuilles* landscape.

The simulation of one entity or another can make possible the credibility of one of the developments of the place whose meaning has been diluted or even destroyed.

Thus the significance of the canal lock at the edge of the site of La Villette, with a ten-meter variation in level: odd for a terrain considered flat in the plan! If that difference of level is added to the hundred-meter variation between Belleville Heights and the Seine, one understands that a reconstructed slope gives a renewed meaning to the canals, to their location, to their intersections, and, through that, also to a ground that has been metaphorically reconstructed.

The landscape entity is the result of a negotiation between the entities' scales, which have come to light through inventive analysis and which as types of different scales do not necessarily tally.

Inventive Analysis / 1989

The place under study is often a surface area that is being pushed to the limits of its luck, since it carries, at the moment when its free development is envisaged and especially if it is a "favored spot," the dreams and needs of the neighbors and the population, as their representatives consider it anyway. Without ado, we establish that numerous images haunt both the sites to be developed and the person of whom everything is asked at the same time: what to do, how to do it, and quite often, how to place too much together in that location.

Inventive analysis consists in going beyond first ignorance, with its feeling of absence or of disorganized accumulations, in order to approach the site in its singularity. This is done, first, by "floating attention": to become impregnated with the site and its surroundings, in the course of long visits at different hours and in different weathers, to soak it up from the ground to the sky until boredom sets in, or almost. To visit that place frequently does not mean to be eager to capture it, but to live a few moments by and with it in its shade, and lights, to read and chat there. Then, to look for the preferential points of view, to discover the micro-landscapes and the perspectives that bind them, to identify and test the visual and tactile scales . . . all the while consulting its memories, localities, tales and local legends, stories and history.

To analyze the existing is also to discover in the use of the places what has been hidden by the erosion of time and is in the

16a. New garden of Mr. Wiesniewski, a "dweller-landscaper."

16b. Mr. Sulek's garden: the mill and town hall of Bruay-en-Artois.

16c. Mr. Pecqueur's garden—"into the forest."

16d. Mr. Pecqueur's garden—Snow White looks at the railway and earth mounds.

process of disappearing. Is it not fitting to rediscover it? To avoid having to reconstruct it immediately or in a few years' time and eventually to maintain its potentiality for new presences. Then to follow the newfound threads, to meet some person bearing precious information, to consult specialists, to invite them to visit the place, be they, for example, musician or ecologist, acoustician or hydraulic engineer . . . but separately so they will not influence each other. It is also necessary to bring to the visible traces of new practices not yet identified: as the non-visible, from the visible to the evident.

Thanks to research funds and the Délégation Générale à la Recherche Scientifique et Technique, gardens since the gardens of the dweller-landscapers have shown us the actuality of the de-measurable, therefore the importance of the poetic in daily life.

Inventive analysis is at no time the renewal of the semblance of system that would begin with what one pursued through rapid enumeration. Rather, it will facilitate, I hope its locating in the presentation joined to some projects.

It is by repeated trial and error, since particular cases are concerned here, that we have to initiate other approaches, or to conduct them according to the circumstances, therefore researches and studies for new hypotheses. Those hypotheses, selected, specified, and tested, become orientations which, strengthened by studies that anticipate the lived experiences of the realization, in particular its conduct, can lead without discontinuity to the organization and its forms (the project), which will enter dynamically into the chosen processes. The invented analysis is the rough plan. Pierre Donadieu in his presentation of our studies in 1985, said: "The form does not come first, it is induced by the articulation of intentions."

Substratum—Support—Contribution / 1989

The problematic of development carried through with respect for the existing can be put in three words.

First, the maintenance of the place's potentialities, of everything that can come out of it (object or momentary state), is the *substratum*, a dynamic patrimony that can be reestablished if degraded, or enlarged to other possibilities.

After exploring the most precise or the most vague dreams carried by the collectivity on those places, considered as less vacant than they appear to be, one can go back in an inverse movement, to the substratum, by looking again at the process and the directions now influenced by the hypotheses of chosen activities, and by sketching the structures of reception (constructed or not).

Sometimes that temporary rupture in the movement does not have to be, because the activities come directly from the substratum, even if they imply reinvesting differently or even partially destroying the abandoned equipment. Then it is fitting to consider what is necessary to dig or to build up again: the whole forming *the support*.

This has to be done, obviously, in the perspective of what the places have already induced by their various lived experiences and are going to induce in the future. The *contribution* aimed at must be not that of a degradation, too usual today, but that of a valorization, which can prove unexpected, from the landscapes of the place and its concrete space.

Is not the best metaphor of that contribution the "concern for beauty" revealed by the presence of the dweller landscapers' gardens in response to the deficiencies of what surrounded them, deficiencies still considered by some of them as equal to visual pollution? The individual critiques represented by these gardens constitute a reproach, as if they were speaking out loud their regret for the total absence of beauty in all that surrounds them.

In the games of "red dots" and "cut out papers" the problem of the "integration" of a new contribution was placed in opposite ways. What does the use of the term "integration" imply, in fact? First, a willingness to receive, by allowing the supposition that the new contribution is partially different from the elements that constitute the existing landscape, and that the contribution is based on as many of the elements as possible by formal similarity in the landscape context.

Consequently, one uses the term "integration" to predict an eventual difference, while at the same time rejecting it even before knowing it, since that difference has to be kept, so that we can avoid considering the implications of a new presence . . . The contribution can then reduce or increase the receptivity of the place. Thus it is not the constitution of a homogeneous landscape, each time reinforced by contributions whose characters are similar to the characters of the constituent elements of the site, that can provide the most favorable reception of the different, thanks precisely to that difference. Only a landscape substratum sufficiently heterogeneous permits the reception of original contributions.

The heterogeneous is more receptive

than the homogeneous.

Landscape Recognition / 1989

To reveal the poetic conduct employed by a good number of the residents in their suburban gardens, between façades and fence, is also to propose other landscapes in the suburban habitat.

To present a set of photographs showing the aspect of a beach or the barks of a group of pines at every moment of an afternoon, or to make people hear a walk in the Foire du Trône, is also to try, by a sensory approach, to suggest an immeasurable moment.

In order to suggest a landscape, it is not therefore necessary to modify a relief even slightly, to plant a few trees, or to enlarge a river.

To say, to show, to make heard, means to propose other readings of what surrounds us, without modifying the physical presence.

To develop a site is also to try to substitute landscapes we perhaps did not know how to perceive, imagined landscapes. However, we do not know sufficiently what those substitutions deprive us of, or provide us with!

The foreseeable transformation of the elements that form an existing place leads to the proposition, parallel to their direct observation, of some hypotheses on their possible evolution.

An intervention, even a very slight, minute one, can bring landscapes to light from a series of objects, or challenge a usual landscape reading of a place.

From the beginning of the study for the recreation area in the new town of Marne-la-Vallée, I realized, while walking in the Parc du Château de Champs-sur-Marne, that we could hear the continual noise of cars in the middle of that garden *à la française,* which was surrounded by numerous trees. Therefore I proceeded with a series of sound surveys on the whole future area, which revealed the passage of the numerous airplanes, the level of the noise of cars and, above all, the sounds of a power plant, situated on the east of the site.

Subsequently, I questioned the people who frequently visited the site: fishermen, people who had discovered this place over the years and who came on Sundays for a walk. Those people did not hear the cars or the planes! In any case, it was probably unthinkable for them to be able to hear those noises, insofar as, having been lucky enough to discover a "wild" spot, in which they could spend their Sundays with their children, to be aware of those noises would have ruined their discovery and forced them to observe the deteriorated banks, the abandoned car wrecks, the greasy discarded papers . . .

Another point: if we imagined that this place would really become a recreation area advertised by leaflets and signposts, where visitors pay 10 francs for a ticket, would they not in that case hear the sound of planes while having their picnic on the grass?

I had put forward a proposal to place a little further in the wood, in the center of the wildest zone of the site, located not far from the famous Meunier chocolate factory on the bank of the Marne, a panel that announced: "Courtesy of the west wind, chocolate mousse." In reality, via the wind, a delicious smell of chocolate extended into the undergrowth.

Thus it was out of the question to isolate the fraction of the site called "wild," even if extended, from those smells and noises, particularly those of the power plant, which invaded a third of the site's surface.

par vent d'Ouest...
MOUSSE AU CHOCOLAT

17. The recreation area at Marne-la-Vallée, 1975–78. Located along the Marne, the succession of ponds and woods that constitute the recreation area is situated downwind of a famous chocolate factory. The smell of chocolate mousse, via the west wind, pervades the woods and replaces the smell of leaves, mushrooms, and moss.

I planned to build, facing the power plant, a high ramp that would have minimized the noises and would have been topped by a crenellated tower, partly collapsed. As with the trumpets of Jericho, the power plant, with its noise, would have succeeded in destroying the tower.

Theory of Faults / 1989

Today from the lowered window of my car, parked at the "viewpoint" (just as yesterday from the concave bench of the belvedere), my broad gazes are followed by more focused looks that bring back to the domain of perception some fragments of the concrete space (according to Malcolm de Chazal, it is the look which is the greatest rake), a fragment of cloud with a suggestive shape . . . a height of foliage . . . a fleeting brightness, that reflection on a smooth surface, the water of a pond or a slate roof. Thus some cracks enter the landscape, up to now a unity, cracks that urge us to imagine what is hidden by the shade of those tall trees, or the mist in the hollows, or the terraced superimpositions of the hill slopes. The abstract surfaces, green or chestnut-colored, become by those attempts at recognition fractions of objects more guessed at than visible. Beneath that mist . . . swamps or a river. Behind that roof and that hill . . . other houses probably . . . perhaps even a town.

Curiously, in an instant, that vast visible expanse has split, revealing wider and more numerous, darker, and deeper cavities: fluid boundaries of a game between the "seen" and the "hidden," between the imaginary and the recalled, boundaries depending on my status as foreigner or familiar to those places.

One discovers then the importance that the sound of an unseen torrent can have, or the scent of flowers hidden by an undulation in the terrain. To the subtle enmeshing of the shown with the hidden add that of the near and the remote. Why not, then, as in the Lainé warehouse, suggest landscapes to the visitors, in turn and with different sounds, since they are contemplating only one, and that no more than a camouflage netting.

In that moment, smells, sounds, and images connect with my memories and with my state of mind to create something else, THAT LANDSCAPE, conclusively disconnected from the objects that have made it possible, but not entirely dissociated from them. Because, despite the expanse and the distance, I still vaguely think of being able to step forward here and there, to verify, with my hands and feet, whether the substance promised is real.

It is precisely between the factors of the "disconnected" and the "dissociated" that THAT LANDSCAPE is situated, since at the precise moment when it dissociates totally from the concrete space it becomes more general: THE LANDSCAPE, the one of the camouflage netting and, if it moves still further away, the one of the cassette tape or the painting.

In some paintings by Nicolas Poussin, representing landscapes that are unknown to me, I discover characters that illustrate the crucial moment of a scene referring to the Old and New Testaments, or to Greek mythology. Since the moment evoked by Poussin has not for the time being triggered off the mechanism of memory, I am looking at places that are as unknown to me as the characters. What monument is that on the top of that rock cliff? Where does the shady river that it overhangs come from? What does that high hill conceal? If, on the contrary, the story is recognized, what a pleasure! The global recollection of those adventures carries along in its wake, by its very movement, the evocation of different places where it could have happened, and makes identifiable certain hidden places in the painting. Let us proceed no further than the hypothesis of the story not recognized or known, in order to explore the paintings of Poussin through play and as homage to the painter, but play of the hidden and the shown . . . in 1980.

A visitor enters the square room where *The Four Seasons* is exhibited. According to André Félibien, each painting shows a subject drawn from the Holy Scriptures. For spring, it is Adam and Eve in the Garden of Eden. For summer, Ruth, who, having arrived from Bethlehem with her mother-in-law Naomi at harvest time, picks ears of corn in Boaz's field. For autumn, two of the Israelites, whom Moses had sent to reconnoiter the land of Canaan and bring back its fruits, return laden with a bunch of grapes of extraordinary size. And, for winter, Poussin has painted the Deluge. In that painting the sky, the air, and the earth are of the same color. Men and animals all seem soaked with rain and the light is only visible through the thickness of the water, which falls with such an abundance that it prevents the daylight from getting through.

Coming closer, the visitor discovers that the painting is slowly changing: while the foreground moves almost imperceptibly, the middle ground moves, too, but in an opposite direction and slightly faster. As for the background, it moves still more rapidly than the foreground and in the same direction. Thus there appear progressively one after another all the hidden elements of the painting. Of course, at the same time, some of these elements are temporarily hidden. Let us add that in that movement the characters, interdependent with the ground on which the painter has placed them, only rediscover their initial places at the rare moments when the relative positions of the ground are again in agreement with the original composition and merge into it.

This kinetic project permitted me to suggest an interpretation of the hidden element of the paintings of the seasons, but that investigation remains solely visual. Therefore I will not return to my belvedere under any pretext if I wish to discover concretely what lies behind those tall trees.

The Faults

The revelation of faults in order to separate, to dissociate the fractions of entities, is linked to my hypothesis that we can only act at present in the encirclable, by which I mean in a world that has become limited, in which there no longer exist truly unknown spaces to explore. Consequently, we have to try to find in terms of the places themselves the possibility for a spacing out, more or less encirclable, extending from the most concrete to the most imaginary.

Let me return to the concept of a fault.

In a stained glass window, the lead encloses colored fractions both to dissociate them from other colored surfaces and to associate them within the same colored surface. The lead that separates thus makes possible the enlargement, otherwise technically impossible, of a fraction of colored light.

If we transpose that phenomenon into the field of landscape, we see that the intensity of the fragment of blue and red glass corresponds to a concern for creating a thick space, completely present but a place whose boundaries are determined in relation to the treatment of its "colored surface" (the entity whose part it is), or to the choice of multiple entities and the way they are arranged in sequence.

Now it remains to study thoroughly the problem of the limit between two places, a limit that I have chosen to call a "fault." Unlike the stained glass window, it must be, as far as the landscape is concerned, not "lead" simultaneously separating and uniting "colored glass," but the disjunctions and the plurality of disjunctions between fractions of entities. But, since the entities of a world from now on encirclable are totally limited in their boundaries, their co-existence necessarily makes them associated: so the Ocean is no longer an unknown dimension indefinitely deferred but a small surface of salt water visible in its entirety from a satellite. A forest is no more a den for wild and ferocious beasts, a place where it is impossible to venture without getting lost, because we know that wolves run away from human beings and that roads and towns are always nearby. No need, therefore, to homogenize the different fractions present in a place in order to emphasize their common features facing an immeasurable absent horizontal, and so humanize them, because their entities are already homogenized.

If one lingers a little bit longer on the role of the "fault," one can show that it allows several ways of proceeding.

Representing an "emptiness" opposed in relative terms to several "fullnesses," the fault not only offers the entities' fractions the possibility of becoming isolated in their limited surface and on their own scale; but furthermore, through the discontinuity it installs, it offers the opportunity for those same fractions to invest (as fractions belonging to entities) the adjacent fractions, at least for some of their factors.

The painter Georges Rouault has already enlarged the "lead" to the point of rupture between two segments of color in order to remain on the two-dimensional plane while stretching the surface. I propose here to introduce the same kind of rupture. The horizontal spacing thus changes into a vertical tension.

What will come out of the faults? That started in 1972 with "The Well."

We can already note that faults can be constructed according to two basic modalities. The first modality is based on the choice of stratifications: the faults are then horizontal, separating the diverse strata into thicknesses and allowing the interlacing of adjacent entities, because their fractions in a place do not have a scale linked to these fractions. The other modality results in a fault in depth created in the dimension of verticality and magnifying the isolated elements. An answer to the encirclable would then be the creation of stratified isolated elements separated by ruptures. Therefore one sees clearly that this process is situated in the vast movement of the return to the local.

The different entities of the place, from the most intimate and precious refuges to the widest expanses—let us consider them now as identified. Little by little, between the concrete fractions of landscape entities, and from their faults, will emerge, by minute sensory suggestions, entities that are entirely imaginary, with all their spaces, from the closest to the most remote. The deliberate absence of transitions and the importance of dissociations will allow visitors to introduce, as they please, some "presences," whether successive or simultaneous, concrete or imaginary. I repeat, heterogeneity is more receptive than homogeneity.

At the beginning, nature was wild. That first nature, progressively, has become "second" by the human conquest of the horizontal. Would it not become "third" as a result of the reinvention of all its strata and the sensory appropriation of its depth?

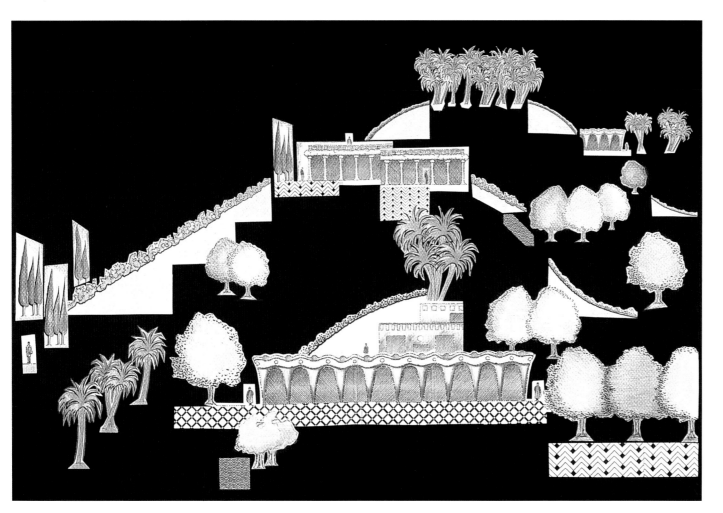

9. General principle of landscape development, City of Nimes, 1989. In diverse spots of the city of gardens will be images of the city of Nimes, all linked specifically to their district. Schematically 50 percent of their surface would be treated in response to the most local issues, and the remaining 50 percent used for building up the image, "Nimes garden." The shade of the trees will be the color of their flowers; thus under the *Paulownia tomentosa* the ground will be blue, and . . .

10. The Garden of Returns, Rochefort-sur-Mer, 1982–87. From the seventeenth century ships sailed from Rochefort to America, returning laden with plants that today are acclimatized to France. The former military arsenal, the Corderie Royale, has become a botanical arsenal and symbol for a new Horticultural activity, through one plant, the begonia, whose name is taken from that of a Rochefort governor, Mr. Bégon. Since the construction of the garden, Rochefort now describes itself as a "horticultural town." (a) Between the luminous vegetable loopholes, a moment of shadow; (d) the mast of the sailing ship rebuilt as before.

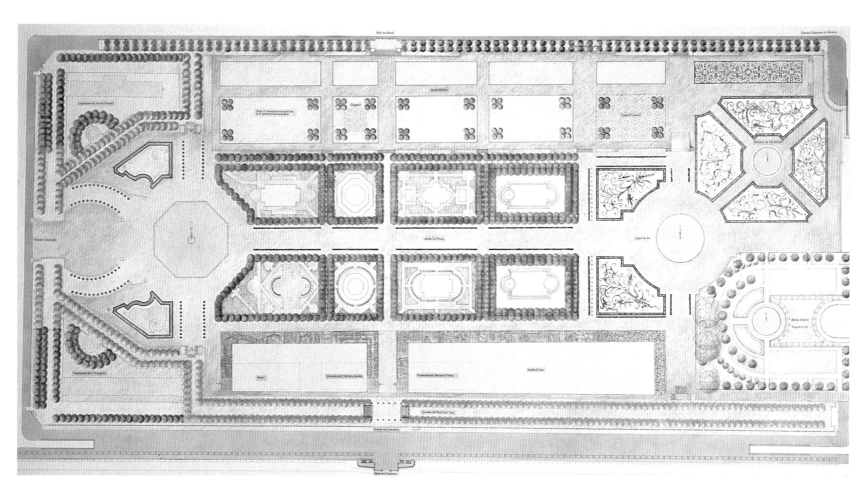

11. The Tuileries, a re-invented garden, 1990. Through the passage of time, in the center of Paris, various gardens are layered over this surface. All have to be present and brought together in a new proposal: a poetic archaeology. (a) The contemporary contribution, besides these historical strata, would be a water garden seen from the riverside terrace and a series of fountains seen from the garden. (b) Evidence of the various strata; cross-section at the bottom. (c) The garden of the Tuileries is not set out in relation to the Seine. (d) Along the rue de Rivoli, some colored hedges.

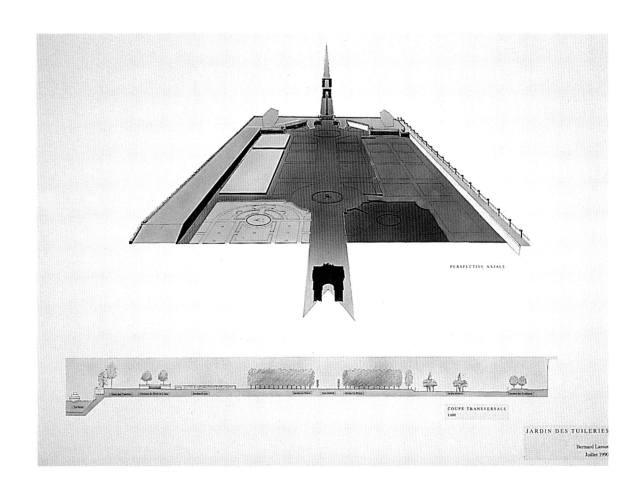

PERSPECTIVE AXIALE

COUPE TRANSVERSALE
1:600

JARDIN DES TUILERIES

Bernard Lassus
Juillet 1990

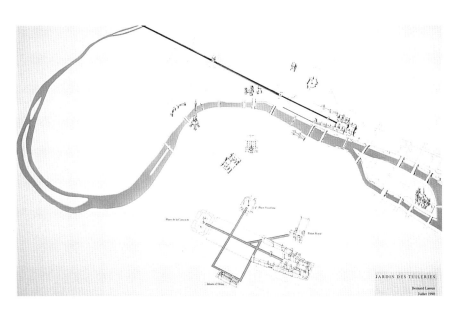

Place de la Concorde
Place Vendôme
Palais Royal
Musée d'Orsay

JARDIN DES TUILERIES

Bernard Lassus
Juillet 1990

12. The park at Duisburg-Nord, 1991. To symbolize the Ruhr revival by giving a new meaning to the water, between ice and steam, the possibility of an everyday life. (a) The river Emscher is very polluted, and because the water symbolizes the Ruhr, . . . (b) The A areas correspond to the demands of the inhabitants who are neighbors of the park; B corresponds to the museographed factory; C is the reconstitution of the river Emscher before the factory was built; D corresponds to a series of experiments between ice and steam. (c) Tomorrow. (d) Yesterday. (e) The time before yesterday.

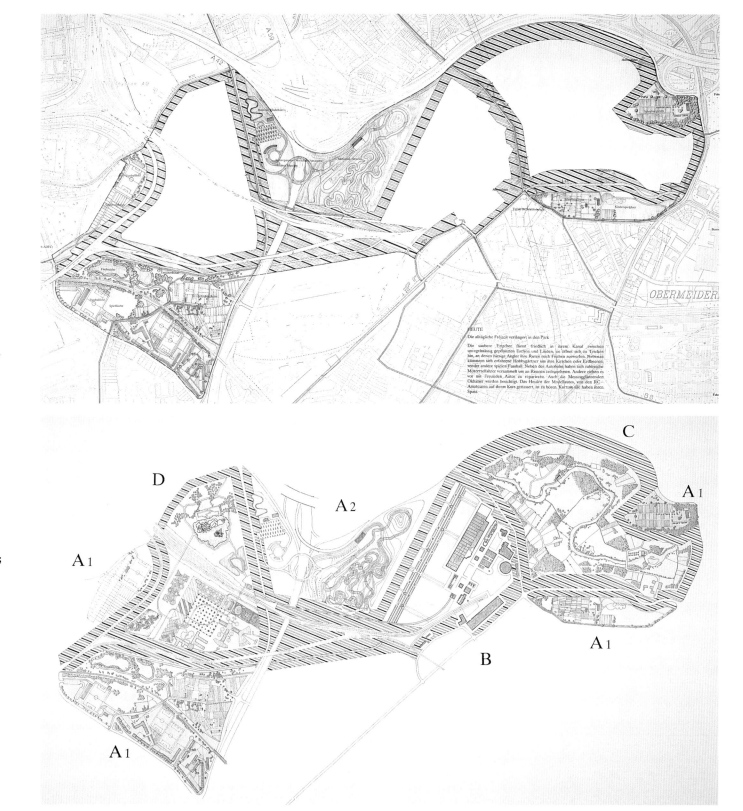

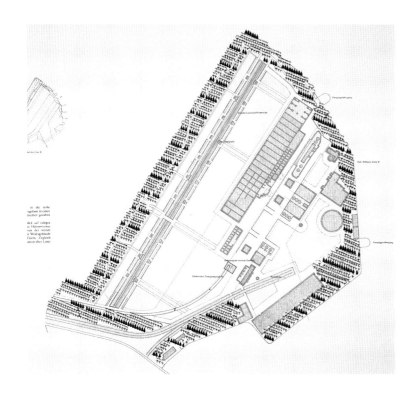

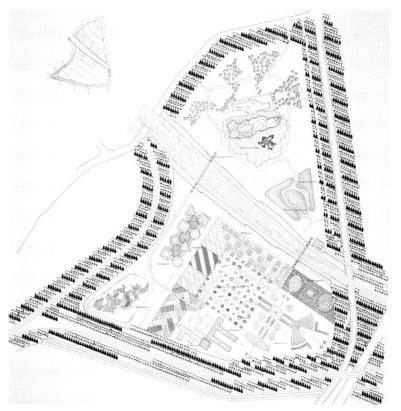

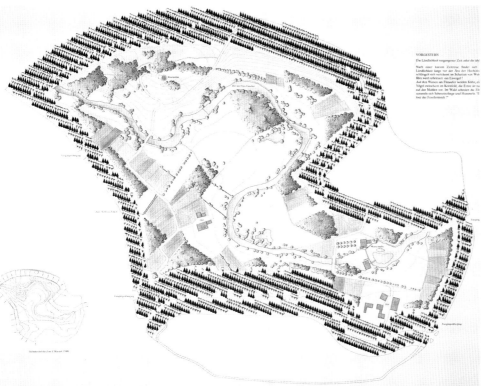

VORGESTERN

Die Ländlichkeit vergangener Zeit oder die idy...

Nach einer kurzen Zerreisse findet sich
Ländlichkeit lange vor der Ära der Hochtec...
schlängelt sich verträumt im Schatten von Weh...
Blitz wird reflektiert am Eisvogel?
Auf den Wiesen am Flussufer weiden Kühe, e...
Vögel zwischen im Kornfeld, die Ernte ist na...
auf den Matten vor. Im Wald schreien die El...
sammelt sich Schmetterlinge und Hummeln. "F...
fort der Forellenbach."

13. A landscape slope, the rest area of Nîmes-Caissargues, 1992. The rest area must serve not only travelers and their cars but the highway; it must urge travelers to discover the land as they pass along. An avenue 700 meters long (twice the size of the green carpet at Versailles) crosses the highway and captures travelers' attention. The authentic theater columns of Nîmes (the town close to the highway) and the metallic belvedere, whose silhouette imitates that of the Tour Magne (one of the oldest monuments in Nîmes), where one can also see a stone replica of the same tower, are mirror games of Nîmes.

14a. The optical bushes,
1993.

14c. A mirror placed obliquely ensures floral continuity from one line to the next.

14b. Study on the theme of the spectrum, 1962.

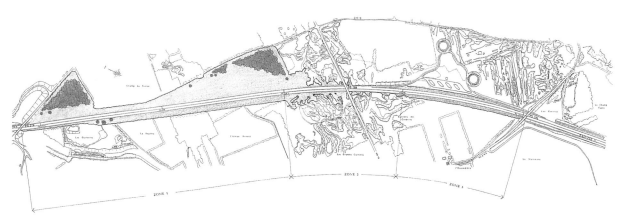

15. Plan of the crossing of the Saintes-Rochefort highway at the place called the Quarries at Crazannes (Carrières de Crazannes).

The Heterogeneous / 1989

Once vision, the only sense that was capable of covering the full range of the measurable and showing the horizon, was a metaphor for unique power.

Once the most measurable elements of the wild and the immeasurable had been clearly pointed out, it is from, and for, that privileged sense of sight that the following could be represented in subtle variations and differentiated symmetries: the taming of unsightly and barren ground, the domestication of the odd tree, of shapeless rock and impetuous waters.

Nowadays, it is the control of man over nature that is valued in the process of being illustrated. To be more precise, we can almost separate in two the distance distinguishing "the château" from the horizon. The first distance, which is closest to the building, is clearly treated in terms of visual dominance, but with essential references to the tactile, the second, leading to the wild, almost uniquely on the visual scale.

For the first distance, we follow a progression from more to less measurable as we move away from the château, hence an elaboration of transitional elements, like the trees, from more to less clipped.

The arrival at the final limits of the immeasurable horizontal corresponds to the triumph of the process of the art of the classical garden. In other words, the representation of new states of progress in the conquest of nature by the elaboration of new transitions toward the wild horizontal dimension has now lost any connection with the real world. Indeed, the Earth is now completely discovered.

The initial importance in the horizontal plan of the contrast between an omnipresent immeasurable and a slightly extended measurable, a real gap to fill, involved the necessity of developing a style. The style of the classical garden proposes to move forward by successive levels closely connected with one another from the most certain to the most remote, from which is discovered, close-up, the horizon . . . the unknown.

The measurable now being closed in on itself, many people acknowledge that a utilization for internal use of what had been elaborated to symbolize the movement of discovery did not suit that concrete limited space, which proved to have fallen to pieces (an apparent paradox) when it was taken up again.

That reversal has meanwhile given birth to other inventions, but always in the visual field. If the changes of view were formerly linked to the changes of the horizon, and thus to the progress of the discoverer, the present position is a seated one as the discoverer follows the development of moving images on the television screen.

Although obviously very different, these processes both imply the greatest variety of sensory forms. This postulate is not far from what I have called since 1966 a certain "complexity." I remind you briefly here that simplicity can be complex and complexity simplistic. Thus, in order to avoid prolonging this debate, I shall stick to the term "variety." It is also the term used by Fernard Léger to explain his procedure.

I have already made it clear that no site is ever a blank surface; thus it is not possible to apply to it a unifying organization, which, in order to reduce the heterogeneous, would tend to destroy the knowledge of it still more.

Let us be precise. How can we proceed if we are always desirous of using plastic possibilities for the creation of variety? First, we establish the heterogeneity of the various disaggregated components of the place where it is planned to intervene. In that way, we have identified and sketched the limits of the most obvious "scraps," others will perhaps emerge in the progress of the study. All efforts then work toward discovering the most specific potentialities connected to their own specific spaces. The principal characteristic of each "scrap" once chosen can be designated henceforth by the term "fraction." That characteristic will be consolidated by one or more secondary characteristics selected because at the same time they reinforce the contrasts already present from fraction to fraction. That mutual valorization of each of them, by amplification of the contrasts, will tend, while dissociating them still further, to transform each fraction into an isolated element surrounded by faults.

In that approach resides the movement of the return to the local and the search for new specific places.

The Obligation of Invention / 1993

From Landscape to Successive Ambiances

The dissociation that has now become widely established between landscape and concrete space hides another one, between appearance and concrete space, and that for two reasons: one relative to their respective scales, the other to the omission of the evocative power of appearance.

Now that daily life has been overwhelmed by this process, would it not be time to try to illuminate the relationships between landscape, appearance and concrete space, for those who are interested in landscape through development?

Visual Appearance and Tactile Discovery

If, while walking in 1961[1] along the quays of the port in Stockholm, I suddenly saw before me the silhouette, which had remained until then invisible, of an imposing warship, it is undoubtedly because, in the background beyond the ship was the landscape of the port. That had helped the thin layer of paint (akin to a paratrooper's battledress) covering the ship to play the role of camouflage, that is, to destroy, through mimesis, the appearance of the boat for the benefit of an ensemble in which the vegetable element dominated that of the port all the way to the horizon. Such a silhouette could only be perceived in that port, because it appeared suddenly in the same line as if it was a piece of that landscape, and revealed its scale at the same time. In the open sea it would not be the same.

To that first shock was added a second, the fact of seeing, over against a mass of several thousand tons of metal, a thin layer of paint. Then a third, necessitating that I retrace my steps in order to assist it, because of the change of distance and point of view of that disappearing, which I recorded with three indissociable photographs: two showing the landscape in which, although omnipresent, the ship was not visible, the last one revealing abruptly the shape of the ship alongside the quay. In the case of that ship, irrespective of the camouflage colors relating to the vegetable world in lights and shades, it is the scale of the fractionalization as well as the dominant colors that induced the obliteration of the limits of the "ship" outline. Thus there was a scale of common reading between the internal fractions of the camouflaged ship and the port as far as its horizon. The fractions as isolated appearances were vaguely reminiscent of numerous objects built or planted, indeed, but they were also an ensemble of numerous specific shapes, although with indeterminate meanings. Hence the gargantuan shock of the ship entity appearing suddenly, in its own scale, out of the landscape of the port. If the port had been covered with snow and the ship painted white, there would probably have been also the elimination of the proper limits of the ship, but that effect would have been fragile, resting only on the common denominator of the white. The slightest shadow produced would have revealed its presence.[2]

In that movement of retracing my steps, standing back, then coming forward again toward the ship, began the discovery of concrete space, a movement that incites us to go and check with our finger whether, in entering a landscape, some object,

---

[1] *Landscape Journal* 12, 21 (Fall 1993): 103, 181; see "Stockholm: The Landscape," this volume.

[2] Heterogeneity is more receptive than homogeneity; Lassus, *Jeux* (Paris: Galilée, 1977).

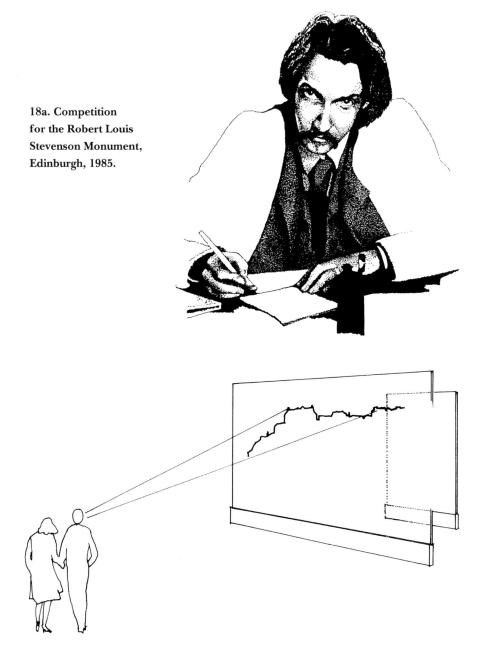

18a. Competition for the Robert Louis Stevenson Monument, Edinburgh, 1985.

guessed from a fragment of its appearance, corresponds truly to our expectation.

From a wider look, the landscape is thus a reading that crystallizes the fractions of appearances. Halfway, one can wonder about the nature of these fractions, of that toward which one is making one's way: that maroon stain has the appearance of being the roof of a house, but can be the appearance of a truck's canvas cover or the autumn foliage of a chestnut tree. Close up, it is just a simple wall in the sun, with the distance of the wall of a few moments ago in its appearance, which is superimposed in my memory on the fraction of the previous landscape.

The elaboration of the appearance can thus be oriented as well in its relation to the object as in its relation to the possible landscapes by a play of fractions between appearances.[3] That notion of an ensemble of fractions of appearances forming a landscape is a drawer full of imaginary landscapes, whose concreteness is not verified, nor, obviously, its visual appearances in situ.

I explored that inversion of camouflage in the project put on at the Lainé warehouse in Bordeaux in 1979–1980 (the Entrepôt Lainé, now the Bordeaux Museum of Contemporary Art), where I combined a huge camouflage canvas with, placed before it, a desk at which, by pushing buttons, it was possible to select a sound: seagull cries, wind in the pines, etc. Thus by summoning up his own memory, the experimenter with the mechanism could transform the camouflage canvas into a succession of imaginary landscapes, chosen according to an ensemble of landscape possibilities suggested by the sounds.

[3] Lassus, *Villes, paysages, couleurs en Lorraine* (Paris: Mardaga/Batigère 1990).

Now I go back to my approach in order to confront the visual appearance with what will be apprehended in tactile terms, that difference between visual appearance and tactile discovery of the concrete results in a "going toward."

I move forward in the direction of the current, evaluating at each step the spot on which to place my next step.

At certain moments diverse choices are posed. Here I prefer a more linear progress, chopped by vertical ruptures, or there, a more horizontal, though extremely sinuous, course. Compared to those of a walk through town, these movements have length and depth at the same time. With each step, in varying proportions, and/or interchanged.

The question is rarely posed as clearly, since the nature of that on which I walk is not given, but there to discover. Reflections, dark depths of water . . . luminous bottoms . . . at what depth will I strike the bottom? Will it support my weight? Hence the preference conceded to what appears the hardest: rock. And, will this rock be slippery in spite of my striated rubber soles?[4]

Why that insistence on tactility, if it is not because we know that new landscapes will no longer be offered to our sight, extracted via the discovery of oceans, as were those of Cook?

Nowadays television is giving us access to many things; therefore as landscapers we really have to make contact, to be interested in things, to encounter them in order to create them out of the dominance of visuality. The finitude of the world leads us to go beyond the nostalgia of discovery in order to approach the effective invention of things, of materials, of their sounds and their new appearances.

That new concrete space will thus be available for perhaps new landscapes. On the contrary, one could also start, for the elaboration of parts of that concrete, from specific landscape hypotheses.

The revelation of the necessity to give shape to the concrete world has led me lately to consider a distinction between tactile scale and visual scale, that is, between a scale where it is possible to confront the visual information with physical presence, and another where the phenomena are only visual.

That the tactile scale is linked to everyday life by a direct encounter with things, I shall take, for example, perception in an urban milieu. The tactile scale is the one in which we move, in which it is required to locate ourselves with precision: to park our car, locate the stairs, and open our door. This tactile scale is the zone within which the confrontation of imprecise information, transmitted by the eye, must correspond to images registered in our memory, in order to allow ourselves to move easily. The space may not be faked, but at least it may be animated, with the proviso that what is there remains subject to everyday requirements of judgment on distances.[5]

Above and beyond the tactile scale is the visual scale, a zone in which phenomena, even if they provide us with various sensations, are only visual.

When one goes in search of landscape's objects, diverse things offer themselves for verification. Simultaneously those things,

[4] Lassus, *Fluidités*, Urbi VIII (Paris: Mardaga, 1983), 74–75.

[5] Lassus, *Polychromie architecturale*, Cahier 423 (Paris: Centre Scientifique et Technique du Bâtiment, 1961).

by evoking others and participating in them, can be inserted in other ensembles, not obvious at the beginning, and be reminiscent of strata of entities not necessarily present in totality on the places of exploration, but which, nevertheless, each take a certain extension, more or less well-defined.

Those objects, regrouped in categories, belong to proper and different scales corresponding to entities that are spatially abstract, that cannot be grasped by a broad look, as can a landscape. In certain conditions, however, they can evoke imaginary landscapes, as the dweller-landscapers have discovered for themselves on the scale of their tiny gardens.[6]

The Landscape Entity

While studying a project for the third phase of the Parc du Roi Baudouin in Brussels in 1984, I was able to see that the surface of the park was composed of fractions of very different elements: one of the oldest woods on the outskirts of Brussels, an old reed bed, places considered as the image of the typical landscape of Brabant (meadows, hedges of poplars, and cows), the whole lot on a slope. Instead of constituting the park as a new object on that slope, the aim of my proposal was to dilute its limits so that the fractions of the elements would be fortified in their differences. My proposal allowed that surface to be the public fraction of a public-private space: the *landscape entity* of the slope of the valley of the Mollenbeek, the local river.

In that way I avoided adding a supplementary object in that place (the park) where there were superimposed already, in addition to the fractions of tangible elements previously mentioned, fractions of other elements, imaginary this time, like the old mills and the archaeological remains of the Roman occupation—those elements being themselves fractions, or rather, remains of different superimposed moments of that site.

My proposal was, at that moment of my process, not to add another fraction (or object), not to destroy one of the previous remains, but, on the contrary, to reveal their successive and simultaneous presences in a chosen expanse (the landscape entity[7]), by the very existence of its characteristics linked to a morphological fraction: one of the portions of one of the slopes of the Mollenbeek valley.

Other places: other entities, rarely linked with the surface planned for the intervention. At the beginning of the study of the recreation area of the new town of Marne-la-Vallée,[8] the general hypothesis was that the image of a recreation area can correspond, before any notion of activity, to the notion of a place called "natural." While walking across the park of the château at Champs-sur-Marne, I realized that in the middle of that garden *à la française*, surrounded by numerous trees, a continuous sound of cars was clearly audible. Therefore I proceeded with a series of sound surveys on the whole area that revealed the passage of

[6] Lassus, *Jardins imaginaires* coll. Les Habitants-Paysagistes (Paris: Presses de la Connaissance/Weber, 1977).

[7] Lassus, "Les Continuités du paysage," *Urbanismes* 250 (September 1991): 64–68; "Le Choix de l'entité paysagère," *Urbanismes* 215 (August–September 1986): 143–45.

[8] Lassus, "Schéma d'ambiances paysagères—Ville nouvelle de Marne-la-Vallée," 1982.

18b. Gibellina, Italy, 1982. After the 1968 earthquake the town was rebuilt some distance away. What shall we do with the ruins, which must bear witness to the old Gibellina?

numerous airplanes, the intensity of the noise of the highway, and a thermal power plant, situated on the east of the site. Subsequently, I questioned the people who frequently visited this place (fishermen, people who had discovered this spot through the years and who came on Sundays for a walk). Those people did not hear either the cars or the planes! It was probably out of the question for them anyway to be able to hear those noises. Having been lucky enough to discover that "wild" place, to be attentive to that sound nuisance would in effect have destroyed their discovery and forced them to see the deteriorated banks, the car wrecks, the greasy bits of paper . . .

Let us imagine that this place would really become a recreation center advertised by leaflets and signposts at the entrance: would they not hear, then, the sounds of planes while eating their picnics on the grass?

In the center of the "wildest" zone of the site, located not far from the Meunier chocolate factory, beneath the breeze a delicious smell of chocolate spread through the undergrowth.

It would not have been judicious to isolate the fraction of the site called "wild" of that rather extensive area (of the order of 350 hectares) from those smells and noises. Rather I was tempted to exalt its presence. Facing the power plant, a high ramp crowned by a crenellated tower, partially collapsed, would have produced a critical response stigmatizing the noises and, just as at Jericho, the power plant, with its noises, would have succeeded in destroying the tower.

Further, in the wood, in the center of the wildest zone of the site, a panel would announce: "Courtesy of the west wind, chocolate mousse."

Minimal Intervention

The fact that a place exists before one proposes to do something to it has repercussions on the nature of the intervention and poses, in a radical way, the question of knowing whether or not one has to intervene. On September 14, 1981,[9] Senator Ludovico Corrao had confided in Lucius Burckhardt and myself, at a conference in Gibellina-Nuova, in Sicily, in order to try to determine how to preserve the ruins of the old town in the mountain a few kilometers away, which had been entirely destroyed at the time of the 1968 earthquake. To try to evaluate the possibility of a

[9] Lassus, "L'Intervention minimale," *Traverses* 26 (October 1982): 148–51; "L'Intervento minimo—Il giardino del passato," *D'Ars* (Milan) 99 (July 1982): 12–23; "L'Intervention minimale," *Archivert* 12 (2d trimester 1982): 28–31; "Minimal Intervention," this volume.

physical intervention, we proposed the concept of *minimal intervention*, and to introduce that concept I chose to mention my work on the tulip.

Belonging to the family *Liliaceae*, the tulip has a caducous perianth shaped like a bell and divided in six. It blooms alone at the top of its erect stalk. Let us say it is red. But is there anything else? To try to enlarge on what I know about it, with a pair of scissors, I take a sheet of white card and cut out a narrow strip whose width is less than the internal diameter of the flower. This allows me to insert it right to the bottom of the bell while still retaining a part of the card outside. I hold the strip delicately, in such a way that it neither brushes against the walls or the petals, nor touches the bottom of the bell. This action allows me to ascertain that the white surface plunged deepest into the floral volume has become rose, a rose which, as it approaches the upper part of the flower, becomes lighter in color. "Un air rosé."

That reflection of light inside the tulip reveals to me, in a flash, that the rose hue is only the sign, the mark, and that it is the totality of the volume into which I have plunged that strip of card that is rose. The reason is very simple: the light reflecting on the petaloid divisions from one to the other, in a play of multiple reflections, each time coloring with a little more red, has formed a volume of colored light.

Then I just as delicately withdraw the card from the tulip. If the flower appears to be the same, it is not and no longer will ever be.

Is not also the landscape a deepened knowledge in the tangible of what the concrete, a certain apprehension of what is and was there, can offer? It is not thus necessary that a physical transformation occur for there to be a landscape intervention. From that point of view, the minimal intervention is to bring other tangible dimensions to the already there.

But must the cardboard be left in the tulip? And if it has to be, on what conditions? Those questions appear to me all the more interesting because in the tulip of France itself they propose to develop a national highway network.

The Indivisible Places

To intervene in a place, to find a form for the passage of a highway, for example, has nothing to do with the fact of passing through there or not. To create a highway, however beautiful it may be, in a place where it should not pass, does not solve that problem of passage, which is the most important factor, and makes it into something else by cutting it in two. In other words, there is a value of identity particular to certain places, which makes them for a moment indivisible.

Thus the decision to pass or not to pass through a place, which is of a symbolic order, must not be confused with the fact of finding an artistic solution for that passage, a solution which can, after all, be a success or not, but is dependent on another problem.

An example: the difficulties raised by the passage of a highway near the Puy de la Nugère, at one of the extremities of the chain of puys, or extinct volcanoes. I gave advice at that time not to venture into that landscape entity. That entity, by its geological nature, must be considered totally unique, on the national and even the European scale. Besides, it corresponds approximately to a national park, the park of the volcanoes.

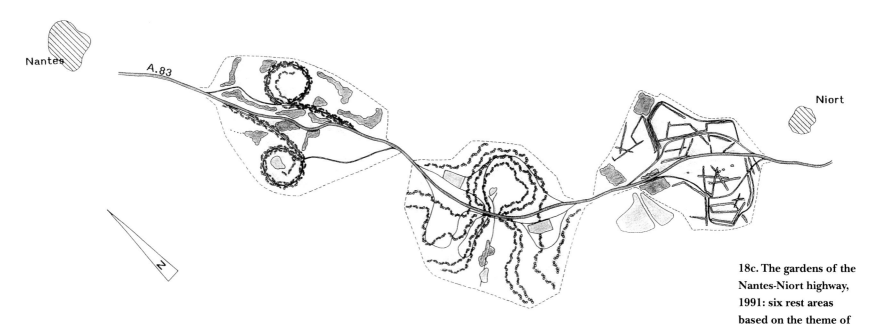

18c. The gardens of the Nantes-Niort highway, 1991: six rest areas based on the theme of hedgerows given their freedom.

Another example: one would no longer dig a tunnel beneath Mont Blanc, as we did a few years ago for a number of reasons at that time held to be convincing, because today one no longer seeks to oppose the human mastery of the technical to the natural power of Mont Blanc. Our actual mastery is rightly not to dig and not to breach that natural power. For that more subtle mastery, the taking into account of new values emerging from a place is part of the decision to make.

Nature and Displacement

The passage of a highway thus supposes a thorough knowledge of the places in their specificity. But what are these places? If one refers to the maps of the sites at the Ministère de l'Equipement, one establishes that they are just as much places where man has introduced no construction, as places which man has more or less modified, either as visitor or as producer of significant non-natural elements: villages, monuments, bridges, etc.

Now, if one places on the same level what would be in the category of the natural, or is wished to be, and what is undoubtedly the result of human presence, let us implicitly suppose we give a similar landscape value to a village or a cascade, for example. Now from the point of view of the possibility of making a passage for the highway, the value of nature is not identical.

In that connection, to distinguish the natural from the artifi-

cial is not as simple as one could first think because the choice of a place as natural is already in fact a human intervention. Furthermore, close to apparently natural cascades, there might have been an earlier clearing of certain views, plantations of trees, etc.

Then the natural would be in that new scale what has been less modified, but such a definition would not take into account the effects of the *displacement*, which can tip mixed places into the category of the natural, by the simple fact of adding obviously artificial objects.

> If you introduce a new element into your visual field, it will be inserted either between the natural and the artificial, or it will become the most natural element, or the most artificial: whence displacement of one or several earlier elements. More or less natural, more or less artificial, it is an identification that leads to a classification.[10]

When we are faced with the question of addition to a site, it is the value of nature of that site which is displaced, or, more precisely, impelled toward the most natural. To pass around or through—these are interventions that have to be considered in

[10] *Jeux* (1977).

relation to setting categories of appreciation of places by referential or dominant factors; in the circumstances here, classifying places from more to less natural, insofar as the factor "nature" takes more and more weight.

Thus, in that way, before the effective passage in a site, the plan of the highway can, in the visual field of the affected residents, make them perceive that site as still more natural; hence a still stronger attitude of rejection of the highway. The project thus helps despite itself to constitute locally a visual field that appears more natural. The effective passage poses then either as a force opposed to the natural power, or, beyond the passage in the visual field, as a destroyer of the entity of nature infinitely vast, of which that visual field is only a fraction. In both cases, to pass is to scar. The identification of the residents with the entity of abstract nature evoked in that way, an identification that is sometimes confined to anthropomorphism, will make the passage be experienced like the destruction of a loved one.

That explains why the concept of landscape entity, here as in nature, cannot be approached only as a visual problem, since it is situated at symbolic levels. Besides, that explains the importance played by maps in the actual debates on the passages. The map indeed represents, with its diverse irregular spots of a certain color, the surfaces and forms of the entity of nature associated with that color. That designation by a colored surface with precise limits is a choice. By that choice, the value of nature is revealed. Over and above this, does not that delimitation join what is shown by the ring of Rouault's paintings or the halo of the saint, by giving it the character of the infinite? Thus it is that one cannot clip off the marshes at Poitiers at their *margins*.

Literality

Literality, which is not (like minimal intervention) a renewed reading, but the action of leaving places in their state, in total respect of their possibles, must be challenged. First let us distinguish between concrete literality and mythical literality.

The first would consist in conserving nature in its biological processes.

The second would signify to protect the acquired because how does one know if what one wants to do is better than what one destroys in the name of the new.

Now even if it is not a similar notion of time that underlies those two positions, do they not both suppose a common idea, the idea of reversibility? On one side, the feeling that one can go back to a pre-human, natural state; on the other, the imaginary attempt to reconstitute human history, to make again, nostalgically, the journey that seemed to have succeeded so well.

In the end, these two literalities are both mythical.

The Inventive Analysis

It appears to me quite clearly, in the particular cases of the Garden of Returns and the project for the Tuileries, that it was necessary to make possible an interpretation that would not deny the natural given, or the patrimonial given, or the social given. It would then make clear the necessity of the conception, provided that one include the importance of *inventive analysis*, both in order to make an account of the physical and historical places and to identify the process of physical evolution and practices in those places. And, through those diverse times, in order to be able to discern what would be most appropriate to the specific relation between a place and practices of that place, the place reflecting the practice, and vice versa. The current grand debate on conservation and rehabilitation is linked to the difference between fixity and the process of evolution.

That question was raised in the course of consultation for the restoration of the garden in the Tuileries. Should we privilege Le Nôtre to the detriment of Mollet or de Dupeyrac, the nineteenth-century garden or the site as it was before the Revolution, or, on the contrary, opt for the present? I did not want to choose by elimination because each of these strata had a reason to be present on the spot. Therefore I preferred to perpetuate through fractions the interventions of the different landscapers who had followed in turn in that garden. In other words, it was about, at the same time, respecting their contributions and remaking them in another form—what they had themselves made in other times and what I have called *interlacing*.[11]

> One reinvents while pursuing a contemporary creation (*at the scale of the whole site, and not only by a simple formal localised adjunction*) the logic of the articulation between successive compositions of the site in the course of its development [. . .] The progressive development of the garden does not result from successive adjunctions of new parts, but from a succession of rewritings on the same space and from reinterpretations, by the society which uses it, of the sense of the garden at each moment of its history [. . .] It is thus that multiplicity of the site that had to be made poetically tangible and to be followed in the present.[12]

The Inflection of the Landscape Process

The term "process" itself designates the ensemble of the interactive movements of the place. It indicates how it is necessary not to stop the place, not to fix it. One could almost say that it is required to catch the place "on the move."

Consequently the role of intervention, which for diverse reasons has revealed itself to be wished for, will take form in that movement and in the game of various processes. It can also tend to reanimate the movement of certain fixed factors and eventually to add others, all of that joining in the process of what is already in place. I call that type of intervention of a landscape project the "inflection of the landscape process." I intend that way to escape the usual term of composition, installation, which implies a reversible and therefore reconstructible temporality. It claims that the landscape process, usually called the project, is situated, that is, participates in the various movements of the concrete. Facing interventions which would be inserted in a successiveness, an agglomeration of objects, would it not be better to choose the reinvention of elements or fractions?

The treatment of each new fraction is therefore concerned

---

[11] To extend the expression used by William Gilpin about the characteristics of the landscape in Great Britain.

[12] Lassus, *Le Jardin des Tuileries* (London: Coracle Press, 1991); "The Tuileries—A Reinvented Garden," this volume.

by revealing the totality of the chosen moment/moments of that given. Taking into account that movement, what I suggest today is no longer to have a plurality of fractions which, unrelentingly moved, end by losing their meaning. Hence the emergence of a certain international art, not the art that results from making modernism banal, but another, split by aestheticism, less temporalized, neutral, and despite everything extremely popular. It is most frequently considered trivial because a priori it is nothing but agreeable and comfortable, whereas I think it is *insipid* in the sense intended by the old Chinese painters.

In a new optics, each fraction is not only an object situated in a horizontality in relation with others in the same temporality, but a fraction of its own time. Beyond the displacement of a given, one finds oneself no longer before a juxtaposition of objects that are able or not to gather in a landscape, but before a simultaneity of different moments, of vertical fractions each having its own necessary space, so that it results in an ensemble of associated structures mutually valorized by their temporal differences. That is what I proposed for the park at Duisburg-Nord.

This last project distinguishes itself from the one at Brussels in that in Brussels I only posed "colors" that were naturally present, when what seems important to me, actually, is to create "spectra," that is, ensembles of "colors" valorized in their individuality, reconstructed and reinvented in their autonomy by cuts, by faults. This renewal in a "spectral" whole, endowed with its own scale, is therefore not a literal juxtaposition of "colors," too concerned with the "natural given" that it mystifies.[13] For each intervention it is necessary to understand each time if we have to

reinvent the "spectrum" and the "colors" that correspond to it. In that "spectrum" the "color" is reinvented in a triple relationship: to itself, to its neighbors, and to the "spectrum" where it is located and which it makes possible.

Therefore, the problem of landscape is not to bring in one or several new elements, by thinking in terms of coherence, integration, insertion, but finally to put in place a new "spectrum" in a system of structures. The common denominator is, indeed, from the moment, the structure, since we can have structures with different dominant factors. Let us take the example of the superimposition of several jigsaw puzzles whose motifs, the sizes and shapes of the pieces, would not be identical. Each puzzle would furthermore be incomplete: here and there slits between pieces would correspond from puzzle to puzzle and create narrow breaks, some deeper than others, suggesting regroupings, both horizontal and vertical.

At the present time, when the finished appears ineluctable, any contribution appears as inevitably destructive and the real extent of that destruction is never known. Nevertheless, one has to choose, hence the necessity to envisage an inflected conception fitting into a history, a given multiple, undulating, unpredictable, resuming or opening other potentialities, especially those so important to daily life and the economy which cannot be dissociated from it.

I shall take Rochefort as an example, for there, in connection with the project of the Garden of Returns, a politics of horticultural production takes place progressively with the development of that garden. That production, centered on the begonia, has a profound connection with Rochefort because it is there that the species was named, in other words, invented. That birthplace had thus to be selected for its production, and that production

13 "Les Buissons optiques" (Niort, 1993); see "The Optical Bushes," this volume.

in turn gains from the relation of the symbol that is the notion of "return." Besides, that connection has incited the European authorities to help start that production. The existence of the garden and its frequentation as a place of daily activities are still other expressions of that symbol.

It is inventive analysis that has made possible those various propositions because the sensory choice of the landscape entity gathers in it numerous factors nourished by the processes of the place itself, processes that find themselves inflected in return. Thus the military arsenal of Rochefort has now become a botanical arsenal. By that progress, the preservation/improvement of our patrimony has allowed a process of production to emerge.

Beyond the symbolic landscape, we have nevertheless to cross the road each day, to take paths by walking on slow or fast grounds to get to work, to hurry or to wander around in passages of light or shade, of sun or foliage, later on to walk in the garden, to breathe its smells, to listen to its murmurs. That, we do by *successions of ambiances*,[14] a concept it is difficult not to evoke as soon as we understand that where a landscape appears, we are already in a place.

[14] Lassus, "Schéma directeur d'ambiances visuelles du secteur II de la ville nouvelle de Marne-la-Vallée Bernard Lassus," 1975.

The New Spirit of the Place, or Taming the Heterogeneous / 1993

When I was a pupil at the Lycée Blaise Pascal at Clermont-Ferrand, I was proud to have in my country the highest mountain in Europe, Mont Blanc, but on the other hand I was very sad that we had only extinct volcanoes in France—the Puys. In the near future, a child who is asked to name a volcano, will be sure to reply: "There is one which is still active: Etna." For twenty years or so, we have been taking part in a movement that leads in two directions. In one respect, our sense of scale has altered completely, with the department being swallowed up in the larger unit of the region, and the region being absorbed in Europe as a whole. But at the same time there has been a contrary impulse, leading in the direction of a return to the local, with places that have a specific character, or are in the process of acquiring it, being enabled to emerge and receive support and reinforcement. The points of reference in terms of which the concrete spaces surrounding us can be read as landscapes cannot remain the same in these circumstances.

The present problems in defining the scale of the department in relation to the region, for example, testify to this; and whether at this level or on another scale there is always the question of identity, which people never stop talking about. The problem of the identity of the region lies in being able to bring to light, through inventive use of analysis, the various places in the region and, working through them and taking them as the basis, to construct or invent a special kind of entity. This is not given at the outset, simply as a result of the accumulation of places; it is necessary to reinvent the different components of a region in order to invent the identity to which they will all contribute.

Identity is here like a kind of perfume, that is to say something that is not only lavender or violet but an entirely new entity. By choosing this metaphor, I intend to show that we must start from the heterogeneity of places and invent a new scale, which will be the regional scale (but can regions in fact be discussed in terms of perfumes?): a specific and concrete one that brings out the value of each of its components.

What is the consequence for the most local elements, for example, the Cognac area with its vineyards? The Cognac area is first of all a place that forms part of the diversity of a department, the Charente, but has its own specific features, on the one hand, in relation to the department as a whole, and, on the other, in relation to other wine-growing areas: Bordeaux, Burgundy, etc. Cognac is at the same time, of necessity, part of a specific territory and a delocalized element—this is a measure of its success. Given that these places are by an immense degree more rural than urban—this is indeed a surprising enough fact for it to be worth mention—we must try to analyze what is happening at the moment and identify some of the factors that are changing the present picture.

The first is the extraordinary transformation in the way in which the rural scene relates to the territory as a whole. At the same time that construction is being extended, but on a vastly greater scale, the process of turning farmland into uncultivated land is gaining speed and becoming visible everywhere. It is almost tempting to suggest that, whereas in our culture formerly the forest was our reference to the wild, with cultivated fields separating it from the town, today the forest is perceived more and more as a place that produces wood, as opposed to other surfaces which the hand of man has abandoned, that is, the fields and meadows that are left fallow. So will not these fallow lands come to seem like the new standard of wildness, or the new myth of the wild?

In contrast to this tendency, there is another movement, linear in direction: the development of the highways. These highways are becoming so numerous as to form a network: one of the aims France has undertaken has been to put them within a roughly equal distance of all the inhabitants of the country. It is an inevitable hypothesis that the network effect, in relation to which each individual component is merely a fraction, has the global consequence of ensuring that there is no longer a simple addition of separate highways but something quite different, which we shall have to discover and invent at the same time. This involves a simultaneous modification in the status of the individual highway, which becomes a fractional part within the network, and implies, at some stage, a change in its basic nature.

Another point: urban culture has vanquished rural culture because it has confronted it with industrialization. Paradoxically, this victory is the cause of nostalgia since urban society requires what is left of rural society to remain in conformity with its former image—which obviously no longer corresponds to reality. One thing that will emerge from this process is a further development in the relation of the new highway network to the town—itself preoccupied with successful attempts to revive its centers and more difficult, often uncertain policies toward the areas being constructed on its periphery. Another result is likely to be a development in the relationship of the high-speed trains (TGV) to these same towns. This will take place in the same measure as the transformation of the countryside that has just been mentioned, and in response to the change in the desire of urban culture to have a stable image of rurality from before the period of its own industrialization.

I agree that this image of the rural world makes it impossible to establish a genuine linkage between the highway network and what it should be bringing about: a new form of habitat. At present people regard as brutal and inhuman the various forms of construction connected to the highway system at its usual arrival and entry points into towns. But we should consider not being so hasty in our rejection of what we now see as the spontaneous urban development taking place not far from the highways and as a consequence of them: we should observe it more closely in order to understand it. This urban development, which is at present seen as negative, could in fact (we suggest as a hypothesis) form the premise for a new way of organizing space, one that leads to yet a further means: that of a habitat that is linked to the highway but at the same time includes the rural within itself. The consequence would be, in a certain way, "town-landscapes" interposed as new structures between highways and "classic" towns on the one hand and between successive towns on the other.

These town-landscapes, created as a result of their accessibility to the highways, seem to me to have quite a lot in common, oddly enough, with the dual plastic system invented by a miner of the Nord region, Mr. Charles Pecqueur. This man had installed at the bottom of his garden facing a mine-spoil heap a statue of Snow White in concrete, life-size, which looked beyond the garden and so on to the spoil heap. I was intrigued with this for a long time before he revealed the significance of this arrangement to me. For him, Snow White was not looking at the spoil heap but at the forest. In fact there could be no question for this miner of abolishing or covering with green carpeting these hills of rubbish, which were the mark of his labor and that of generations of miners.

So he had made the decision to keep the spoil heap and at the same time to annex it poetically on another level by making it into a forest. In the same way, the town-landscape, growing up in rural landscapes or uncultivated areas of the countryside, would be capable of revealing once again these former landscapes, of preserving them while at the same time allowing them to become something else.

I want to say a few words about the confusion that reigns between the concepts of environment and landscape. Let me give a simple image. The fact that we are solving the various problems of pollution that face us does not mean that we are bringing landscapes into being. It is all too easy to imagine having perfectly clean environments that are not attractive at all. By contrast, it is quite possible to appreciate landscapes that, from the environmental point of view, leave a lot to be desired.

To clarify the distinction I am making between these two terms, I would point out that a healthy environment is a "degree zero"—obviously a child who is playing in a meadow must be able to drink the water of the stream that meanders through it—and that from building on this substratum alone will we be able to invent landscapes, that is to say, our culture.

The concrete space we call "rural" or "countryside" is being transformed out of all recognition, and in these circumstances I need to give a further definition of what I mean by landscape.

Landscape is a cultural reading that renews the concrete space and what surrounds us. It is all too easy to forget the temporal nature of this reading and the ways it has been transformed in consequence. In the nineteenth century, mountains were first viewed as being boring or even an abomination, in landscape terms, and yet, while they remained physically the same, they ended up as places for tourists and alpinists. The same goes for the sea, where I could take as my example the Promenade des Anglais at Nice, which was in the strict sense invented by the British visitors. Today we are witnessing the birth of the marshland considered as a support for landscape, on various different scales. In the same way, and on the European scale, the Loire—which has provoked demonstrations by the Germans in support of what they call "the last wild river in Europe"—has been given a new identity.

The way in which rural places are being transformed at present shows, indeed reveals to us, that new landscapes are capable of being developed in concrete spaces that remain fixed. On the other hand, places that were formerly rural and now have been completely transformed by urbanization can still appear legible through the works of painters like Monet and his fellow Impressionists, or the more recent practitioners of Land Art. There is thus an uneasy relationship between the concrete places, which remain relatively stable in their physical organization and the continually changing readings, which are in the process of altering their significance. An uneasy relationship also exists between the places that are changing and being transformed, and the fixed images, such as those provided by painters or postcards, in terms of which we continue to read them.

Uncultivated land, which is a kind of diffuse, indeterminate instance of the concrete with no obvious boundaries on the national scale, cannot be a determinate object like Mont Blanc or the marshland. Its specific character is a result of the fact that, the moment it has been abandoned by man, it takes leave of the proprietorship exercised on a daily basis from ages past. All this can be understood by reference to the different types of scale that are at the basis of different forms of identity and reference. Here we have a relationship between a concrete space, which is more or less fixed, and a landscape reading of the same place, which is more or less mobile. In this case, we need to invent new landscape concepts and new ways of apprehending the very notion of landscape. This brings us back to the great debate in the eighteenth century, which tried to make a distinction between different categories in our surroundings: people of this period devised terms like the *ferme ornée*, or *paysage de pays*, which today seem curious categories to us but indicate that there was indeed a debate about different types of scale at that time.

The return to the local as a constitutive element in the ulterior construction of landscape can be understood within a cultural and economic context, which is at once pre-existent and at the same time subject to being broadened and transformed by its particular contribution. The example of the begonia at Rochefort-sur-Mer is an instance of this. The genus *Begonia* was observed for the first time in the West Indies in the seventeenth century by a royal botanist, Père Plumier, who gave the first description of it. At a later stage, the plant was named for Monsieur Bégon, then the governor of Rochefort, the place from which Plumier embarked for the Indies. If we look at the matter on a European scale, it is obvious that Rochefort, which gave the flower its name and also has a good local climate, would be more suitable for the cultivation and production of the begonia than the Dutch and German plains where it is mass-produced at the present day. This success depends, however, on the fact that Rochefort possesses the instrument to reveal these facts, in its Garden of Returns, which becomes the reinvention, through the aesthetics of the garden, of the notion of the horticultural production of the begonia. Otherwise, you will have the same kinds of begonias everywhere—in a banal and senseless fashion. So, through this kind of process, the return to the local can contribute to the reinvention of a rural culture which is firmly rooted in the specific place, and it can also support the reinvention of values which are more than visual.

The specificity of Rochefort as a place also implies an interaction between culture and economics, which now begins to make sense on the European scale, just as Etna could be in the process of becoming the European volcano.

The Paths / 1994

When William Gilpin invented walking in the eighteenth century, it was not only a new country, Scotland, that began to exist perceptibly through his look, but also a way of traveling across a country, choosing a route, in a certain weather, exploring grounds of different degrees of roughness, all sensations that participated in equal parts in the rise of landscape.

In my own work "Journey in Alaska," I introduced an explicit reference to that great inventor of Scotland in order to reveal how that vast northwest extremity of America sprang up in pieces, at different scales, by means of all sorts of vehicles of transport: ship, small plane, airliner, train, car, walking, between extreme mobility and immobility, between sky and earth, between land and water, between water and ice . . . That work reveals a fragmented Alaska where each view, each perception, remains independent and also at the same time participates, precisely through what it proposes, in a vaster entity, an Alaska present by its very dispersal, a landscape that exceeds and includes at the same time the picturesque landscape invented by Gilpin.

That the landscape is formed through walking, and no longer only through the fixity of belvederes and viewpoints (that is, walking as link, as underlying continuity, forms landscape), implies for the art of the gardens an interrogation that I have constantly resumed in the course of my different projects.

The garden path is obviously related to walking, to the temporal scale, to the sensations felt by the foot: ascents, descents, obstacles, mountain tracks, roughness or softness of materials, fluidity or firmness of their foundation, variability of ground according to atmospheric and seasonal changes. But the possible combination of elements of the path also depends on its width,

and one cannot see why it should stay fixed for the same walk—as in most past or contemporary gardens, where those same paths maintain clear relationships with their neighboring surfaces.

The path does not exist only for itself, as a particular sensory experience, and only rarely to "cross a zone" by going from one point to another, as if that zone did not exist. It is also a plastic tracing offered for view, which hides in order to reappear according to the variations of the ground and what it supports.

In my proposal for the Parc de la Villette, "The Garden of the Planets," I proposed, with my team, that the various parts of the garden be recognizable by particular treatment of the ground of their paths, texture and color of materials being thus intended as the constitution of a recognizable, clearly identifiable ambiance. Too often, in fact, the various surfaces of a garden merge one into another, lose their limits, because a uniform way of walking imposes its continuity on those surfaces. So that what results, really, is the display of paths which often have nothing exceptional about them and thus take up an unmodulated existence.

Now, by evoking a classical register, the picturesque path is an integral part of the picturesque landscape and does not break free from it. Therefore, by proposing to differentiate the paths of La Villette, I had the intention of placing the accent on the different surfaces of the project, to emphasize their mutual differences.

That idea of differentiation is found again in the project of the Garden of Returns in the Park of the Corderie Royale at Rochefort-sur-Mer, though deeply enriched, in that the walkways also partly play the role of significant limits of chosen strata

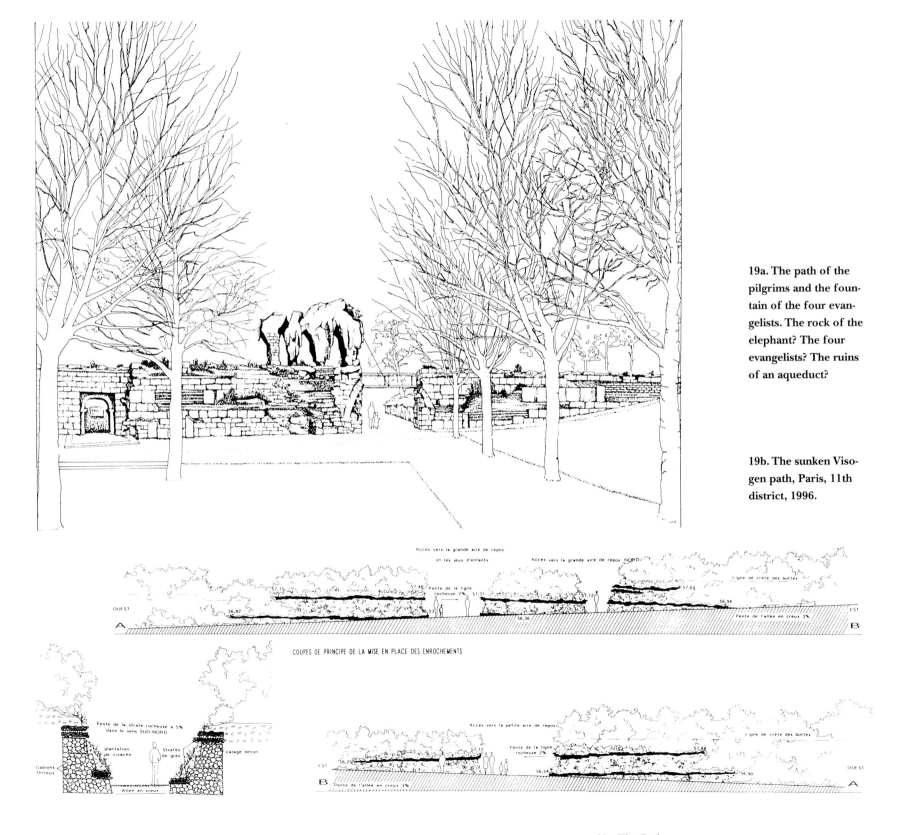

19a. The path of the pilgrims and the fountain of the four evangelists. The rock of the elephant? The four evangelists? The ruins of an aqueduct?

19b. The sunken Visogen path, Paris, 11th district, 1996.

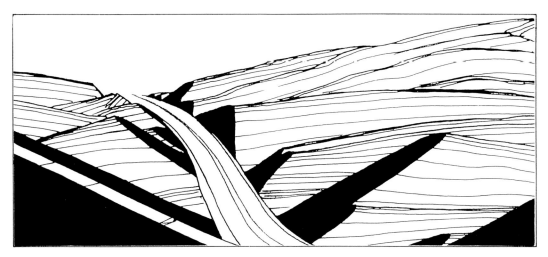

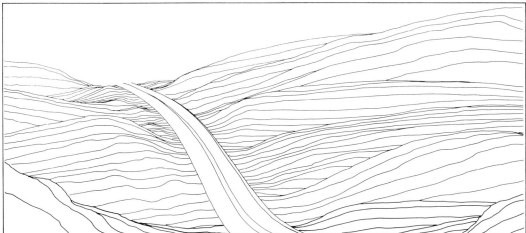

19c. Highway A20, Brive-Montauban. The surfaces of the sunken slope are transformed into movement by following the contour lines.

in the continuum of all those superimposed on the places: a poetic archaeology. A stratum of paving stones reminds us of the industrial period of Corderie Royale nearest to that historic building. When that stratum is next to the one claimed by the vegetation that took possession of the places after their abandonment in consequence of the closing of the Rochefort arsenal in 1926, the question of the relationship between these strata and their superimposition is also posed. I made the decision to bound the recent meadow leading to the Charente River with a dark brown border imitating the texture of earth lumps. Furthermore, in order that one can at leisure imagine that the expanse of paving stones continues under the meadow, that small border inclines slightly to define a shadow, as a result of which the context between the two strata dematerializes. Thus

the meadow becomes floating in relation to the paving stones, and the contact of those two strata pushed back by that shadow creates a temporal fault likely to stimulate a form of interpretation. Other dissociations are proposed to the walker who decides to follow the path along the Charente. It is possible to walk either through the riparian vegetation or in parallel between that vegetation and the line of limes that mark the boundaries of the meadow. If our only aim were to be functional, the idea of a single path would obviously have prevailed, but when it is the meaning that is important, as here, the possibility of experimenting with a dual solution relating to two differing ways of seeing the Corderie gave me the idea of those two deliberately parallel paths, a clear invitation to compare two perceptible universes.

This conception of the path as limit and place of experience is still more thoroughly studied in the project of the Emscherpark at Duisburg-Nord. Was it not imperative to respond on several levels to the plan: saving a part of the terrain for sports activities, workers' gardens, and other local requests from the neighborhood residents, thus permitting, posing on another level the question of an actual park? As a matter of fact, people usually include in the concepts of park all those components, which dissolve in advance the apprehension of the park as a space of its own since one tries in advance to integrate it into the urban tissue. The Park at Duisburg proposes to separate what is purely urban and by contrast adjacent with linear-ring spaces, sorts of vegetable screens. But these screens only take on meaning in connection with the fractions of space included in the park, three dissociated periods, themselves in interrelation and relative to the day before yesterday, yesterday, and tomorrow, the today corresponding to those peripheral spaces required for the activities of the various riverside residents. The day before yesterday is idyllic nature, with its fields and farms, as it was before the installation of the first industries. Its paths are rural, sandy, sinuous, circulating between the patches of meadow or culture, and one follows them on foot or in carts drawn by horses. Yesterday is the industrial phase with its factories. There one follows very geometrized paths, harder, evoking a simple technological functionalism. Each stage receiving a particular treatment; the screens of vegetation also resolve the difficulty of the passage from one period to another, because that passage, which dates neither from yesterday nor from today, is in fact theoretically the analogue of those transmitters of temporal material, those doors on the strata of space-time invented by

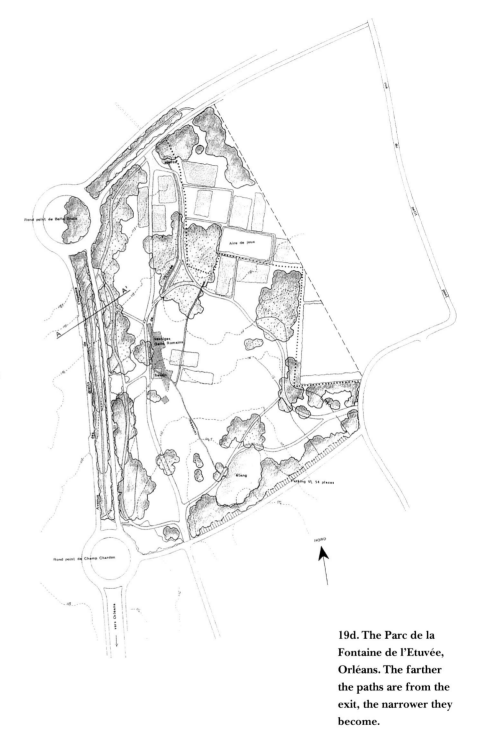

19d. The Parc de la Fontaine de l'Etuvée, Orléans. The farther the paths are from the exit, the narrower they become.

19e. The garden of Mediterranean plants. A different kind of path for each country.

Etang de Bages et de Sigean

Sallins Tallavignes

Halte Nautique

Chemin des marais

Parking

le Rieu

Parking sous pinède

Vers Sigean

Parking sous pinède

Cimento

Chemin de la

Yougoslavie

Château

Bergerie

France

Albanie

Syrie

Vergel

Italie

Liban

Espagne

Turquie

Israël

Algérie

Grèce

Tunisie

Maroc

Egypte

Libye

Bergerie de la Tutie

Garrigue

Jardins des plantes de la Méditerranée

Métairie de Rivals

Carrière

Carrière

Carrière

science fiction. Thus there are lines of blue trees between which the light grows darker, with the ground itself dark blue. Those walkways are also at a different altitude, heightened in comparison with those of the ground of the different strata, so that by following them the foot notices that what it steps on does not resemble at all the other paths, those of the components of yesterday, the day before yesterday, and tomorrow. Thus, contrary to the Garden of Returns at Rochefort, where the contact of the strata opened into an imaginary gap, the passages metaphorically bridging time in the Emscherpark include in their abstract unity (the least local possible) the fractions of the park with a sort of ring in order to isolate them clearly one from another. Therefore there is no continuity here, no smoothing from one period to another, but real isolation.

In that metamorphosis of the concept of walking, I managed to clear a supplementary step by reinventing the access points to the Parc de la Fontaine de l'Etuvée in Orléans. From what one most commonly sees, the walkways of a park lead, wherever it is, to the different parts that constitute it, as if they were a geometrical network pressed and plated from above. From the park to its fractions, however, there is a passage from a particular global scale to an equally particular scale of fractionation. Thus is posed a problem of dimensionality in proportion to the walkways which are distributed in a park. For the new park at L'Etuvée, the idea has been to associate the dichotomy of the paths with a narrowing of their width, from *bronchi* to *bronchioles*, to use an image from the human body. The parts of the park to which access is thus given are then miniaturized in relation to the global scale of the particular space. This indeed preserved a characteristic of the space proposed for intervention before it was made: small orchards, postage stamps of a few dozen

square meters covered the surface of the park, like a patchwork of square clumps of trees. Homogeneous walkways in their dimensionality would thus have annihilated its apprehension in advance.

From a symbolic point of view, that concept is also interesting in that it calls attention to the irrigation of the park, as if the visitors were the blood flow or the air stream from which the park could start to live. The tree plantings there also attempted to develop in another way a relationship between the real and the symbolic tree, also from the proper to the symbolic scale. Did there not exist on the site the buried remains of a temple dedicated to the nymph of the place, the goddess of the spring who fed the aqueduct intended to quench the thirst of the old Gallo-Romans of the city of Orléans?

Landscape Values / 1995

Process, Fixed Images, and Entities

For more operational clarity, I had proposed, a while ago, the dissociation between environment and landscape.

The purpose was to grasp that landscape's nature was cultural, a construction of the mind, resulting from the perceptible and aesthetic considerations forming on a natural given, while the environment was a state of things able to be improved technically and scientifically.

That dissociation has allowed the understanding that the landscape did not reduce to the picturesque, as has existed since the nineteenth century. Related to that first proposition, a new fact appeared recently: if a polluted landscape could, until today, be considered beautiful, it is not certain that that will be the case tomorrow. The end of the Immeasurable horizontal mingles, in a way, the garden and landscape.

Is it not indeed at this moment a profound change of attitudes toward nature that leads to the notion—it is precisely because of its clean water that a meadow and its river would be considered beautiful?

Let us halt for a moment. The fact of saying "clean water" does not necessarily mean that one accepts subjecting oneself fundamentally to nature, but that, in the first place, one simply wishes that that water could be drunk on the spot after having run through the meadow, and even that it had an agreeable taste.

Then we must distinguish naturally clean water resulting from an ecological or biological, and local process and the water resulting from an artificial and delocalized process.

Here I stand with the option that the notion of landscape is linked to the fact that what makes it possible is an ensemble of natural elements supposed positive and in interaction on a sensory level, that is, smell, visual quality, richness of tactile contacts, etc.

But how can that landscape be obtained, since what constitutes it is built on the sensorial agreement that one has had, and will have, while visiting the concrete space itself—support of that landscape? That agreement could then be generated artificially through the restoration of a natural system: the idea called by the Germans "renaturiert."

That means, consequently, that there is an intermediary stage in which the elements of nature cannot be necessarily natural in the sense of the ecological and living process of the ecosystem (independently of man).

The question becomes more complicated for each one, or at least many people,—I should add here a reminder of one of my old studies on the dweller landscapers—and carries the necessity to situate things between natural and artificial.

For example, the geranium occupying a place of honor on the refrigerator in the kitchen is the natural standard, or can be, of all the objects of the apartment. The refrigerator, or the family computer, is considered as the most artificial object and the geranium the most natural—the wooden table and the jar of raspberries being in the middle.

The question asked for that geranium, so that it can be effectively the standard, is that of the credibility of its naturalness. To use the previous image again, what must be the credibility of that shady meadow with a river, if what is wished is to make it appear really natural? In both cases, geranium and shady meadow appear intrinsically natural, that is, they are spontaneously appreciated as natural, whether they are organized by man or not.

One could, however, question temporarily that confidence

which drives us to believe that clean water, like the geranium, could be assimilated into the natural without any further question. Is it not well known, indeed, that a perfectly natural water can be full of sulfur and quite undrinkable!

The system of security, with the importance that it acquires, appears to work in favor of naturally clean water, but we know that this is only one of the different forms that nature takes. Should we not look closely, with more wonder, at that assimilation between nature, quality, and safety? Because behind all that, there is obviously the wild. (We situate ourselves here, in relation to what appears as a general attitude, in order to pose some questions on the subject.)

Would it not then be the case, because of the very fact of its rarity, that the natural process would become beautiful? In what concerns the art of gardens and landscapes, we would then be in the process of attending to a reversal of perspective, since in the past it was the order of the controlled garden that was the most rare. Today, the awkward, clumsy, and disturbing mastery of nature is the most current natural and free process. Other approaches, being far more rare, become thus more sought after. Would it not be in that way that the richness of the landscape process could become an aesthetic phenomenon dominated by the myth of rarity?

Would a new abusive relation, between rarity and beauty, tend to be established, although we know, however, that one is not the other?

In fact, the geranium only becomes beautiful in the apartment because, in the visual field of daily life in which it is placed, there is no other element more natural.

To come back home after a walk in the woods with mush-rooms and moss, for example, would be sufficient for the geranium to appear, in relation to the mushrooms and moss, more artificial, and because of that, less beautiful, if only for a few hours.

That consideration leads me to suppose that, since certain people consider clean water as nature itself, there is implicit acquiescence in the established fact that it is no longer nature but, primarily, a safety imperative that is involved.

If one persists in placing oneself in that system, one finally reaches the point where the most poisonous mushroom would then be beyond the natural, the wild, since to accept that natural wild leads us directly to respect the socially poisonous as being part of the natural organization. The real natural would result in the confusion of the wild with safety, by objecting to the wild in order to exclude it.

That is what could well lead us to the myth of clean nature, under cover of the acceptance of poisonous nature as model for the wild. That is, besides, what had led me to consider with the greatest reservation the ecological gardens of Louis-Guillaume Leroy, who seemed to me, with his biological battles between kinds of vegetation, to be organizing what I called "Roman circus games."

Indeed, beauty can be poisonous, perverse, but it is not the same with the use of the places or objects we have to work with. Places can really be impossible to live in—as the events of these last years have amply shown—exactly the same as poisonous mushrooms are inedible.

Once again reappears the necessity to situate oneself that I had taken advantage of in the development of ships like the *Mermoz*. I had noticed with closed places that they always harbor a cursed spot, a place that all those who live on the ship, like sailors or, temporarily, passengers, agree to avoid. The problem for the ship owner is easy to understand. The owner has to create that cursed spot in advance, in order to give value to the other developments in relation to that one. Otherwise, complete disorganization of the proposed spaces can result. I have noticed also the presence of that phenomenon in gardens, as had earlier the landscape gardeners of the last century.

The necessity to consider these negative spaces—and there also will be posed, sooner or later, the question of their different scales—takes on the greatest importance when the total occupation of the Earth makes them all the more interrogative to our eyes, because we have not chosen them and we could imagine one day having positive spaces everywhere. It is thus the question of topological classification of these spaces which is posed. I have already evoked the classification that goes from the natural to the artificial, which appears to me as having to be replaced by that vaster one which goes from "more to less." The necessity of those classifications is not finally other than the metaphorical expression itself of the movement. Indeed, one goes from more toward less in order to understand them in relation to each other.

In that movement of "to go toward," a possibility of meaning is automatically established, which only becomes explicit when one determines the two extremities of that movement. Inside the actual movement going from the natural to the artificial, it is then possible to see that we actually have two sorts of wild between which the actual question of meaning seems to move: on one side the proper natural, on the other the proper artificial, because we have to consider the fact that the artificial destroys

the natural. There is thus profound modification of the classification in which we were situated just a little while ago, and which placed the artificial facing a nature which was completely independent from it.

That permits us to understand that we could have had an aesthetic position that completely accepted electric pylons as being a valorization of the landscape, when now one buries these same pylons. Are we not facing so much of the artificial that a profound imbalance is felt on the part of nature, which causes us to ask for more of the natural? That natural of course is no longer the same as the natural we had before, which was in reality the last white blot on the map of the globe.

In that new system of relationships, the meaning of the object has obviously changed. It is the end of the classical age for which the system of relationships was exterior to the object and was imposed on it. At present it is the object itself that is imposed on the system of relationships, because it contains the system already. Following that I can say that today's proper natural constitutes a value not because it would permit understanding of the proper artificial but because, being a value in itself, it contains its own movement, is by itself meaning. Therefore progression is no longer from the natural to the artificial, that progression being a conquest of one more meaning on nature, but to better juxtaposition. That explains why the system of their relationships has to be built over and above, that the landscape possibilities are no longer given but to be invented.

What is the landscape, then, in relation to that new classification? It always remains, I think, the moment when the object, becoming integrated in a system, an ensemble, passes under that ensemble, some of its qualities making thus function a new sensory unity that becomes superior to that object. The actual change I propose is that the object does not disappear in the landscape as before, but continues to coexist with it.

The actual insistence placed on the object has consequently to accentuate the heterogeneous sensation, but, as the homogeneous is no longer possible either, the problem of the minimal organization of that heterogeneity is posed.

But what are today's landscape values? One could keep the landscape propositions of Leroy as being a kind of poetic ecology, but, for myself, I think it would be advisable to look for other forms of that poetry as future landscape values, by trying, for example, to make elements of the nature of nature itself leave. Did not Mr. Addison already advise the English aristocrats of the eighteenth century to let the trees occupy their full form, to emancipate them from their struggle for survival, so that they could acquire "still more" nature?

There was a poetic metaphor for the new protective agriculture that tended to isolate the plant from its predators in order to make it reach its platonic ideal and better productivity simultaneously.

Perhaps the fact that man "imposes" his law on the form of the tree has been exaggerated. Was there not, there, precisely, a pure poetic ecology insofar as, in the natural state, the oak does not care whether in its growth it smothers whatever species grow beneath its shadow? To each its own torture!

Most often landscape values are defined in relation to fixed images: postcards, paintings, photos, and, finally, films, which themselves only result from a succession of photos. These fixed values are linked to memory; they are "places of memory," to use the phrase of Pierre Nora.

The current rediscovery of the body, which is substituted for manual work as compensation, seems to me also now to open the way for other values. That rediscovery leads the person who intends to look at a concrete space no longer to be able to extricate from memory having already lain down on a certain patch of grass, or having walked in woods. There is a memorial value of the use that has now been established which brings the one who tries to visit a space no longer to be able to appreciate it, if, in order to do so, he must get caught on barbed wire or walk on broken glass while ambling across brome-grasses and fescues. The end result is that future beauty could well depend on that absence of roughness.

Thus I go back to certain observations I was able to make in 1967 on the generalization of the use of asphalt in towns, which appeared to me at that time as an attempt to free town-dwellers from tactility so they could become more interested in the city view. That asphaltization was also a way to break with the countryside, by opposing what makes it rich: the astonishing variety of its textures, the soft material of muds, silts, and sands, the pliability of the grasses, the chaos of scattered stones on paths, hillsides, abrupt ditches, spongy and treacherous under foot . . . In contrast, urban tactility has found a refuge in apartments and the softness of carpets. The study of the gorges of the Aradin, which I made at approximately the same time, helped me to understand better the connections between tactility and visuality, because it is precisely in those moving milieus, where the ground is indistinct and uncertain, that the view plays an exploratory role, a role of evaluation, what I called optical tact. A preliminary sensation, somehow, which would have, finally, to be confirmed by the touch of the foot. A place, far from being only visual, had thus, in order to be real, to manifest itself according to the senses of touch, smell, and hearing.

The reality of places is also their evolution, their transformation, which can be of a catastrophic nature. When, in 1981, we decided with Lucius Burckhardt to organize a conference in Gibellina on minimal intervention, I think because it was in that place profoundly transformed by an earthquake that the conference had taken on all its importance. There precisely, where, faced with a maximum intervention by nature, it was the minimal action of man that better affirmed its essence, the modern expression of the sublime. It was also faced with Hiroshima, another form of maximalism, that this conference founded its aesthetic opposite, in order to state better that minimal intervention not only opposed those two extremisms, but wanted to be a contrast and in between. Thus, later, I was able to say in Duisburg that water, to be the milieu of life, must be midway between ice and steam: the milieu of a separated existence and in direct contrast with the other two.

That particular virtue of contrast, we find once again facing a phenomenon particular to our twentieth century, which has not still been properly explored: public housing. Insufficiently thought through, it has first been seen as a momentary palliative, something provisionally installed next to the town and which the town thought perhaps later to reintegrate into its urbanity. One sees what has happened: the separation has been more and more accentuated, to the point that, by juxtaposing spaces culturally very different side by side, one has only succeeded in accentuating their contradictions. For my part, I think that not only can the housing complexes not be brought back into the traditional town, but, by trying to perpetuate the traditional town beyond what constitutes it on its own, one has cut off in advance the new chance that these ensembles could represent: another form of urbanity. When participating in a call for ideas for the development of the future Tremblay en France near the airport at Roissy, the necessity appeared to me not to fear heterogenous urbanism, to organize a system of contrasts inside that heterogeneity by separating the space bearers of those heterogeneities, in other words, by putting in place different scales of heterogeneity.

I reached that sudden awareness while working on the recoloration of old industrial cities of the Lorraine, where very large complexes of buildings, all identical, were threatened with desertion by the residents of those municipalities who wanted to live in a more agreeable habitat.

The recoloration of the façades of those buildings and the recovery of their exterior spaces helped me bring other qualities to those buildings, which were very poor from the sensory point of view. The matter of recoloration is in itself not difficult. The most delicate task was to create a varied plastic system that is a sufficient bearer of meaning for the residents of those buildings.

The question is not easy to solve, because the conceiver is not necessarily conscious of cultural systems different from his own, by which his work will be confronted. By chance, I have been interested for years in the gardens of those I called dweller-landscapers, and in clarifying the systems of reference and the plastic mechanisms on which they based their argument in order to organize their spaces. Those systems are themselves interlocked in the structuration of meaning about which I spoke earlier, which leads each of them to classify what surrounds it in relation to a scale of meaning that goes from the most natural to the most artificial.

In applying those discoveries to my own activity as conceiver, I could verify by myself the validity of those premises. Mr. Schilling told me recently that on his visit to Uckange he was guided by children living there, desirous to show him the variety of painted scenes that surrounded them. But the most astonishing for me was to understand, through his story, that by re-making those façades, by redefining the exterior spaces in that way, I had, while looking for the maximum diversity, contributed in valorizing a certain type of habitat whose residents saw by themselves that it had something different of which they could be proud.

Uckange shows that the question of forming landscapes is extremely important and that it cannot be understood if it is confused with the question of environment or vegetalization of exterior spaces. The landscapes are not an add-on of a decorative order, they are the possibility itself to understand, and to make one's own, the space that one inhabits. When that space is perceived as repetitive, the possibilities to appropriate it for oneself are accordingly diminished, from which my actual position to reject the systems of composition derived from painting or photography, which only praise the sempiternal formal unity. That unity always should be placed again in the social and cultural context where it has a meaning.

Another landscape element deeply linked to the specificity of places is slope. Facing the geometric and technical systems, in other words, the formal, which ceaselessly seek to flatten the terrains in order better to establish forms that are first of all abstract, the slope appears accordingly evocative of diversity. I tried to express it several times in diverse projects, notably in Uckange and on different highway parking areas as in Nîmes-Caissargues, among others.

The terrain on which that parking area had to be developed was an old quarry, a wide open hole dug into a hill for the needs of motorway development.

From an academic point of view, to occupy that quarry, to make it into a poetic cavity, would have been logical. In doing so, one would forget that there had been landscape moments before that digging. In remaking the initial terrain and rediscovering the original slope, one could give back a meaning other than technical or strictly ecological to that terrain by creating a belvedere area. The reconstructed slope of that area, hardly perceptible by foot, but visible because of its 700-meter length, now indicates to the road users the very reason for their halt, Nîmes. One notices here how the terms of integration or preservation are to be considered with the greatest caution because they can give rise to serious landscape misinterpretations.

The very possibility, as in Nîmes-Caissargues, of an evolution of places seems to me interesting, at a time when there is a persistent ecological upsurge. It is indeed remarkable that the movements of ideas at the start of that opening, have introduced the notion of irreversibility of process, and in a vaster sense, the movement of nature itself, when we know now that we are living on a planet whose resources are limited because its dimensions are fixed.

The evolution of landscape values that will result will undoubtedly include a loss of influence of the painting and the photograph, to the benefit of something still vague but essentially focused on movement and time.

The art of gardens would therefore seem, in that perspective, to be the very medium particular to the expression of those ideas. Before that is completely acquired, however, a game will still be played between fixed and mobile images, and landscapism will have to integrate those values in order to end in a relativization of fixity.

Part 3   Inflecting the Landscape—Studies and Projects

Study of La Coudoulière / 1967–71

The Municipality of Six-Fours-la-Plage

The reason I had been asked to study the operation at La Coudoulière, the municipality of Six-Fours-la-Plage, next to Toulon, is that the municipality wished to establish 195,000 square meters of housing on a very particular terrain. That site, on the seashore, was an old tile and brick factory that had worked the quarries on the same site. Gradually, those quarries had been abandoned.

The mining had produced three types of places:

- spots that resulted from the extraction of the first materials, that is, the quarries, but abandoned at different periods;
- tips, that is, places on which earth had been dumped;
- finally, untouched places and ground, that is, neither tips nor quarries.

Those three types of surfaces inclusively constituted a landscape whose logic could only be ascribed to the presence of the factory.

What could one possibly make of a site like that, if one had to establish 195,000 square meters of new buildings, the surface area planned at the coefficient of occupation of space of the zone?

The problem was not only to analyze a phenomenon called "natural" (I say "natural" in relation to the built ground), but to try to see how that substratum and that contribution of 195,000 square meters of housing could live together. Thus the question was to imagine a certain number of hypotheses concerning the future utilisation of that terrain.

At one of the limits of La Coudoulière were situated the factory and a path leading to the port. Located before the factory, that port had permitted the shipment of its products.

How to try to understand that landscape? The first thing to do was to go and walk across it, to make several visits.

Through personal experience, I am always suspicious of an opinion based on one solitary visit, one that lasts only so long. I prefer multiple short visits in order to see the site in different seasons if possible, at different times of the day anyway, and to be myself in different states, in order to control the kind of situation in which I would be experiencing reactions that were too dominated by impressions gathered at one precise moment.

Therefore, multiple visits, and I should almost add, a little bit disorganized, and with "wavering attention," that is, without particularly trying to concentrate on some aspect or other, because the point is to try to let oneself be invaded by the presence of the place. Besides, when my students want to see an exhibition for which they could feel a priori certain reservations, or which they think they are not able to understand, I advise them to go after having partied all night or when they are very tired. In short, the opposite advice to what one would think: indeed, it is required that a certain number of preconceptions in which we believe have fallen so that we can receive, understand, and return to what is proposed to us.

To fix and understand the places better, I also take a large number of transparencies and make drawings from them. The transparency is very interesting in that it allows us to project at the same size and scale as the drawing that we want to study. We just have to adjust the equipment, project the slide, and then draw. That drawing has the advantage, in relation to the sketch, of being more precise despite the reservations we have against photos. With photos, one can have a flattening of planes, so it is imperative to pay attention to that fact in the interpretations we give with the drawings. It is in that way that the drawing re-

**20a. Toward the sea,
toward the land.**

veals itself as very useful for studying the modifications of a landscape in terms of displacement. The practice of sketching obliges us also not to stop with a simple photographic recording. It would be indeed imprudent to totally rely on the fact of having photos alone.

Therefore, when one has taken a few shots, one moves 30 or 40 meters away and starts on another series. That allows the careful study of the modification of the places in terms of a slight displacement; then we can notice the transformation of the land-scape according to that movement and its eventual "fragility," while calling fragility a transformability that is too important or excessive.

The photos so taken are never made to be shown, nor is the ensemble of the documents. Consequently, the photos can over-lap each other to great extents. In general I shoot far more than I need in order to be sure not to miss anything.

In that apprehension of places, the presence of the factory, an important visual mass still visible on the occasion of my first visit, but which had to be demolished, was perhaps going to modify my judgment on the visual aspects of the bay.

It was difficult, even for professionals, to grasp the height of that factory at first sight, because it was not composed of conventional levels, which, as we all know now, are all three meters high. But one could at least suppose that that presence would considerably confuse my judgment relative to the scale of the place.

Then I sought to take photos in which the factory would not appear, in order to try to imagine the places without it. Quite often, I also took a series of photos from nearer, and at differ-ent scales into the distance. On the same spot, seen from the quay, the port concealed a stretch of water, that became visible from closer. I took that surface, shot and reverse shot, isolating it from the dyke that appeared in the visual field.

That dyke was literally eating that stretch of water, since, from a high position, the aquatic space was not visible. The slope con-cealed that fact and I could only see the edge of the dyke.

Until now, that water surface had not manifested itself visu-ally. Compared with shots taken on land, it did not thus play a very big role, while being however very important as a plane. The interest of the approach as a walker and of the photographic approach is, as we can see clearly in this example, to provide dif-fering modes of appreciation between the plane and the photo. Some surfaces, which may in fact be very important, do not always have a visual role proportional to that importance.

This example concerned a stretch of water. If it had been another type of surface, for example, more marine, would it perhaps have had an interest? But from the moment that it resembled a pool, as a closed stretch of water, it lost its sea character, clearly linked to that expanse. So I took note that the sea effectively began to be perceptible in visual terms as a place, from the point that plane indicated. What is more, the intermediary place—a mere meaningless pool where paper rubbish drifted in and accumulated—could be transformed in spite of its small size. It would acquire a new interest if it was enlarged as a port for small sailboats. A beach might also be created there.

Now let us come to the problem of the tip. Without the factory, it appeared very different. It ended up constituting a kind of incongruity, because once the factory disappeared, one could no longer understand the presence of a tip in those places.

Thus I had to find for that landscape a different logic from the formal one, centered on the presence of the factory, to explain in ultimately different terms the quarries (which in the

future would be no more than holes) and the tips in order that, precisely, those quarries and those tips would lose their awkward significance in the future.

The tips would acquire a quite astonishing height, since the factory would no longer be present, because that building, with its chimneys, flattened the scale of the landscape and environment. Another thing, the tips implied a natural element: a little wood next to the beach. As soon as the factory was demolished, there would be an intrusion of a high mass that would reach the edge of the sea, as a kind of perpendicular to the beach. Luckily, that mass, by its artificial character, could be cut down from inside the site. Moreover, it was quite narrow.

A site of 55 hectares is a rather large surface area when we need to represent it in plane. What I mean by that is that when one draws plans that have to be held with both arms outstretched, one is inevitably tempted to have a scale that is not always compatible with the recognition of differences of low levelings. However, we know how for a pedestrian, differences of level of the order of 50 or 60 cm, or even a meter or more, on relatively short distances, are significant and strongly felt. The movements of the site had to be understood both in relation to the human scale, and in relation to the scale of the buildings to come.

Generally, for a better understanding, I draw almost systematic cross-sections of the site, of the whole site, so that I can figure out all the differences in level and the successive steps. I proceed in that way so that I can better understand the movements of the ground, but I do it without a precise purpose, without knowing for example if one will establish houses with low roofs there, or something else. I am simply trying to learn how

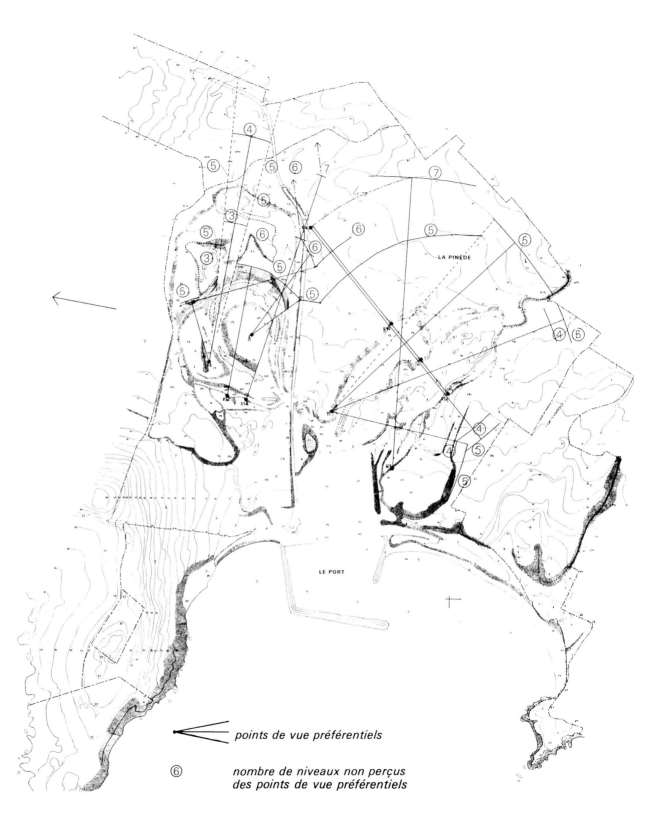

20b. Preferential points of view. (6) number of levels not visible from the preferential points of view.

LA PINÈDE

LE PORT

points de vue préférentiels

⑥   *nombre de niveaux non perçus des points de vue préférentiels*

the sensations one could have while traveling on foot over the places can be translated, in terms of height, in a clear way.

As a general rule one sometimes has the impression, while walking on some terrains, of a rather important movement, but in plan it can be revealed to amount to nothing. In a cross-section, one sees clearly the nature of the movement experienced and thus can more easily realize why, at a certain spot, one has an impression of falling, of slope movement, when at another spot nothing similar is experienced. The confrontation between a relatively precise survey and the impressions experienced can lead to a better understanding of the visual organization of the landscape.

For preferential points of view it is necessary, then, to determine what residents of the future buildings, situated, for example, 12 meters high, in other words, looking out of their window, will or will not see. Thus one tries to get an idea, at the global scale of the site, of what type of buildings could be established, considering what one wishes to see and, on the other hand, the way in which one will be overlooked.

As a general rule it is necessary to observe in detail what happens at two heights: one at a meter and a half, another at 12 meters (that is, the third floor), because at that altitude people can sit near their window and look outside. Several schemes are thus obtained, but at that stage it is a good idea to avoid going for the best possibility, and to fix straight away on a number of ideas.

On a terrain like La Coudoulière, it was realized that one could establish houses of 6 levels without their being visible from certain strategic spots of the terrain, even at a height of 12 meters: interesting information. That way one discovered that

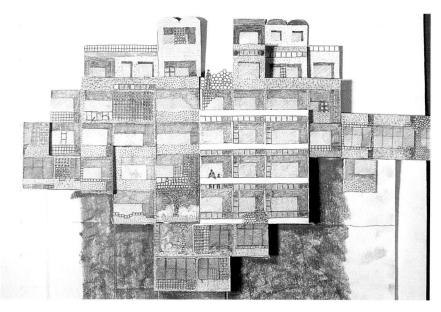

20c. "Fake rock" building.

this site on a relatively fragile relief, without precise character, could encase a presence of housing perhaps superior to what one would have thought at the outset, and without those buildings even having a very significant visual presence.

What, ordinarily, can those preferential points of view be? Spots from which one imagines that a relatively large number of people will be able to examine the site. That can be highly hypothetical since, as long as the indications are not specific, as long as the landscape modifications are not determined, everything remains in the domain of conjecture. For example, it appeared to me that from the back of the port and behind the factory, that is, at the beginning of the big quarry, there was an interesting point of view. I noticed that, from there, one could build at a relatively high level without the constructions invading all the landscape.

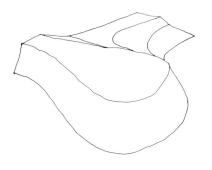
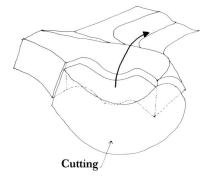
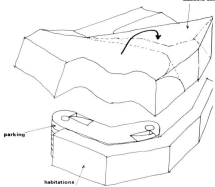

Embankment

Cutting

parking

habitations

Terrain — actual state	Terracing	Constitution of the rock building

I mentioned, some lines above, the road along the beach that had to be displaced. As it was not possible to displace it outside the surface of the property, there was an obligation to accomplish it inside the site, therefore cutting back the tip that was perpendicular to the beach.

From the moment when the road would be laid out and pass through, it would affect the tip by reducing it to the size of a molehill. It would become a road with lateral splaying, since the ground at the back of the tip would be higher. That way, the ground would be dislocated and, consequently, lose still more of its meaning.

In order to avoid that unfortunate effect, it was necessary to create a false logic: to build a tunnel (a fake one because buried beneath the earth that had been brought there) in a continuous mass, to ensure the eventual continuity of the planting as far as the end of the tip so that the displaced road did not seem to cut that mass. Moreover, to establish a wide footbridge would allow trees to grow, hence a vegetable continuity between the two sides of the displaced road. I persuaded the property developer to look at the possibility of building a vegetable passage, imagining it as 16 meters wide, fixed after study, thus large enough to plant trees above the 12-meter mark.

Besides the port and the factory on its way to being demolished, there was also present on the spot an original quarry, encircled by a pine forest. The quarry was modifying the character of the coniferous wood, because it lowered the visual level from 7 to 2 meters. There was also another quarry, an older one, which I had named "the ring" for the simple reason that there was water in the center.

The two quarries were separated by the pine forest and a path. I proposed not to use that path so that a reservation of vegetation could be created there. Why? Because the flat surface where the ring was situated was much more ecologically fragile than the pine forest and it was likely that later, the crowd, the public, would be required not to go there, if only by constraining and precise footpaths. On the other hand, the pine forest could be left to the public.

If I had not succeeded in joining those two vegetable ensembles, there would have resulted a certain frustration for people, who visit that area in great numbers during the summer, because they would not have access to that zone. Besides, there would have been a hope of partly transforming that zone into a botanical garden or something similar. That place was thus made to coexist with the pine forest, which remained accessible to the public.

Another problem was the problem of the pine trees with which the quarry was bordered. On a vague sketch the architects had planned to establish buildings at the top of the quarry, in place of the foliage, so that people could see the sea. However, a study from the Tourism Center at the University at Aix en Provence, which had also been made, following my advice, permitted us to discover that the eventual residents of those places slightly removed from the sea would not have attributed very great importance to that sort of view. It is easy to understand that this had direct repercussions on the project. Thus one knew that the people whose housing would be 200–250 meters from the beach would attach less importance to a direct view of the Mediterranean, at least in that maritime region.

Let us imagine that towers or high constructions had been built there, in the pine forest. That type of solution would have visually killed the site, because those trees, seen between the houses, would no longer have managed to form a pine forest, even if they were kept in great numbers. Indeed, as the pine forest, some of which was planted, offered a through view, if housing had been built on its edges, the lower parts of the buildings would have been visible between the trunks, which would have destroyed the pine forest as well as the curve of the ground, an idea that had to be rejected.

By contrast, if, through the pine forest, the light, the sky, and, further away, still more trees could remain visible, that transparency would preserve its meaning for it. In that case, if the pine forest was bordered by houses, it became trees seen through. If the possibility offered by those visual extensions thus gave meaning to the pine trees as an ensemble, it was not the number of trees which was important, but those extensions.

But, even if one wished to safeguard the pine forest, it was still necessary to find a place to erect the buildings. To look for a good foundation led to placing dwellings at the bottom of the quarry, that is, without a view of the sea, in a blocked-up place.

It was indeed a solution: to build housing, but to allow the residents to see the pine forest in the interior direction of the land, because the roofs did not show above the level of the surrounding ground.

Next to the existing port, I also suggested digging a second port to extend the first one, and then a third, to create a visual interest and make it more lively. Ports of a small scale, of course, since the eventual habitat would be of small height and proportion.

Thus I wanted, on one side, to safeguard the pine forest in itself, that is, as a visual phenomenon and as a presence, and, at the same time to add interest to a place, insofar as the people would have suddenly discovered a port in the middle of a wood with houses beneath.

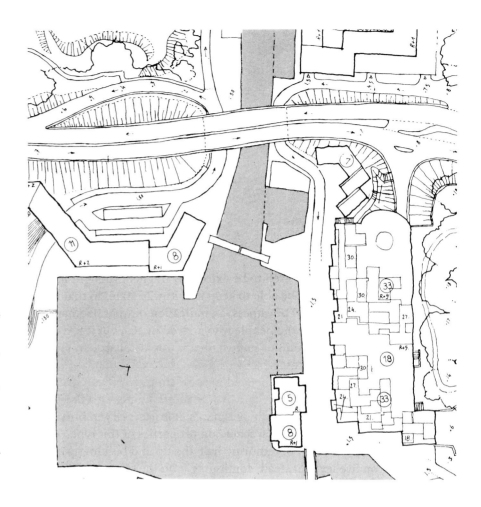

20d. Study of a fragment of the rock building.

As for the people circulating on the road, they would have seen, on the one hand, foliation above the footbridge in continuity with the foliage of the trees of the tip, and on the other hand, foliage on the ensemble of the buildings. Indeed, the fact of being overcome by trees could fundamentally change the presence of those buildings. The property developer having accepted that hypothesis, the ring, the pine forest, and its extension were safeguarded with a displacement of the road.

It was a reasoning starting from the micro-landscapes: the landscape of the ring, the "tree" landscape, the landscape of tree-houses at the back of the wood, and the landscape of rock-houses.

The tip showed itself to be extremely fragile. I thought initially that I would be able to keep it in its wild state, so that we should have a kind of witness, an indication of what had happened before, for the people who arrived by sea, but it was confirmed that it would not survive, that it would collapse by gradually falling to pieces.

A proposal was also needed to solve another difficult problem, the problem of parking. At the present time, with the regulations and the frequenting of places, it is necessary to provide for considerable parking spaces on properties of this type.

Thus I thought of removing half the tip and building parking on five levels instead, continuing it on the side with housing while quite straightforwardly making that tip by contrast a fake rock: in short, transforming that tip-parking into rock, a logical continuation of the nearby cliff. I created a kind of constructed rock, surmounted by houses, while resolving the problem of the fragility of its ground and the problem of parking.

But why that new landscape and those new designations? Because the existing landscape was weak, and one could not sustain the argument that it was possible and desirable to insert oneself into the original site.

Besides, the expression of "insertion into a site," too frequently used, has no meaning in the sense that the simple fact of bringing a construction into a site, however large it may be, generally creates a new landscape. One can rarely speak of insertion, except for exceptional cases. There is more frequently a creation of new sites on which the buildings take on a heavy presence.

Bringing a sand-building next to the rock-houses permitted helping the construction of other buildings near the beaches. The fragility of the site had led me, because of the importance of that fragility, to go in the direction indicated by the existing landscape, but on the condition that the construction help reinforce that landscape. At that level of options, I also thought of building some housing around the ring, but that implied knowing better about the state of the existing vegetation by calling on the services of an ecology expert.

I have already referred to the intervention of experts concerning the tourist study made by the Center at Aix-en-Provence. Before having to defend the idea of micro-landscapes, I wanted to know if the eventual constructions would modify the local biological conditions, which could lead to the disappearance of what, on the contrary, I wanted to try to make survive. I considered indeed that I could only present my study if the experts said: "Considering your interventions, one can suppose that the vegetation of the pine forest and the ring will continue to flourish, that the water inside the ring will not disappear, etc." Furthermore, I had asked a society specializing in the study of ports to try to calculate the work to see how that work could be balanced with the costs of construction and also to calculate all the art works at each stage, since their construction is very expensive. I also had studied the problems of drainage and circulation of water, because, with regard to a terrain so close to the sea, some concerns existed on that level.

Generally, the landscapers working on development occupy themselves on more important surfaces, whose development cost permits consideration of extensive expert reports on certain points, but when operations of a relatively small extent are concerned, as here in La Coudoulière, I consider that the problem is to express a certain number of hypotheses from which the specialists can tell if it is possible or not to continue in the directions considered. Of course, hypotheses are needed, otherwise one finds oneself with studies extremely and, in fact, unnecessarily heavy. It was not possible to take soundings on the entirety of the terrain in order to know which zones were constructible or not. One could also make a complete ecological study, but this would not perhaps be necessary. The production of hypotheses, I insist, thus enables one to ask for advice on precise points, which avoids very important costs and unnecessary studies.

It is of course also for the expert to determine the importance of the study to make. In certain cases, a single phone call is sufficient, when, in others, longer studies are needed. One cannot know in advance.

We have seen that the pine forest posed a certain number of problems. With the proximity of the sea and the small expanse of trees, the problem of trampling feet was to be found, since, with the arrival of summer, thousands of visitors would pass through. How was I to make it withstand that treatment? To that was also added the question of the ecological survival of the ring. It could be interesting to safeguard, at 100 meters from the sea, that landscape so different from the landscape of the pine forest or the rest of the site. There herons could be observed, as well as giant horsetails and vegetable rarities of that kind, which it appeared to me absolutely necessary to protect. Thus it was not possible to allow the people to go to that spot, which would have disappeared beneath their feet. Therefore the ring had to be imagined from afar. I think, indeed, that to see such beautiful giant horsetails a few hundred meters from the sea could certainly present some interest for people on holiday.

I also had planned in the middle of the ring a tiny restaurant with an extremely low roof, and some animals in cages, so that

no one would think it was unoccupied land. In fact, it has been well known for quite some time that it is necessary to give so called empty terrain some use from the very beginning; otherwise, pressures to use it can occur later. That is a well-known phenomenon. Thus it is necessary to think in advance of neutralizing those eventual pressures. Another difficulty is that of the visual extensions in relation to the scale of the site. I had tried to find a middle way between the forest and the sea with successive passages of habitat—rock-houses, sand-houses, reflection-houses—linked to the diverse characteristics of the site, but once the project was done, one would no longer understand the contrasts that existed on the sides and at the back of the ground, where habitations with four levels were erected, habitations of high density. As I did not think that such high buildings would be authorized, taking into account the coefficient of occupation of space and the closeness to the sea, I was led to modify my proposals and to create screens to control the visual extensions, though not seeking a complete saturation, which would have been absurd. Thus I was led to close visually, in a certain way, a shell corresponding to the surface of the site. An identical problem had already been posed for my study of the 600 hectares for a recreation area in the new town of Saint-Quentin-en-Yvelines, for which I had asked for the benefit of an area of protection to stop the pressure of the built zone, which would have completely undermined that natural space.

I would like to come back once more to what I call an architectural problematic in order to understand better the sense of the diverse architectures I wished to see on the site. What do we usually do in an operation of this kind? A cell is created, which is a certain type of building, and that unit is multiplied to fit the

20e. General plan.

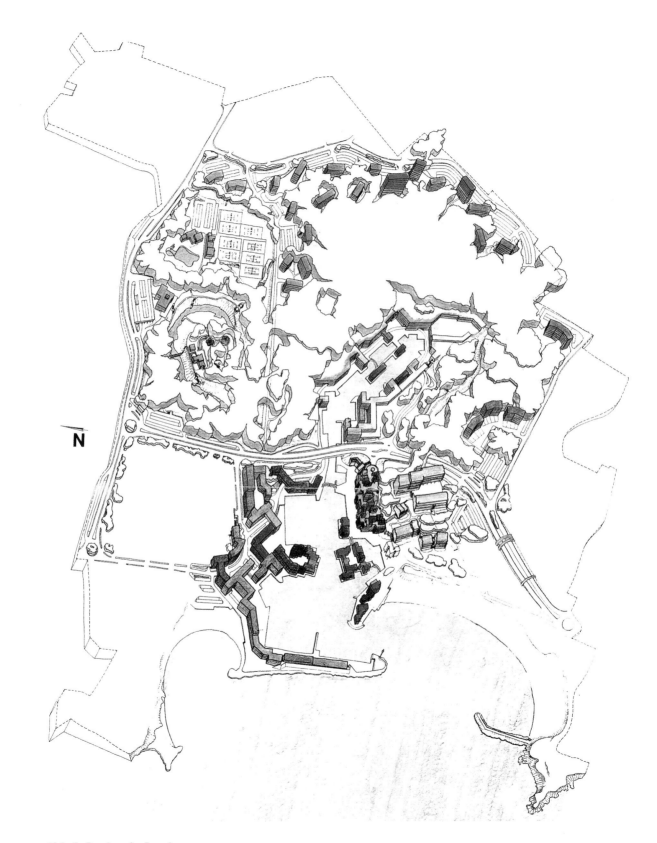

N

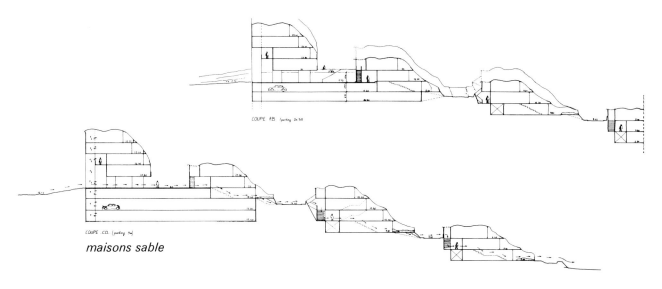

COUPE AB (parking 2e 30)

COUPE CD. (parking 3e)

maisons sable

maison végétale

20f. Sand (top) and vegetable houses.

scale of the surface to be treated. Thus a contradiction can occur between the characters of the site and the architectural elements that are built independently. By that I do not want to say that all sites require an architectural variation like this one. Indeed, this concerned a particular case linked to the problem posed by that quarry, which had to be made plausible after the disappearance of the factory. What was to be done?

In the case of a real site, truly natural or more or less truly natural, a house appears obvious, but in the present case, where naturality was wavering, it was imperative to pull out the evidence, or rather, to reinforce it.

If one wanted to create here a rock, I mean a fake rock, more artificial houses would have to be built on it, so that the significance of the artificial material would be displaced from that fake rock to the natural rock, along with an effort not to oppose those houses against what would look like a dressed-up parking spot. Indeed, without a clear opposition in the material,

the dressed-up parking and the houses would immediately have in common the constructed concrete, and so resemble one another. It was thus a necessity to draw attention to the houses themselves, by differentiating the houses from the rock, in sufficient contrast, by not directing the eye to the difference between houses and fake rocks. Thus I proposed to introduce artificially a certain number of contrasts between the rock-houses, in order to orient perception on them, and so to make more logical, more natural, the pseudo-natural elements of the rock parking area. Thus I planned houses which, by being very flat, gave the rock a higher scale, and, by being brightly colored, seemed definitely more artificial than the rock.

The relationship of "artificial" to "natural" had to be structured at several levels, to give a precise sensory situation to each of the elements in play: classic plastic problems but never seen in practice. In that study of the rock-houses, I diverged thus deliberately from the notion of style, the notions of "beautiful" or "ugly," because the aesthetic character of the architecture did not exist in itself; in fact aesthetic character only exists as global. So that, in that precise case, if the visitors had seen only the houses and not the landscape, they could have said that the development was a success, because the landscape of the rocks would have appeared natural to them.

Such plastic problems are to be found everywhere. In particular, I shall cite one in an unexpected domain I know quite well, the development of ocean liners, because I have had the opportunity to fit out entirely the liners *Mermoz* and *Renaissance*. Now when a lady said to me: "Mr. Lassus, you have painted the ceiling of that room with a really awful maroon color," I was delighted because, in fact, that lady had not seen that the ceiling was only 2.20 meters high in a room of 550 square meters, in other words, much too low. Quite often the clients object over a problem of taste and do not see the technical solutions, in that specific case the concealment by the use of color of a ceiling all too present through its lack of height.

That is why, in a domain that seems to everybody only a matter of taste, I only place myself on a level of plastic technician, a logical technician who brings solutions to specific objectives.

With the help of those examples, it becomes possible to understand that the natural is in fact only a term of a relationship that goes from more to less natural, so that a thing is always placed inside that context, relative to a determined visual field. In a given visual field, there always exists an element that is more natural than the other and thus becomes "the natural." But that classification only exists in relation to a determined field, and has nothing absolute. Consider a shrub in a container, in an apartment. It certainly will appear more natural than the enameled refrigerator next to it. Likewise on that site it is necessary to organize an architectural problematic according to the diverse elements already existing. Thus I had proposed, next to the rock-houses, sand-houses designed to be more in line with the beach, which helped and were part of that line. In other words, buildings that were not built there in contradiction with the elements of the site. Those sand-houses would have been dressed with shells, sand, and climbing plants, and so would have been able to

contrast with the rock-houses by differentiating them still more from the rock. Between the trees, on the other hand, it would have been more interesting to have more vegetable houses, that is, houses where screens and containers would have been put at the disposal of the residents in order to garnish the façades with vegetation. That place was indeed sufficiently removed from the sea. In any case, it was hoped that vegetation could effectively be grown there, which was not the case for the houses on the sea-front or on the port. I call that an "architectural problematic" because the matter is not to determine the appearance of architecture for itself.

By creating in that way micro-landscapes and types of architecture corresponding to those micro-landscapes, the people were led to imagine the links between those different types of landscapes. The residents would have thus established visually, by themselves, the relay between those different types of houses. One finds there the other mechanism about which I was talking before: first pose the terms of the contrast at the level of the habitation so that one can finally fix the passages between the sectors.

Concerning the houses which bordered the pine forest, in the part of the site closest to Six-Fours, and which did not have to be too visible through the tree trunks, I planned to bury their parking and to lift a few elements of relief so that the lower parts of those houses were situated at the height of the leaves, and less transparent than the trunks. In that way the encircling of the built became less obvious. According to that line of thought, one can find architectural expressions of completely different types. I myself give much attention to what happens on the ground because, usually, when one is at the seaside, one thinks that all the problems will be resolved because there is sun and water. So what is on the ground is massacred, when, precisely, it is interesting to prepare the manner in which one arrives at the water, by making people be conscious of that passage.

The houses situated in the port would have been colored with bright blues and greens, on which the movement of the water and the masts of the boats would have been reflected.

I have not mentioned until now the landscapes which surround La Coudoulière. It seemed to me impossible indeed to establish visual relationship with surrounding surfaces whose evolution was uncertain at the beginning of the study. Not being able to weave those visual relationships with the neighboring zones, I preferred to elaborate the silhouettes of the site's limits by preparing a succession of constructions and plantings that constituted a real background for the new landscapes. It is difficult, no matter what one wishes, to find relationships of similarity, to weave passages with the neighboring operations, which most often have the tendency to consider themselves as entities independent of the surface each one may have at its disposal. And this I had myself been compelled to do.

The Garden of the Anterior / 1975

Project for a Park in the New Town of L'Isle d'Abeau

Often we are able to trace the past of a town by looking at the fragmentary remains that date from its various periods of construction and remain visible in its old quarters and its ancient monuments.

The past of a new town, however, does not lie in its buildings. It is in the rocks, fields, and forests over which building has taken place, and in the lives of those who made the region what it is.

To keep the past of this new town alive, we can divide the center into a natural zone and a constructed zone. By means of this contrast, the zone in which construction is dominant will appear more secure than the one in which nature dominates. The latter will seem wild and a little frightening.

All too often the few trees that have been carefully retained in the new built up area merely indicate by their presence that they are the remnants of a wood that has disappeared, and attest to the fact that the constructed area has only been able to develop at the expense of nature. Thus they simply reinforce the brutality of the built forms.

A clear boundary between the two zones will have the effect of sharpening the opposition between the "natural" and the "constructed." But this boundary should not remain the same over all its length. It might take as its basis the principle of dissociation between the tactile and the visual.[1] When an overall view from a

high point is available, physical access would be made that much more difficult, to the point of being impossible; on the other hand, when physical access is possible, there would be obstacles to our discovery of the view and the visual prospect would be much reduced.

The first feature in this boundary might well be a wall or a rampart, whose textural treatment would be different from all the other buildings in the constructed zone, perhaps taking its inspiration from typical old walls of the region.

We can only make sense of the various zones if we envisage the relationship of this secondary center to that of the principal center in terms of overall images. That is to say, the internal contrast between the natural and the constructed zone in no way prevents the secondary center from appearing as a whole more natural and closer to vegetation than the urban center—which will appear even more urban by virtue of the same fact.

Inside the constructed zone, vegetation will be very much to the fore, but only domesticated vegetation: ornamental trees, some of them clipped into shape, flower beds, and perhaps a few fruit trees. On the other hand, plants that have been treated artificially in this way would be totally excluded from the natural zone.

The meaning of these two zones depends on the way the passage from the one to the other is achieved. But it is equally bound up with the various types of relational systems that provide their internal structuring.

[1] From the mid-1960s Lassus has consistently distinguished between the "tactile" and "visual" levels in his architectural designs and projects. That is to say, he holds that there is a crucial difference between the zone within which we require precise information about our environment— in order to park our car, negotiate a flight of steps, etc.—and the zone which is manifest to us only through vision and does not entail the risks of direct physical contact. More recently, he has suggested that this difference corresponds in many respects to the distinction between "garden" and "landscape."—S.B.

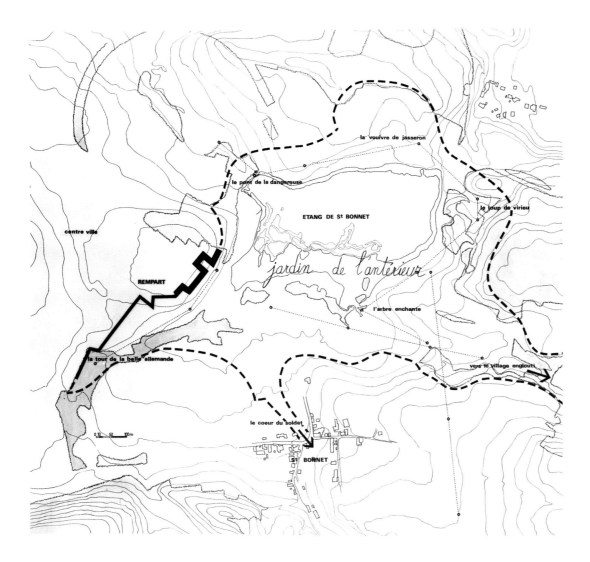

The constructed zone would come to an end at the terraces, which would overhang the natural zone from the wall or rampart. In this section the ground would be treated in such a way as to form surfaces with a high degree of granulation.

The façades of the buildings sited on the principal axis and in its vicinity would be treated as vegetation façades. These façades would have to provide support for the plants that would eventually cover them completely; it would therefore be necessary for deep jardinières and trellises to be installed. Even in the preliminary period, before the plants succeed in covering them, these façades would have to be identified with the theme of vegetation. They might be ornamented with motifs in concrete, cast and colored in bulk in the forms of flowers, leaves, and even animals, as well as simple trellis designs.

In line with the geometrical shape of the buildings, a geometry of jardinières and ornamental trees would grow up at ground level and enable the principal axis to be re-emphasized along certain sections of its length. Huge jardinières would provide continuity and support for some of the urban street fittings, in particular for the public lighting system. A structure of this kind would make groupings easier and also diversify our reading of the principal axis and the façades by introducing other scales.

On the pedestrian level, the vertical surfaces treated with vegetation would give way to more and more mirror-like, transparent, and brilliant surfaces as one approached the central area. Smooth white floor-surfaces would encourage the reflection of light from these vertical surfaces, which would eventually become shops. A vast horizontal network, like a roof above

the traffic, would hold the public lighting system, thus emphasizing the distinction between the "tactile level," which would
be treated in terms of brilliance, and the upper parts of the
façades, which would still register in terms of vegetation on the
visual scale.

In the area devoted to living accommodation, the continuity of constructed forms would be focused on small groups
of clipped trees, themselves surrounded by colored façades that
would form a contrast with the colors of the plants in order
to emphasize their character as objects. Where there were no
trees, the constructed façades would complement one another
through the contrasting vegetation planted according to the
wishes of the inhabitants.

Throughout the constructed zone, entrances to blocks of flats
would be conceived as subtle transitions between house and
street: sheltered places, that would encourage restful behavior,
offer views, and perhaps stimulate conversation, like a kind of
winter garden which it would be necessary to cross in order to
enter the house. As intermediary volumes, with virtually no connection to the façade, these light constructions would help in
setting up a tactile scale, and establish continuities with the network that supports the fitments of urban life. In an avenue close
by the ramparts, there would be a miniaturized micro-landscape
set up around a fountain; this would provide a reminiscence of
the garden of the anterior, which would be one of the most important parts of the natural zone.

In order to carry conviction, the natural zone must be sufficiently extensive for the boundaries not to be visually appre-
ciable, whether from the privileged point of view offered by
the terraces or from that of ordinary pedestrians. There should
be no opportunity for people on foot or in cars to be aware of

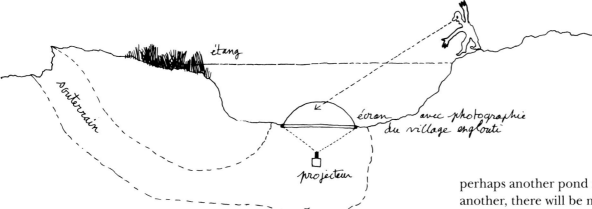

étang

souterrain

écran — *avec photographie du village englouti*

projecteur

making a full circuit of the area. The firmness of the division created by the wall would be emphasized by the lack of definition in the other boundary lines.

The difference between constructed and natural zones would be defined essentially as one between an area in which measurable elements—houses, roads, and street fittings—are brought into juxtaposition, and one which is beyond measurement but nevertheless incorporates a number of measurable elements: for example, a tree at the edge of a forest. But at the same time we know full well that this natural zone can no longer be regarded as altogether outside measurement. It simply serves as a support for the immeasurable of the imagination: for what we term the *demeasurable.*

Away from the foot of the ramparts, there stretches the garden of the anterior. Although there are no walks and pathways, you will discover—as the ground becomes more and more wild—occasional fields scattered with groups of trees, a few domestic animals, almost abandoned fields that retain parcels of earlier cultivation, fallow land, woods, bushes, thickets or briar surrounding practically inaccessible ponds, fringes of the forest where the dead branches are no longer gathered up, and

perhaps another pond further on. Then, in isolation from one another, there will be micro-landscapes, almost like islets, to illustrate the legends and tales of the region. At sunset, you will be able to hear, close to the banks of the pond, the strange tolling of the submerged bells of the Lac du Bar; and a little further on, the image of a submerged village will emerge, in a halo of light, from the depths of the water. To aid the discovery of these secret places and to allow pedestrians to find their way, columns will be installed beside each of the micro-landscapes. At the top of each of them, which you reach by a few steps, there will be a peephole through which one or more of the other columns can be seen: they mark the "location" of the Tour de la Belle Allemande, the Grotte de la Bonne Femme, the Enchanted Tree, the Wolf of Virieu . . .

These visual tracks will make up for the lack of coherent tracks on the tactile level. Once again, when a general overview is offered from a high point, physical access will be made more difficult, and inversely the visual field will be reduced to a minimum if there is easy physical access, so that the process of discovery can take place gradually.

With increasing use, a large number of rough tracks will come into being among the nettles and brambles.

Quite by chance, entrances to underground passages will be discovered. But these will turn out to have collapsed a few yards further on, suggesting a whole network of subterranean galleries.

In the garden of the past, we will be free to play in the meadow, to identify the various plants, to listen to the sound of frogs croaking, or to venture into the woods; and the miniaturized versions of local legends will enable us to dream of the legendary past of the place.

An example:

Toward the end of the afternoon, at the moment when the walker becomes aware that the light has died down and night is on the way, weak, muffled sounds seem to be coming from the pond of Saint-Bonnet.

If the walker wishes to identify them and situate their point of origin more precisely, he will follow them and draw near to the banks of the pond, where he will recognize the sound of the various bells emanating from the pond itself. Before he can get too close, a number of flashes will light up the depths and the surface of the water.

Then some of these points of light will rapidly turn into spots and finally into luminous areas of greater and greater extent, with ill-defined edges; as they grow larger, there is gradually revealed from the center, at the bottom of the pond, an aerial view of the shifting images of houses, streets, and unidentifiable monuments.

The way the luminous areas separate, the form of their edges, and the scale of the revealed landscapes tend to suggest that there are cracks in the bottom of the pond which allow us to glimpse another world—a world that may be submerged but is full of light. The full extent of this world will not seem to be restricted simply to the surface that is presented, but will give the impression of stretching way beyond the pond.

Then, all of a sudden, the images are gone. The pond and its reeds appear once again, but this time they seem darker. The walker, staying in his place in order to be able to hear more clearly, concludes that the bells are in effect no longer sounding. Then he recalls that they grew silent a few moments before the images disappeared . . .

The Garden of the Planets / 1980

Proposal for the Parc de la Villette

The first image:

The conquest of the immeasurable forest and the ocean by a system of measurement: the art of the French garden, which led from geometrical forms to the wildness of nature through a continuum of subtle transitions: from the topiary tree to the tree in its optimum state.

Printed over it, a second image:

"(Down) from the rocks (up) to the water, the field is soaking, breathing in and out, and flourishing" (Francis Ponge).

From the fact that it is situated on the ring road around Paris, this place could also serve as a direction finder between the ingoing and the outgoing city traffic.

And then the aim of the installation would be to give this place a kind of verisimilitude by creating a logical image of the landscape *substratum*—the relief of the land, the water—and the elements which are added to it successively—the canal, the trees, the buildings, a meadow . . .

In this place reserved for science and technology, a sensory approach that involves "making visible" both Nature and our own nature, passing beyond irony, would be a vital means of restitution for the present: an indispensable way of reconciling science and the sensory world.

The cultural prolongation of the symmetrical garden, which is such an attractive form despite its hierarchical quality, should not blind us to the fact that gardens have almost always foretold in advance the relationships between man and nature, and between society and nature.

Thus it is a question of "hypothesis." What of yesterday and today will be maintained in the sensory approach of tomorrow, and what will be the new ways of touching or moving people?

Just because it has lost the measureless quality of the forests and oceans, and become "second nature" to us, the Earth has not for that reason turned into a garden. Shall we have the capacity to bring about a third form of nature, a nature we have chosen and intended: a garden?

Instead of investigating the last forms of measurelessness, or other possible forms of the measureless, some people prefer to bring the notion of measurement itself into open question and make elaborate attempts to avoid a "conqueror's posture" in their elaboration of a new everyday mode: a total landscape consisting in relationships between measurable elements, another order of measurelessness. It is they who have the opportunity, if they wish it, to make use of the forms of activity, known or unknown, which the reconstituted substratum makes possible.

Echoing the situation of the last half of the eighteenth century, this garden should testify precisely to the diversity of present day attitudes to nature and the reflections which they give rise to . . . That is why I originally called it "the garden of dreams."

> The visible landscape before my eyes is, not external to, but linked synthetically with . . . other moments in time and in the past, but these moments are genuinely behind the landscape and simultaneously within it, not they and it side by side "in" time. (Merleau-Ponty)

Let us try to reconstitute a logical picture of the site, beginning with the presence of a canal that will still be used by barges. This canal necessarily passes at the lowest level and breaks the relief only at its least elevated point in a tunnel, on the side of the circular road.

On the Paris side, the point where it joins another canal corresponds to the lowest point in the whole terrain; to the east, is

22a,b. The measureless
vertical dimension.

the highest point, which will enable us to develop the steepest slope and keep the site free from the noise of the road.

The newly adapted buildings would be installed along, and the new constructions at the foot of, this declivity; they would adjoin the canal and the street, so as to be related and connected with the town, and to free the largest possible surface area for the park.

The constructions along the canal, and the spaces which are closest to them, all being measurable, would lead stage by stage to the less measurable; the high points of relief, planted with trees, the verge of the "forest which is now of automobiles," would form a border of varying depth along virtually the entire surface of the terrain, following both the circular and the exterior boulevards.

Differences in scale would reinforce these transitions, while the attempt would be made to open up each one of them to a different form of "measurelessness." There would be a garden of scents, a garden of colors, and then a garden of nature poets,

from Virgil to Francis Ponge and from Jean-Jacques Rousseau to Malcolm de Chazal. A large axis, the Alley of the Fountains, links the group of buildings, opening them up toward the canal and the great meadow . . . each of the fountains would suggest a different treatment of water, incorporating rocks, elements of vegetation and fire . . . with sound accompaniments also varying in each case.

This Alley of the Fountains would be followed by larger and larger surfaces, like the meadow and the high grass garden, whose boundaries would be traced by a border of continuous bushes, approached by way of the Alley of the Winds.

The fundamental difference between the mineral and the vegetable, between the town and the country, is that grass bends in the wind while stone does not: grass, in all varieties from the white valerian to the giant agrostis at the water's edge, and including the yellowish oat-grass at the verge of the wood, the white hair-grass and the brome-grasses.

Beneath the meadow, beneath the large grasses that sway in

the wind along the slope, and beneath the entry to the forest, the Path of Abysses would open up behind the fountain's curtain of water, not far from the tunnel framed by poplars, under which the barges ply their way.

After accompanying the subterranean river, whose murmurs can hardly be distinguished from their echoes, from stalagmite to stalactite, the pathway would arrive at the measureless verticals. And so, under the ground, visitors would come upon the celestial, immaterial vault of a planetarium, with its suggestions of infinity, a measureless vertical, taking the place of our measureless horizontals, the new forest of the classical garden. Then, further on, in a descending gallery, there would be a reconstruction of the visual field of Neil Armstrong, walking on the Moon,

set around one of the stones he brought back: the first flower of this new botanical garden. Successively, we would see other reconstructions of stellar landscapes, what we know of them and what our scientists suppose: one after another in distinct environments: Mars, Neptune, Venus, Pluto . . . the planetary garden.

At the lowest point, with a dull growling, there would be section models of volcanoes, both active and extinct, bordering on a bottomless pit, in homage to Jules Verne's *Journey to the Centre of the Earth*; another measureless vertical which is still beyond our apprehension: the depths of the Earth.

There would also be numerous places, very disparate in surface area, reserved for activities of an ephemeral nature (like letting off hot-air balloons, concerts, training animals), or for the formation of particular areas devoted to solar experiments . . . or for the breeding of *lepidoptera*: "Great Mars" changing to black wings with violet reflections . . . "Day Peacock" with red wings, "Morio" with brown wings bordered with yellow . . . to adorn the meadow with flowers . . .

Postscript (September 1982)
Stephen Bann

Since the election of President Mitterand, the entire project for the museum and park at La Villette has been substantially revised, and a new international competition has been launched to determine the design of the park in particular. Lassus is working at present on a new and very much more detailed version of his Garden of the Planets, which will be submitted for the competition (see this volume).

The Snake and the Butterflies / 1981

The Footbridge

Five years ago, two landscapers for the new town, Istres, situated near Marseilles, on the edge of the Etang de Berre, asked me to design a footbridge with them. In fact, they were developing an urban park between the old town and its new extension, but it came about (let us not enter the debate of inevitable responsibilities) that the area reserved for the park was cut, I should say sliced clean in two, by a four-lane highway, with a central strip four meters wide, and, to avoid the children being flattened by

cars, it became necessary to station police at the start and finish of the schoolday to help them across.

Indeed, the children were living at one edge of the park, and the school was situated at the other end. A pedestrian and

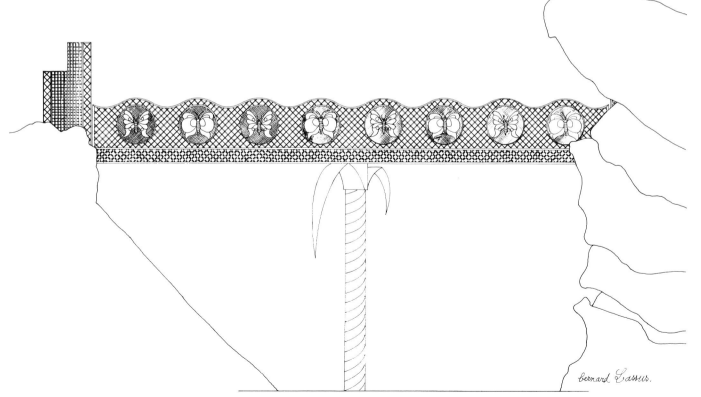

23a. The metallic butterflies fly more easily than the rock.

bernard Lassus.

119

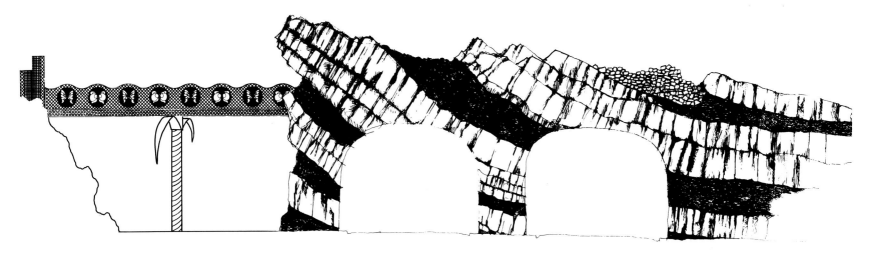

23b. Separation into two elements.

23c. To make a foot-bridge that doesn't look like a footbridge.

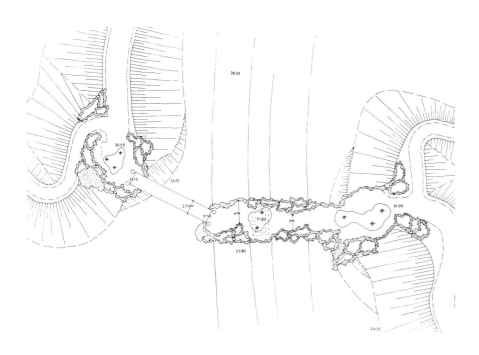

cycle footbridge had to be built, probably in "glued laminae" (in wood) since its purpose was to reunite the two fractions of a park!!!

I will not waste time with the various phases of that design, except to say that the first plan of the footbridge, including in its center a cast-iron kiosk decorated with a frieze of large butter-flies, whose antennae tips bore the public lighting, was, in short, not realized, even though it had overcome all the financial and administrative barriers.

At this moment, the realization of the chosen project is under-way. It is a tunnel, about forty meters long, in imitation rock, embodying the two lanes and the median, coming abruptly to an end and then being replaced by the second part of the foot-bridge, narrower and metallic, with lattice guard rails, about fifteen meters long.

The imitation rock must not appear more "real" than the railway tunnel of my childhood, painted over with cows in a meadow. For those who pass along the road, is it not strange to make the road pass under a rock, when, by a slight diversion, it could have passed under the metallic section? An introduction to how absurd it is, and to what a beautiful well-made footbridge would have hidden, since drivers would have barely seen, with the help of a few pine trees, that they were traversing a park.

To the absurd is it not imperative to respond with still more absurdity, in order to have a little probability?

The Slope, the Meadow, the Vertical Garden / 1982

Proposal for the Parc de la Villette

We didn't feel the moon in the same way as you can be saturated by a terrestrial landscape that you see, that you feel, or that you touch.

Up there we were isolated: our space suit was a barrier between the surface of the moon and us, and the tinted visor of the helmet gave us a false impression of the landscape. (Edwin Aldrin)

The fifty hectares of the site at La Villette, flattened when the slaughterhouses were originally built, is located on the slope of the Seine valley, which links Belleville Heights to the river at Saint Denis, with a 100-meter variation in level. Moreover, on the terrain itself, the lock of the Canal Saint Denis proves the point, situated as it is 10 meters lower than the Canal de l'Ourcq, which crosses it. From the site, the only visible reference to this fundamental factor is the ground one perceives beneath the buildings going up to Belleville Heights. To demonstrate the double adherence of the site of La Villette to the suburb and to the district of Belleville, to underline the logic of the Canal de l'Ourcq and to make it visible, and to be in line with the moats of the museum as well as with the lower part of the lock of the Canal Saint Denis, we plan to establish a slope parallel to the old natural declivity of the ground. Thus the slope constituted makes the place credible. It operates, like a junction, between the Porte de la Villette in the north and the Porte de Pantin in the south, and as a visual metaphor for the Porte de Belleville.

With that slope, the site of La Villette becomes once again a fraction of the landscape entity of the Seine valley at that spot.

It constitutes the fundamental substratum of that place.

In order to play its role, it is important that this slight slope (3 percent) can always be perceived as such, and draws the eye

toward Belleville. Thus it has to remain very open, which would equally favor a view of the canals.

Destined to become a park and, as such, to be a credible partner to converse with the town, we propose to treat it as a grass meadow, a treatment that appears as the most suitable to accompany the water of the canal lined with its poplars.

In the logic of its substratum, the grass covering a surface area of twelve hectares, cut and bordered by canals, permits a vegetable scale to be credible and natural to the place.

The meadow open to the light and presence of the sky also becomes the mirror of those spaces.

Numerous constraints could weaken the meadow, but here we will talk about the omnipresent noise. Between the source of the noise and the meadow we raise a long, high talus that erases the view of the highway totally and its sound impact partially, and forms a vegetable boundary.

The principle of a meadow in dialogue with the town and the suburb led us to propose the establishment of most of the activities of the program at the periphery of the park. Thus, a garden in the southwest section in dialogue with the 19th *arrondissement*, greenhouses in the north in dialogue with those of the museum and thus with the museum itself. On the basin section of La Villette, a few rows of poplars accompany the Canal Saint Denis and the Canal de l'Ourcq and form the equally vegetable west boundary of the meadow.

The only place for which dialogue still has to be introduced is the talus at the peripheral Pantin edge, and this will become the Vertical Garden.

As a skyline, of a constant height, the talus reinforces the visibility of the slope which runs alongside it as it rises gently from

24a. In the vertical garden: the garden of lianas.

the Canal de l'Ourcq. Covered with brambles, whose trailing roots absorb the high levels of sound, and through its length and height, it lures the eye to climb above the buildings of Pantin toward a freer and more spacious sky.

Parallel to the ring road and the boulevards of the Maréchaux, the park is accessible either laterally to vehicles, which it absorbs momentarily, and to pedestrians via its extremities. Walking against the traffic takes place in the most important section of the north-south walk in the park. There, at every moment, the pedestrian can either ignore, or see, and/or have access to the meadow.

The horizontal meadow, a space with its own scale, has tilted in a series of vertical miniaturizations into imaginary spaces.

The talus offers the possibility of being occupied on two main levels by a series of places whose ambiances and diverse functions are organized according to two principles:

1. The ecotopes based on natural light and given sound by acoustic processes. The arrival and the dispersion of the natural light gathered vertically through holes made in the upper level of the talus, levels of grass and light, would be specially designed for each of them.

2. Places with luminous ambiances, which are entirely artificial and given sound by electro-acoustic processes.

The thematic gardens of discovery and initiation, required by the idea of the work, will be grouped around a general theme until now undeveloped in the history of gardens, that is, the vertical dimension. All the elements of the garden will be here tackled according to that dimension. Without prejudging subsequent decisions on the different types of gardens chosen, here is what we propose as examples:

In the *Garden of Lianas* the visitor could climb up and down

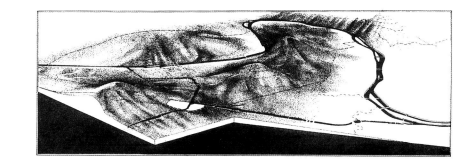

Seine Valley

Slope

Prairie and vertical garden

Walkway

24b. The terrain of La Villette is a slope linking the Belleville Heights to the bottom of the Seine Valley.

and along the trees to observe them in their different tropisms, from their tops right down to their roots.

In the *Garden of Cascades* the verticality would be emphasized by the movements and sounds of the water gathered in the green lake at the subterranean level, a place accessible to visitors.

The *Garden of Ascending Movements* would be the garden of the air, alternatively hot and cold, dry and humid, laden with mist or perfectly clear: the games would be those of the rainbow, the rising or descending breezes, frosts or dew, mosses and alpine lichens, or cacti and succulents of semi-desert ecotopes.

And finally the *Garden of Echoes* would play on the sound and acoustic dimension, thus turning to account the capacity for expression of real or illusory distances through sound and its modulations. Furthermore, that sound dimension would not be limited to that garden alone, but would create an essential dimension to the park, in connection with the famous Cité Musicale to be built.

Going beyond the stage of simple noise protection, the science of acoustics will propose to help the artists and conceivers to animate the park in a real way.

For this purpose, it will try to recreate a silence particular to the park. As silence is not absence of sound, to recreate a silence at the limits of the audible, it will propose a sound screen sufficiently complex to forbid immediate and simple deciphering.

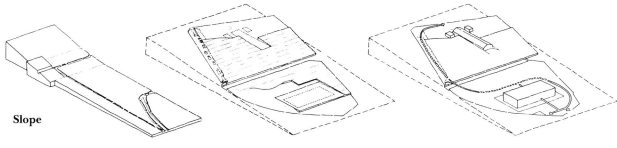

24c. From the horizontal to the vertical.

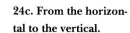

de l'horizontal au vertical

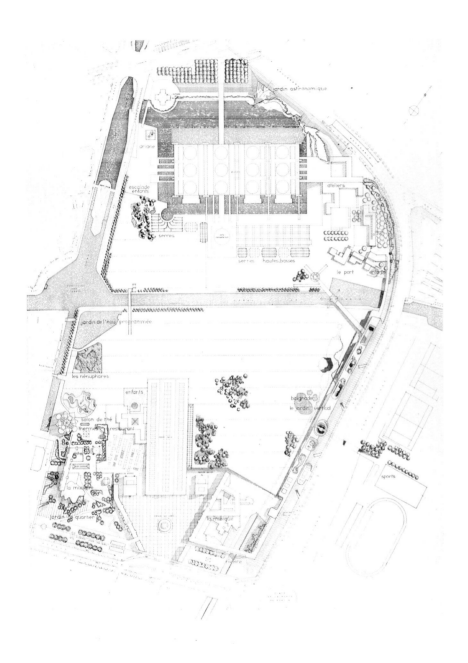

24d. International concourse, Parc de la Villette, Paris.

The memory of the visitors exerted on the complexity of that screen-silence will easily be capable of deciphering, by contrast, the images produced by the acoustic signals on that first plane.

The Vertical Garden will permit the construction of different silences not penetrated by low frequencies. They will go from the almost empty silences of the places where the ear will hear the most minute echoes (cf. the Garden of Echoes), to silences suggesting the natural elements, those ensembles functioning in phase with the creations of artists and visitors. The circulation plan we propose is based on the principle of displacements of bodies following the differentiated rhythms and paces according to *the sequences of heterogeneous places*, the very fact of movement in the space assuring the walk of unity.

The walking is thus never imposed and is opposed especially to the linear principle of urban circulation. All circulation of a certain length that would cross the meadow in a straight line would make the internal dimensions of the park be perceived as inferior to its own length, and would destroy "the effect of the park" perceived by the visitor beneath the angle of possibility for him to appreciate the dimensions by the movement of his own body and not by references of the urban register.

Concerning the surface area of the meadow, we suggest that it will be planned gradually, in accord with the circulation patterns that will be put into practise by the visitors.[1]

[1] For this competition, Bernard Lassus was helped by Pascal Aubry and Alain Mazas, landscapers, Anne Cauquelin, philosopher, Pierre Mariétan, musician, Jean Marie Rapin, acoustician, Pierre Lefèvre, architect, Pierre Donadieu, ecologist, and the advice of Jean Duvignaud, Lucien Sfez, and Jean Nouvel.

The Fountain Way / 1983

Four lanes separated by a central strip, and then a desert . . . if you happen to live in one of the thousands of apartments situated on this side, you will have the greatest difficulty in visiting your neighbor who lives on the other side of the highway.

To join these two areas, it is envisaged that a footbridge two hundred yards long will be constructed, before the railway bridge. But who will want to mount the footbridge and use it? Many people will just keep on crossing the highway underneath, at risk of their lives.

For the people living here to take advantage of it, the footbridge should not look like a hostage, or a new and violent assault on the site, or, if you think about it, like a footbridge. It

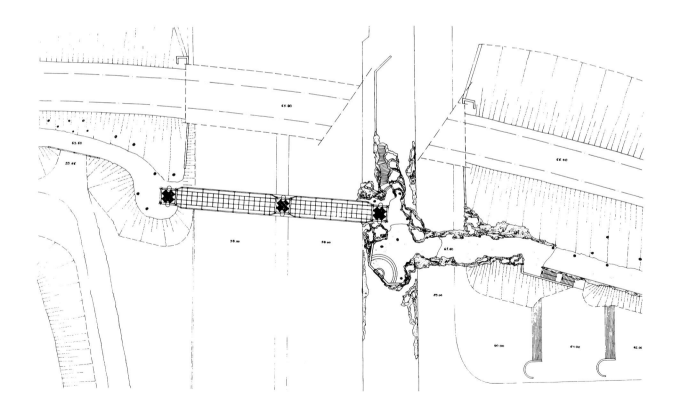

25a–c. The Pytheas footbridge. "I love you . . . a bit . . . much . . . passionately . . . to madness . . . not at all . . ." in order to encourage children to use the bridge.

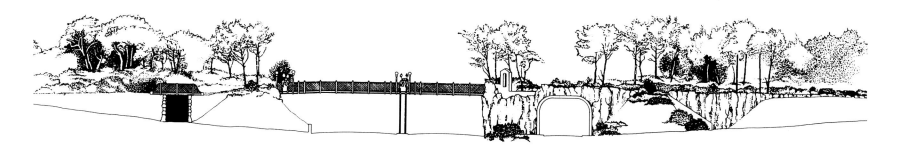

must look as though it could have existed before . . . as if there was then, some time ago, a pathway that became a footbridge at the moment when the highway was hollowed out underneath.

But how can a footbridge be changed into a pathway? Probably there has to be something specific to which it traditionally led . . . a fountain, a Provençal fountain that can easily be recognized as being earlier in date than the other elements from the site.

After all, who would be so stupid as to construct a fountain six yards over a false tunnel and a medley of autoroutes? Such absurdity merited an even greater absurdity, to make this footbridge into a pathway: the "Fountain Way."

Uckange / 1981–87

The difficult and courageous decision made by M. Robert Schoenberger and M. Charles Ruggiéri, to destroy half of the 1,200 housing units that had just been repossessed in Uckange, immediately posed the question: what housing?

From the joint planning pursued by the mayor and the persons in charge of the different residents' associations emerged the choice of keeping the buildings from which the highway could be seen, eliminating the two whose façades looked out over closed spaces (they contained, moreover, most of the empty housing), and, finally, dividing the longest into fractions.

The initial mass plan was covered with long straight lines of circulation bordered by buildings isolating interior spaces, spaces sometimes cut by perpendicular buildings. That plan is now, following the decision to destroy specific buildings and the disappearance of their mass, in an inverted spatial situation. Indeed, it is the totality of each of the two spaces where the operation is situated, which is from now on perceptible. Even if the visual field is limited, here and there, by a building, the ensemble of the new plan leaves a neat impression of an expanse whose boundaries are uncertain.

The objective that was set for me by the concept of the work was above all to do away with the image of that housing complex in whose accommodation nobody wanted to live. In that context the double intervention can be explained of reinstalling the arrangement of the grounds, whether they be garbage heaps or "green spaces" (roughly a dozen hectares), and painting the façades of the 600 housing units that were retained. I will not mention the internal renovations pursued concurrently.

The recoloration work and the movements of the ground started when the machines were engaged in demolition in order to show that "destroy" did not mean "abandon," but the proposition of a new space on the tactile scale as the most concrete and if possible the most appropriate to the place. That space definitely had to be imaginary as well, this time on a visual scale. That double movement led to the formation of light reliefs, with slightly concave stretches changing into slight but long slopes, to take the buildings into wide ground movements, less artificial than the former. That slight emphasis on the natural was meant to try to link the ground to that other fundamental element, the sky, so that this one offered in return a tiny patch of its immensity. If the variations of level have not always had the importance desired, that is due to the passage of networks not deeply buried and thus impossible to move, and to the presence of trees planted at the moment of the original construction, which have become tall and thick. It was indispensable to keep those trees by trimming them back severely because, compact as they were, they created very somber places, dark places not appreciated by the residents. It was also necessary to cut those which had grown against the façades and plunged the apartments into shadow. A few lines of poplars, and clumps of trees and bushes in groups of several varieties, with many more bushes than trees, were planted in place of the old mineral or constructed surfaces. Today, intermediary planes of low vegetation conceal the view of the façade/ground links, and push back spatially the entirety or parts of certain façades, themselves supports of landscape elements, taking into account the position they have to keep in the landscapes of "planted vegetation — painted vegetation." When winter came, the painted trees restored leaves to the bare trees.

But, before mentioning the painted façades at greater length, let us go back to the ground and the implantation of the new

nevertheless separated by a few buildings and a very busy road (the trucks that leave the highway always drive to the factory too fast) made a traffic circle with stop lights imperative in order, finally, to cross safely. A clock, clearly visible from the north and south ensembles, and, especially from the small square situated further, has been placed in the middle of that circle. This year, it juts out over the begonias planted on its conical base by the municipal gardeners.

If, in the north, the few houses painted with intense colors signal the new square from far away, laterally, the perpetuation of the real trees by the fake ones fluidifies the boundaries of the central planted space, by painting out these ones as ambiguous by the conflict this perpetuation introduces between the intangible position of the building and the inevitably vague expansion suggested by the drawings and the colors of the façades. The presence of a vaster, freer park, destined perhaps for even more freedom, escapes from it.

In the south, that ambiguity is not even considered because the surfaces brought together by the demolition are insufficient to disengage the breathing space indispensable for the creation of a park. The area liberated there collides rapidly indeed, except in its length, with the interior façades of the buildings that border the main thoroughfares, which, however, have been fragmented by the demolition. On the street side, the façades present houses of all styles, all periods, and from many places, even beyond the frontiers, all stuck together.

The openings of the windows, whose form and distribution were too repetitious before the painting, are for each decorated house either enlarged or minimized, in any case bordered and rearranged in different configurations. Adding to those differ-

walkway, which traverses the planted surfaces and goes alongside the streets of the two principal ensembles, called north and south, in a flexible but almost direct route. Beyond a ramp and a few stairs, it leads at the extreme limit on the south to the Mairie and, at the opposite, on the north, to a new small square, at the bottom of the widest planted stretch, enclosed on three sides with painted façades of brightly colored small houses, next to the school. The junction between the two housing ensembles

**Appearance of the
buildings before the
intervention.**

ences, some fake oriel windows have been inserted. To alleviate globally the weight of the built, the loggia façades, with loggias that overhang the paths parallel to them, have become skies full of white and pink clouds on which there float from time to time flags of the countries from which the residents originate.

Then, having passed beyond the street and the visually softened angles of the gables, the eye, and eventually the feet, penetrate the new interior space which is enlarged and more open.

The gables and their pointed angles, multiplied by the fractioning of the buildings, have become the essential articulations from the streets to the garden. For example, they form the passage from the drawings of the follies to the planted elements which structure the views that lead there, or ensure the transition between the rotundities, the curves, the ornamental accidents, the vegetation, all painted, and the movements and accidents of a walkway. That is why there are changes of relative heights in the motifs, intentionally too big or too small, heights linked beneath certain angles to the sought after effects of remoteness or closeness. In that way, spaces are inserted where the buildings become close or remote fractions of the suggested landscapes. From most of the other points of view, one perceives a jarring accumulation of images at contrasted scales, of fractions of parks, gardens, and landscapes of all periods and all kinds. Exotic follies, a Chinese pagoda, or the golden cupola of a Turkish pavilion border the flowered portal or the house with a tiny garden of a dweller-landscaper. Further, a fragment of geometrical park with clipped trees fraternally plays with the angle of a gable. At the extremity of a façade, crowning a hill, a folly with a straw roof, surmounted by firs, stands as a tribute to Charles Rivière Dufresny, the famous rival of André le Nôtre. A

remote line of gray-blue poplars, on the horizon of the first floor of the longest façade, announces perhaps the course of a river, or perhaps it evokes some swamps. The central space shelters not only a garden, in which an old imposing cedar is visible from the highway, but also a range of parks, gardens, and imaginary landscapes, from yesterday and today, a "mille-feuilles landscape," but also thanks to the houses and the skies of the buildings-on-street, a "critical landscape."

The simultaneous process of developing the grounds and treating the façades permits opposing tracing with visuality, which thus favors, by mutual induction, a greater adequacy between the appearance and concrete presence of the ground and also an effective dissociation between the physical presence of the façades and the spaces suggested by the painting.

Paint is not a rich material, but its possibilities are vast, and, if one paints, one has to use these possibilities, if only to fit in with

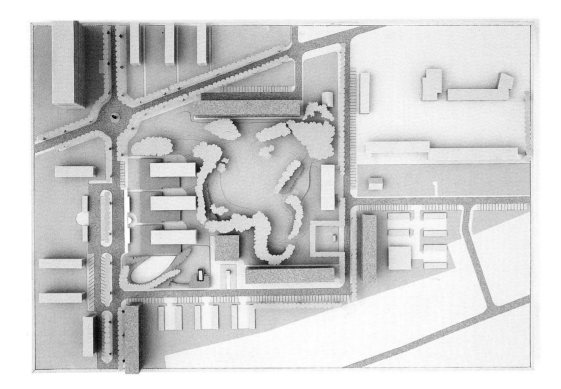

Detail of the exterior spaces restructuring project.

the idea of the work and the residents. However, the point was not to dress these housing units up as beautiful buildings. The buildings are what they are and the first to know that are those who live in them; if not, they will discover it quickly enough. The purpose of the intervention not being dressing-up, it was, however, important that the paint was used with care, because what the residents were looking for was properly finished work, with due respect to them. Concerning the effect of the painting itself, it derives certainly from what we do with it, but, above all, from the way others perceive it.

Early in the morning, each day, the Mayor, M. Frentzel, made his way to the building site and exchanged, here and there, a few words with people encountered on his way, and with the workers, concerned as he was with the progress of the work and the opinion of his interlocutors. From the beginning, the residents had welcomed the double process of demolition and rehabilitation and had followed with attention the evolution of the painted motifs. If they knew about the general principle, they did not, however, know the details of it and, at the bottom of the scaffolding, they arrived to interrogate the painters on the subjects and colors forthcoming.

Those painters were first of all transferring the drawings to the scale of the façade by referring to the plans and then adjusting them according to the openings of the windows. It was more difficult on the pebble surfaces where there were no guide marks. Then, helped by a bigger team, they added the colors. Those painters were volunteers, having years before gone to classes at the Ecole des Beaux-Arts in Metz, at the request of their companies, in order to complete their foundation in drawing and to realize these projects. But it was by trial and error that this organization was put in place, resulting in the realization of the projects of recoloration.

It is not, however, on that particular aspect that it is important to insist, but on the essential role the foreman and the painters of the diverse companies that realized them played and still play by preparing the people to accept the paintings. It is these people, indeed, who announce step by step what will happen, to the young as well as the old, and say the few words that make sure that, after their departure, the paintings not only are there, clearly visible, but also are created in the spirit of those who look at them.

The Garden of Returns—Rochefort-sur-Mer / 1982–87

In 1982, the town of Rochefort declared an open competition for landscape architects to create a park by the Charente River, where an exceptional building had just been restored: the Corderie Royale of Rochefort. Let us briefly recall the terms of the competition, which involved three principal requirements: first the conservation of the site, which also implied preserving its connection to foreign and exotic places; second, the establishment of connections between the town and the Corderie; and third, the design of all the surrounding areas in such a way as to take the industrial character of the building into account.

The team set up by Bernard Lassus, which included Pascal Aubry, Alain Mazas, and Pierre Donadieu, won first prize for their "Garden of Returns" (Jardin des Retours). Four years later, the initial plan is little by little coming into effect. In order to explain this evolution from the original conception onward, we thought it necessary to set out the project as a whole once again, as it was published in the booklet intended for the competition, before developing its implicit consequences. First of all, we simply wish to describe the present state of the works, since the first stage has now come to an end in late 1986, while the second stage is just about to start—not to mention any further stages that may be required in the future. In this way, it will be easy to recognize how the validity of our ideas was supported step by step in the carrying out of the plan, thus demonstrating the relevance of our original hypothesis through its development, which generated its own set of further possibilities.

In the seventeenth century a new town was born: Rochefort. The Anglo-French rivalry at sea and the warmongering lust of the great powers for the New World prompted Colbert to found, in 1666, an arsenal city opening onto the Atlantic but enclosed within the estuary of the Charente, sheltered from the cannons of the enemy. From that period on, the Corderie of Rochefort, which was the first building of the arsenal to be erected, actively produced rigging; nearby, in the forms of the dry docks, the king's ships were built.

From this particular place, soldiers and scientists would sail to all parts of the Americas, Québec, and the West Indies. Later on, the troops of La Fayette would embark on boats built in the arsenal. At a final stage, numerous convicts would sail from this port to their goal in Cayenne.

In 1926, the arsenal of Rochefort came to a standstill and the Corderie stopped working. Burned by the Germans in 1945, the building was rescued in 1950 by Admiral Dupont, and its final rehabilitation was completed in June 1987. Meanwhile, screens of trees have had a chance to stifle the once industrial banks of the Charente and hide the building behind a green rampart. Inside its "shroud" of foliage, the Corderie seemed to have lost all raison d'être. Invisible from the river as well as from the town, it hardly existed any more.

Now unearthed once again, the Corderie is already coming back to life. It houses the League for the Protection of Sea-Birds and the Centre de la Mer, the body concerned with the protection of the shoreline, and will soon also house the municipal record library. In effect, the mission of our garden is to diffuse the newfound life of the building into the surrounding areas. History has changed its course, and it would be pointless to reinstate a monument to the former role of the marine arsenal, or the workshop for sailing ships. But neither do we intend that the garden should be merely an outdoor museum.

The programme of the competition required, as already men-

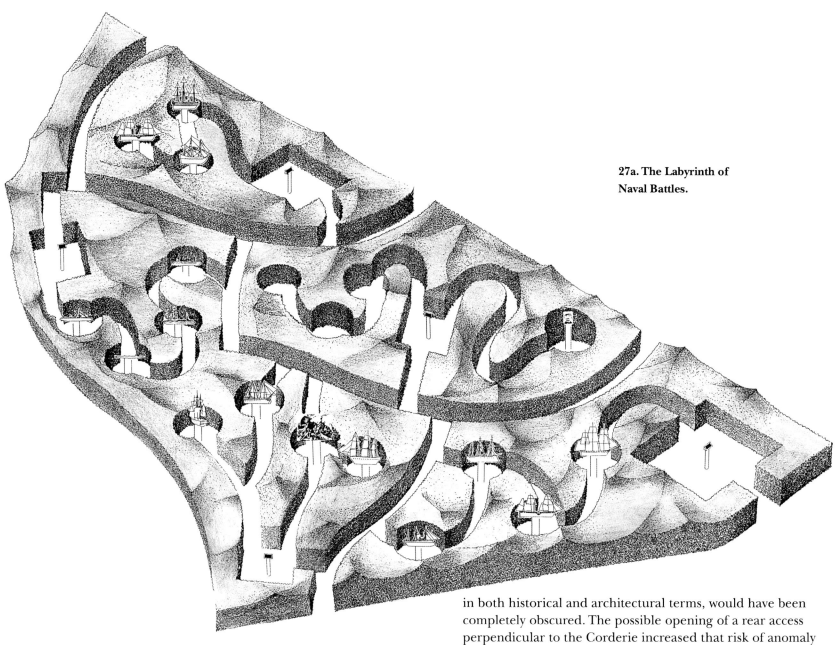

27a. The Labyrinth of
Naval Battles.

tioned, that there should be a connection between the town
and the site. However, if we had contemplated the possibility
of clearing the terrace of the garden attached to the naval high
command and other more modern constructions impeding the
rear access to the building, we would surely have risked transforming the rear of the Corderie into a front façade turned in
the direction of the town. The very rationale of the building,

in both historical and architectural terms, would have been
completely obscured. The possible opening of a rear access
perpendicular to the Corderie increased that risk of anomaly
even more.

Therefore the initial problem had to be examined from
another angle. We took it for granted from the start that the
dominant entity, from which the life of the town of Rochefort
could not be dissociated, was the sea. A voyage along the Charente is quite enough to reveal that the front façade of the building behind its green screen can be glimpsed for at least seven

minutes—as we verified in the presence of the Mayor of Rochefort. That observation impelled us to consider the relationship between the town and the Corderie, within the larger framework of the relationship between the town and the Charente and, on an even larger scale, between the town and the sea, extending far beyond the confines of the park. We therefore took as our first principle the fact that the sea, first of all, and then the river, were the main access to Rochefort.

What did we find from this new viewpoint? That the Corderie Royale was completely hidden by the unchecked growth of the riverside vegetation to such an extent that the authentic Rochefort, which began with the Corderie, had been transformed into an inland town cut off from its origins: the past had been repudiated.

Taking that fact into account, how were we to emphasize the relationship between the sea and the town? The solution was to open up loopholes in the screen of trees, in order to bring the symbolic façade of the town back into existence; in this way, the meaning of the town would once again become perceptible from the river, that is, from its main access. It would be a marine arsenal once again.

For it was surely quite obvious, once the Corderie had been rediscovered and reinstated in its relation to the Charente, that the river itself was at the same time being reinterpreted as the artery which continuously irrigated Rochefort, which established the site and was for a long time the watery rampart of the town—a supple, glittering rampart. So we brought together again two opposing but friendly elements: the rock of the Corderie and the flat stretches of the Charente marshes that extend endlessly out toward the ocean: Rochefort-sur-Mer.

The building—that vast urban façade turned outward to the river—now seems to grow even greater as a result of the multiple and various vistas opened along its imposing length. But is it not in the nature of Power and its attributes to flourish and make themselves manifest? Such an image is accentuated and reinforced by displaying the rigging—the symbol of the industry that developed on the site. Inserted into the river bank, on a level with the North Pavilion of the Corderie, there stood a useless block of concrete on which we shall be erecting the Rigging Area (Aire des Gréements) as a faithful replica of the masts and ropes that were made in the building. These will suggest children's games at the same time that they evoke the past. Near these masts, there will be flowers displayed in wicker baskets similar to those in which botanical specimens were brought back from the islands. These flowers from overseas, duly labeled and described according to the Linnaean classification, come from various species of exotic outdoor plants. Our intention is clear: by showing them in a singular and original way—in other words by reinstating their exotic qualities—we make use of the shock value derived from the sensory impact and resurrect their past through the effect of their presence.

The visitor will now be in a position to enter the eighteenth-century environment with a real sense of scale. Southwest of the park, near the Porte du Soleil, the two forms of the dry docks flank the point of land at the end of which the pennants of the Admirals of Rochefort will flap in the breeze.

Invaded by sludge during the period of abandonment, these two docks have since been cleaned out. In the older one, people will make contact with the once effective presence of the ocean by visiting two full-scale vessels from the past, which are in the

27b. General aerial view.

process of being rebuilt in forms derived from plans in the *Encyclopédie* of Diderot (which assures us, by the way, that these forms were among the first of their type in the country). In the other, more recent dock, a submarine or more recent type of boat may bring to mind the last active years of the site.

Consequently, we have heterogeneous presences in the same place, deriving from a number of equally lively periods: the present, a time of leisure; then the time of abandonment, when the reeds and the trees along the banks became established; and, finally, the time of the origins, conveyed by the Corderie itself, with its pennants and its shipyards.

As if summoned up by two opposing flows, time is established in the form of successive, simultaneously present and contrasting strata in the presence of the building. In a previous project, the Garden of the Anterior, we had posited that even a new town is not without a past, whether true or imaginary, natural or legendary, which implies that the interweaving of different relationships to the past of the town will necessarily contribute to the strengthening of the framework of the present time. Indeed, in the case of Rochefort's industrial past, we were given a number of historical threads, precisely dated and culturally significant, which would allow us to restitch the period of neglect to that of the present. However, the most flexible of these threads, and the one most likely to bind the three periods of the site's history harmoniously together, was once again the province of the imagination. The historical logic of the three periods could only be understood on condition that their basic heterogeneity was admitted and that we kept in mind the fact that every stratum of the past is in itself a total space. A simple glance at the Corderie now calls into question its original vocation as an industrial building: whether we like it or not, J. F. Blondel's classical archi-

27c. Behind the Corderie, along the length of the façade, a line of *Chimaerops* palm trees.

tecture is quite alien to our normal idea of what industry looks like; indeed, it is close to being the extreme opposite.

Let us now take account of the shore. The hard-packed soil of the eighteenth century, on which goods and equipment were stacked, now seems no more to us than an abandoned lot; industry today means a "well-built location." So we made the decision to pave the surface areas without transforming them into true pathways: that is, to interpret them by way of the imagination, and stratify the poetic as well as the sensory presence of the hard-packed industrial soil (which was the reason for the invasive growth of many trees, a sure sign of abandonment). As we wanted to open vistas while making it possible for people to stroll, picnic, and play, we decided to create a meadow—but visitors may be surprised to feel under their feet in that meadow, here and there, the hard shapes of cobblestones, which stand out beneath a slightly unstable, floating, and ambiguous extra layer of ground.

The logic of geography would have given us the meadow alone, possibly filled out with bits and pieces of ecological significance. But landscape architecture involves other considerations.

The landscape entity we had in mind to make the whole site cohere, from the sea right up to the town, involved a relationship between the physical factors and human activities considered in their horizontal development (leisure, economy, culture, equipment) and the vertical sedimentation of the site, that is, its history.

The landscape architect was charged with extracting from that complex space the vital impetus that would restore meaning to all the horizons that were his starting points; harmoniously brought together, these would exchange their potential meanings, create a topology of legend.

Stratification of plants would also have its part to play in this dynamic reworking. The stroller would go from the river bank, with its reeds, willows, alders, and ash trees, to the meadow with its well-tended and pruned trees, and finally to the garden of La Galissonière, which lies behind the Corderie.

In 1711, the young R. M. de la Galissonière, then 18 years of age, brought back from his travels in America the first seeds of the large-flowered magnolia, baptized *galissoniensis* in his honor. In fact, he was carrying on a Rochefort tradition, which had

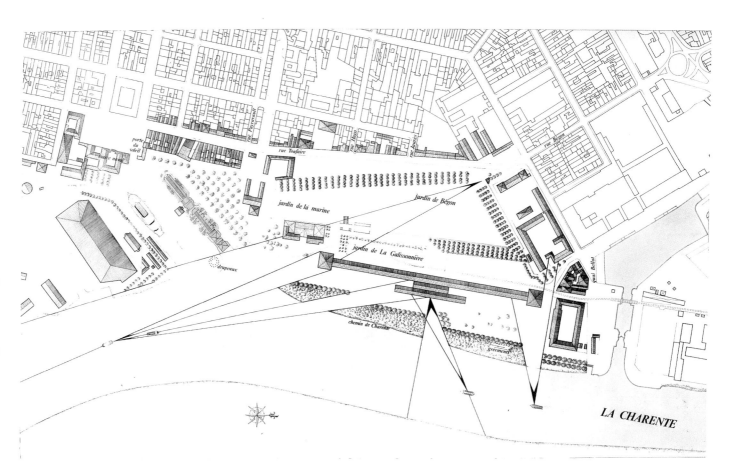

27d. Plan of the Garden of Returns, designed for a multitude of viewpoints. Along the Charente, loopholes cut into the riverside vegetation frame fragments of the Corderie Royale.

started with his grandfather Michel Bégon, who of course gave his name to the begonia. (Their names would also be closely associated with other American plants, such as the tulip tree of Virginia.) For this reason we chose to build—behind the Corderie and in line with the palm trees—greenhouses in which the Millérioux begonia collection, newly bought by the town, could be displayed along with other varieties offered by the Brazilian landscape architect Burle Marx: a set of wild species he had discovered in the Brazilian forest.

In another greenhouse, used as an orangery, we displayed the plants brought back by the Admiral de la Galissonière. Planted in vats, which were kept in shelter during the winter, they would be taken out of doors during the summer: a kind of miniature voyage in the wake of the lengthy voyages by ship that carried them to Rochefort. And, in addition to the botanical and horticultural aspect, these plants would be enabled to display their landscapes of origin: close to the living plants, indeed, a set of video clips would show them in their original environment, a

present-day way of reactivating their historical dynamism, which had been interrupted.

When seen from the sea and from the Charente, the town now makes sense again: no longer an inland city, it becomes a "freshwater port," extended by the fresh waters of the river.

But having unearthed its origins, we still had the task of reviving the dynamic side of it. We were no longer in a position to contemplate the soldiers and settlers departing for new worlds, but we had one solution left, which was the idea of return as a form of *dynamic* nostalgia.

Having drawn the ocean nearer in, we had to reckon with the paradox of a sea port solidly planted on terra firma. For reasons of military safety, Rochefort had been constructed out of sight of the mouth of the Charente, a situation that made it seem as if the port had been transposed or transplanted into the middle of the countryside. And is not the Corderie itself built on an oak raft afloat on the swamp, like a kind of huge ship that protects the town?

This led us to think in terms of the whole of Rochefort, not only the park by the Charente, as being a garden. The idea required us to treat Rochefort, both aesthetically and practically, as a garden, and construct out of the dynamic of the process of return to the site a concept for a garden: the Garden of Returns.

Local history confirmed us in our ideas. From its origins, the arsenal of the Corderie had always had a sheltered garden at the rear of the building, where the Intendant Bégon, and later the Admiral de la Galissonière, acclimatized exotic plants and flowers so successfully that they ceased to seem exotic in the following centuries. The military arsenal was coupled with this "botanical arsenal," both of which, however, had been reverting to wild vegetation until recently. That explains why the concept of the Garden of Returns implies not only the return of the Corderie to the town, but also its return to a garden: in other words, to the very nature of the town as a transplanted site.

To understand the nature of the site better, and to verify our hypothesis, we must now envisage it from the other direction: that is, looking from the sea to the town, with its real meaning evident once again.

We pointed out earlier that the town had been obscured as a result of the neglect of the old wall parallel to the Corderie; the point was to rediscover that wall, the façade of the town turned toward the river. However, we thought it imperative to preserve and even rebuild the wall in several places, preserving its function as a cutting edge, so that the Bégon terrace served still as a promontory from which to cast the eye down upon the Charente and further on toward the ocean. Was not the Corderie of ancient riggings and sails intended, by its nature and its vocation, to open out on to the sea?

27e. Aerial photo of the abandoned site, before work began on its transformation.

What we did was remove the screen of trees between the wall and the building, so that the visitor standing on the terrace, which had been re-established above the wall, could enjoy the vista. In this way, the oblique line of sight that widens as we enter from the Rue Bégon leads the eye across the newly cleared and luminous terrace down to the southern gable of the Corderie, then up to the Charente and out toward the open sea . . . .

That oblique junction point is strengthened by the presence of the pennants and flags of the Admirals of Rochefort: the past is brought alive again in terms of color and sound, interpreted by the mind, at the end of this narrow promontory at the river's bend. Once again, the original building is being brought back to the town and opens onto it.

How were we to set about making a concrete connection between the town and the Corderie? Were we to build an alley "à la Royale," perpendicular to the main façade, which would have ignored the successive parallels running at right angles to it, and perfectly aligning the wall and the building itself with the river bank? To resolve this question, it was useful to take note of the style of the Corderie itself. No matter how splendid and impressive, this building was not a château but an old industrial building. So, when planning the pedestrian link between the town and the Corderie, we risked being led astray by the possibility of a perpendicular route of access. This would have been to make two mistakes—a historical one, as we insist that the Corderie is not a château, and a functional one, as a conventional alley would simply lead visitors to the rear of the building and show them in through the outbuildings—so we had to offer a parallel access route. This has to be a vast ramp, 140 meters long and 21 wide, running alongside the old wall of the town next to the Corderie. From the top of the ramp it is now possible to see the tulip trees of Virginia growing on the steep slope, those "plants of return" that have just landed and are in the process of conquering the territory allotted to them.

Walking down that slope we encounter once again the row of newly planted palm trees that seem to look us in the face. In this particular spot, the plants that had become so trite take on a strange aspect once again, as though we were looking at them for the first time; the proximity of the Corderie, with its impec-

cable classical architecture, stresses even more their disconcerting aspect. Separated from the usual landscape of the Charente, where they grow completely unnoticed, they recapture the freshness of discovery. Before them, we experience the surprise the navigators of old must have felt when they saw them for the very first time. In consequence, the renewed sense of freshness they communicate is extended to all the plants that have become adapted to Rochefort and eventually to the site as a whole.

As we can understand it in retrospect, the whole dynamic of Rochefort starts from here: the wall, the Corderie, and the palm trees; and from this point the *genius loci* takes shape and symbolically extends all over the town. If we maintain the same line of logic, we can assess the needs, functions, and meanings of the other lay-outs contained within the Garden of Returns, as well as the economic consequences they imply.

Near at hand lies the Labyrinth of Naval Battles: drawn from the classical garden, in which it is an almost compulsory element, the labyrinth is a link between the river, on the one hand, and the flags, the dry docks, and the little world of the returning plants, not to mention the Corderie itself. It is an act of homage to the warlike and sometimes stormy age of the ships that were fitted out on the site, and also to the classical era in which those battles took place: homage taking the form of a topiary garden, interspersed with the most sophisticated technology.

The undulating garden is to be explored step by step and from within. We are at sea, as the rustling blue gravel reminds us. A green swell enfolds us, the sounds of the land are stifled, we feel only the breeze that moves the crests of the clipped waves. Suddenly, in front of us, a specifically named ship is manoeuvering to attack: transformed as we ourselves are into ships, thanks

27f. On the town side, a ramp planted with Virginian *Liriodendron* slopes toward a row of *Chimaerops* palm trees.

to a helmet and a control box, we are ready for action. A wave concealed the foe from us. Now here he is, all set to scuttle us with his infra-red rays. While playing this naval battle in the open air, we are told by a voice that we have just begun the battle of *La Bayonnaise* with the British frigate *Ambush*. Further on, beyond the unpredictable bend in the wave of yew trees, more heroic exploits will draw us into the heat of the action.

Did we enter the labyrinth as one would enter a page of history? Or are we at play like children, criss-crossing a miniature sea in which the circuits of the present coil up, like sea snakes, around the past? In any case, we are now plunged into a weightless world, whose dimensions flow into one another. One step too many into the magical garden and visitors could easily find themselves back in the actual past . . .

So, simultaneously and on the same ground, there exist two scales: in real terms, the history of ship building; and in miniature, that of the sea battles—a contrast that aims at enhancing

the importance of the true scale. The garden, moreover, overcomes its natural tendency to get enclosed within limits (even imaginary ones) by virtue of the docks that offer a direct passage to the town. In this respect as well, the garden becomes associated with Rochefort itself. To encourage this conjunction, we thought it extremely worthwhile to create these various convergent elements, which are of a very different nature, in the living presence of the site. Far from clashing, the various components in fact tend to form a consistent unity, like that of lock and key, which only makes sense through the simultaneous coexistence of the reciprocal lives that feed on one another.

Symbolically cut off from its past by the closure of its access to the Charente River, Rochefort was in fact cut off from its dynamic roots: it continued to live on its past, but it was a phantom past, the object of obsessional longings. Now that it has been reinstated and reinvented through the mediation of the garden landscapes, the past can breathe again.

Is not the arrival of the Millérioux collection—an arrival in the true sense of the word—a shining sign of this return? Augmented by the diversified genetic potential of the new collection, the Rochefort horticulturalists will now be able to create new varieties of begonias and other so-called exotic plants.

We know the economic significance of an ever-growing supply when confronted with a public avid for strangeness and novelty. So far, in France, the begonia has not had the success it enjoys in other countries like Germany, the Netherlands, and the United States, where there are a large number of enthusiasts no less interested in the begonia than—to give an example—the French are in the chrysanthemum. This still unexploited area will of course benefit from the image of the Garden of Returns, as if from a prestigious label. Not only will new activity be created, but it will be linked to the history and poetry of the site. On the flower market, the image greatly influences the appeal of the product, and a situation like this could start a kind of cultural fashion. Some species in fact only grow in limited areas and territories that give them their character, just as they lend character in return. Could this not be the role imparted to the begonia in its relationship to Rochefort, acquiring its cultural meaning in this one town and lending its character to it?

Every species in nature links up organically with the neighboring species; in the same way, commerce can participate in the symbolic presence of the begonias at Rochefort, as in all the activities more or less closely connected with horticulture: fairs, flower shows and everything that could be gathered under the title of "Begoniales."

The support of the Garden of Returns is, of course, essential in offering commerce and industry the opportunity of exploring such an interesting market and developing a prestigious image. This could lead us to think about possibilities for a new kind of tourism and use of leisure time.

At Rochefort the town lost its soul on the day it lost its way to the ocean. Who, for example, still remembered that the forms in the dry docks had been among the first of their type in France? But meaning cannot be built up again from outside. It is deep down in the cultural entity that the recuperative movement must take root. Our task was simply to clear the ground in order to disclose the depths of the level of the surface. For logic cannot be imported.

In contrast with Disneyland, the Corderie can now stand for a new, pluralist attitude to our cultural resources. It offers an arsenal of ideas that seek to link our patrimony with the economic world of the present day. It was from Rochefort that people left with their myths and gave birth to the New World. Disneyland is one of their offshoots. The Americans can rightly take pride in the form they gave to our legends. But shall we allow our own humus to dry out, and repudiate our own resources in favor of their spectacular displays? If Rochefort takes on its past once again, it does not only excavate it, it reinvents it. And the idea of Returns, generated in this specific place, is the mold through which that reinvention can take place.

The City of Nîmes / 1989

General Principle of Landscape Development

To its diverse historical stratifications of development, whether it be districts or monuments, the Municipality of Nîmes is adding another at the moment, created by districts and particularly remarkable "architectural objects."

These "new monuments" contrast with the old ones in a movement of mutual valorization: thus the pairing Arènes/Stade, and thus, still to come, the pairing Maison Carrée/Médiathèque. The repetition of the theme "Let us contrast the most beautiful objects built yesterday and today" is one of the current constituent elements of coherence for the city. It functions, too, because, for example, the Stade is as beautiful as the Arènes—and as square as the other is oval.

The principle of those sensory oppositions must be retained in order to understand what would be the principle for a landscape development of that city. The ensemble of the city gardens, existing and future, has to be created and recognized as such, by the differentiation of its internal components and by detaching itself, as an ensemble, from the ensemble formed by the diverse architectures of the city.

The principle which advocates that the accompanying plantings should soften the existing architecture goes, however, in the direction of a weakening of contrasts between old and modern architecture, and also smooths down the other contrasts, which would oppose the plantings, and the gardens themselves, to the architecture.

To preserve all the contrasts of those different ensembles seems to be the basic principle of landscape development in Nîmes.

What would be the particular characteristics of the landscape spaces destined to form the specific ensemble of the gardens of Nîmes? To list them, it seems necessary to understand first what constitutes the most distinct and remarkable element built/planted at this time: the Garden of the Fountain.

Its analysis shows it is composed of several *plastic* terms:

- an oblique "wild vegetable": the slope that leads to the Tour Magne;
- a horizontal that is "controlled": the designed garden enclosing fountain and canals;
- a vertical "mineral": the Tour Magne;
- a vertical "planted": the trees of the garden and the palm tree that figure in the arms of the city;
- and the water (spring and fountain).

Those *plastic* terms permit the appearance of the elements, four in number, which, once organized, would form the planted/built objects in diverse districts of the city, that is:

- a horizontal "design": for example, a black and white ground, with varied motifs, different in each place, planted or not with trees;
- a vertical "built": but, to avoid its being assimilated into other walls and partitions, and to be specific, it would be covered with a colored tiling, particular to the spot, on which would figure vegetable motifs;
- an oblique "wild vegetable" element able to lead either toward a concave slope, or toward a convex slope planted with thick bushes, with varieties favoring the presence of small birds;
- a vertical "planted" element: trees in groups and each group with a different variety . . .

The formal presence of the water would be a resource connecting with the constraints and the cultural values particular to each place of the city.

Combinations of those elements, each time different, would permit the formation in diverse spots of the city of "gardens," all images of the city of Nîmes, and all linked specifically to their district. Schematically, 50 percent of their surface would be treated in response to the most local issues, and the 50 percent remaining used for building up the image, "Nîmes garden."

Each district could thus ascertain that it owns in its own right what the others have, and would verify its connection to the urban ensemble. The effective presence of common *plastic* elements would facilitate, moreover, the impression that the "rich or poor" districts are treated in the same way.

The built elements of the gardens would make possible, moreover, the development of diverse activities, especially schools of gardening and the selling of plants, plus cafes with terraces . . .

Along the routes, the accompanying trees would also become "planted objects." Their presence would be reinforced, for example, by giving a color to the surface of their shade and by selecting for this purpose the color of their flowers.

Thus under the *Paulownia tomentosa* the ground will be blue. And in May, at the time of their flowering, the blue of the flowers would multiply the blue of the ground, and the passerby would move through a bluish light.

From colored surface, the ground would change here and there into diverse forms of benches or urban furniture.

Each type selected would feature its own variety of tree, its own color, its own form of urban furniture, and just so many new objects planted for the image garden of the city.

For the city cemetery, let us insist on the fact that it is a remarkable monumental ensemble, because of its richness of vegetation as well as the originality of its funeral constructions.

The Tuileries—A Reinvented Garden / 1990

To give concrete form to the new mythical axis of Paris from the newly erected Pyramide to the Arche de la Défense, the garden, in accordance with the policy of the Louvre, will develop by longitudinal strata the image of a space exploring time within its successive layers, while maintaining a strictly rectilinear axis. This showcase among French gardens offers a landscape in depth to be reinvented by anyone who looks down onto it from its terraces.

The recent construction of the Arche (de la Défense) has given Paris a new axis, from the Louvre Pyramide to La Défense, thus supplanting in the mind of the public André le Nôtre's axis. The disappearance of the Château des Tuileries opened up the possibility of this new geometry, which superimposes the axis of the modern world on that which survives from the classical age. In the Tuileries Garden the pedestrian walks on that axis. It is therefore necessary for the garden to become associated with this new geometry from our own time and to reinforce its effect through its own distinctive contribution.

Axis: The Symbol Conquers Geometry

When the Château des Tuileries was still in existence, the discordance between Le Nôtre's axis and that of the Louvre was not visible; it eluded perception and could not even be guessed at.

This element of discordance created a delicate problem for the first time during the construction of l'Arc de Triomphe du Carrousel, and it has become important again with the establishment of the liaison between La Défense and the Louvre, since the visitor coming from the Champs-Elysées now looks for the

top of the Pyramide, which is displaced to the left of the axis. At the moment, from the terrace of Mr. Pei, the visitor can see clearly the top of the Pyramide, which is out of alignment with the Arc de Triomphe du Carrousel. Pei's project, transforming the courtyard of the Louvre and the garden of the Carrousel surrounding the Pyramide, allows the visitor no sense of this lack of alignment. The garden must therefore make up the deficiency in the scheme by offering a continuous route for the visitor coming from the Place de la Concorde in the direction of the Louvre. The sense of touch as well as the other senses must contribute to the symbolic effect and be in accord with it, so as to reinforce the identification of the Louvre axis with that of Le Nôtre and establish the axis between the Arche de la Défense and the Pyramide.

To accomplish this, the route from La Concorde to the Arc de Triomphe du Carrousel will be given a threefold definition in our project:

- first, by connecting the octagonal pool to the large round pool, where spatial symmetry will affirm the connection of the Arc de Triomphe du Carrousel with the axis that joins it to La Défense;
- second, when, moving around the large round pool, it will be possible to see the discrepancy between the *jardin réservé* and the *parterre de Mollet* placed on either side of the central avenue. In this way the asymmetry of the parterres, helped by a slight difference in level between them that makes the ground dip from the south to the north, will help eliminate any sense of the angle between the Louvre and the Tuileries (as Le Nôtre had realized, it is the way the two sides obviously fail to match when seen from an oblique angle

that draws attention to the central axis that separates them);
- third, by changing levels and revealing the Arc de Triomphe du Carrousel, as visitors will not be able to walk on the axis itself, but only on avenues parallel to a central lawn that comes next to Mr. Pei's terrace.

This displacement of pedestrian traffic to the sides of the lawn will make it impossible to register the difference in angle between the Le Nôtre axis and the Louvre axis until one stands at the foot of the Arc de Triomphe du Carrousel itself: at that point one will see the Pyramide in its entirety.

History: A Poetic Archaeology of the Art of Gardens

Archaeology has revealed how densely history is packed in layers within the Seine's banks. Likewise it is the depth, the very thickness of the ground opened by the Pyramide that now gives access to the Louvre, inseparably bringing together the museum and the ancient Palais du Louvre, whose origins are now exposed. We are seeking to reinforce the unity of the Louvre and the garden that was projected by Henri IV, by emphasizing the garden's own identity. Le Nôtre arranged for the garden to be enclosed by shutting in the axis between two terraces, thus making it the pinnacle of Parisian civility, to remain so for three centuries. To give expression to this poetic rootedness in time in terms of sensory space, we have carved the depths of the earth in such a way as to reveal a kind of mythic archaeology.

Therefore we propose that the garden should reflect, albeit in an extremely schematic fashion, the history of the art of French gardens by bringing together the main epochs as they are displayed in the site of the Tuileries. As a matter of fact, to give more importance to one epoch to the detriment of another would be to take no account of the multitude of attentions that have been successively lavished on it by different artists. The very site of the Tuileries is the sum of the thickness of places and events, each as significant as the other.

In order to bring out the many different original features of this site, we had to define the concepts of *restoration*, *rehabilitation*, and *reinvention* in a new manner:

- *Restoring* what is known within the limits of the historical sources available.
- *Rehabilitating* what is less well-known so as to facilitate the complete restitution of the space: by reconstructing known layouts, by creating spaces where the layout is not known; and by making ground available for new uses that are more or less ephemeral. The aim is to evoke by material or by design the period of origin.
- *Reinventing*, that is to say, using contemporary creation to establish a logic of articulation between successive compositions of place that have been used throughout history, a process we call *intertwining*.

The way the garden developed in the course of history is the result not of successive additions but of successive rewritings on the same spot, of reinterpretations carried out by the society using it, of the meanings attached to it in each moment of its history. There is therefore no essential truth or origin to which one can return. On the contrary, the garden's truth is historical, the result of the intertwining of the various transformations of its space, of its uses, and of those imposed by Parisian society; so it is the multiple significance of the place that we had to render poetically perceptible to the senses and follow into the present.

Hence our recourse to an archaeological metaphor which yields successive strata, a pattern whose organization is understood by the public, functioning in the same way as an archaeological excavation which gives access to the history of a city by simplifying it:

- the stratum of the Medici garden (−80 cm under the present ground surface);
- the stratum of the garden during Mollet's time (−20 cm);
- the stratum at the time of Le Nôtre (0 cm);
- the stratum of the nineteenth century (+50 cm);
- the stratum of the contemporary epoch (+170 cm).

In each stratum it is necessary to adopt a distinct attitude of conservation:

- restoration for the strata of Le Nôtre and of the nineteenth century;
- rehabilitation for the Medici stratum;
- reinvention for the Mollet stratum and the contemporary stratum.

However, the design and conception of these different strata itself necessarily depends on reinvention since we only have at our disposal fragmentary documents that reveal no more than a part of a reality we seek to interpret.

Consequently we are dealing with a reinvention of the garden as a whole: we are trying to develop its contemporary existence without breaking with its history and without making it a monument to a time already past.

A Landscape Enshrined with the Total Landscape of Paris

If one sees the Louvre and the garden as two complementary expressions of place, interdependent by their historic and spatial community, and if the Louvre gives onto the garden area, as is the case in Pei's scheme, the garden must by contrast be closed off so as to preserve its unity (the structure of which is formed by the Défense-Pyramide axis) from this risk of becoming too fragmented by a transverse emphasis. The involvement of the Louvre with its neighboring districts must make the Tuileries even more of a garden. However, because it is impossible to enclose the garden more than it already is, it is in its apperance only that it must find itself more enclosed, whereas the reality is that it must be open to the Musée d'Orsay and to pedestrian traffic, both perpendicular to and diagonal to the Seine.

What attitude should we adopt with regard to the large terraces bordered by noisy thoroughfares that form its boundaries?

These two raised terraces are meant to look into the interior of the garden, even if they allow sight of the Rue de Rivoli from the Terrasse des Feuillants, and also the embankment—overburdened by cars and bordered by trees through which the river can be glimpsed—and of the Musée d'Orsay from the terrace by the water's edge. Dézallier d'Argenville confirms this idea in his trea-

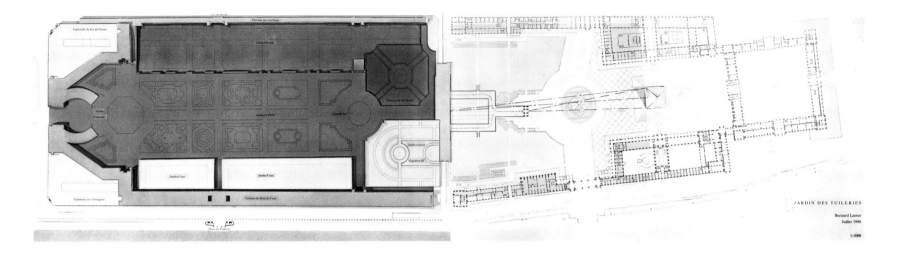

JARDIN DES TUILERIES

Bernard Lassus
Juillet 1990

1:1000

tise, where he says that, for a flat piece of ground, it is fitting to raise terraces around it, so as to make it visible. We can therefore imagine that the Tuileries terraces were specifically constructed in order to permit looking down onto the garden from above. This has now become impossible due to the present density of chestnut trees along the south terrace.

In our judgment the wall of this terrace, which extends the façade of the Louvre as far as the Place de la Concorde, constitutes the main front of the city, bordering the Seine like a cliff and creating one of the most characteristic settings in Paris.

This line seems to separate the garden from the flow of the Seine, the geomorphology of the ground confirming this impression, since the lowest point is not located at all in the Tuileries, not even at the Place de la Concorde, but rather on the ground surrounding the Grand Palais. The terrace by the water's edge that Le Nôtre raised to protect the ground against floods not only fulfills this function but also seems to deflect the course of the Seine, by its impenetrability redirecting the very flow of the river. This line cannot be disturbed unless it is intended to transform a major Parisian landscape.

Moreover the Tuileries garden has always been set apart, with a strong identity, so that the public went specifically to see the Tuileries, or to see the gatherings there, and not to have a view onto this or that part of the city.

We have therefore sought to reinforce the perceived autonomy of the Tuileries, so that from the heights of the terraces the visitor will be impelled to turn toward the interior of the garden and the Pyramide-Grande Arche axis that now determines the form of the city.

Our Proposal

Let us turn for a moment to the inward part of the garden as it is at present, which is, in essence, the place where a succession of gardens are stratified and intermingled. Does one not still today find Medici design in terms of Le Nôtre's layout, since he preserved the layout of his predecessors' paths, reused the echo motif to superimpose his octagonal pool, and reused the bastion Renard had transformed into a garden in order to build the

**29. Must the mythical
Arche de la Défense-
Louvre axis be per-
ceived in its totality as a
concrete axis?**

diagonal terrace along the octagon on the south side? His successors have taken the same principle, as one can find still in the
two circular pools of Le Nôtre at the side of the Louvre, in the
middle of the *jardins réservés*, which now take on a completely
different meaning.

As we have underlined, the garden is based on two ideas,
superimposition and intertwining. In this regard our project
proposes a new stratification, which, while accepting that the Le
Nôtre axis must be retained, will not cancel out or give undue
precedence to any particular period of the garden's history.

With regard to these successive gardens, we have a variety
of kinds of information at our disposal. We have only a few elements for the period of Henri IV–Cathérine de Médicis, but
for the Le Nôtre period graphic documents as well as texts are
more numerous. From the end of the nineteenth century to the
present day the documentation is precise, even if the works of
sculpture have come down to us in poor condition.

The very idea of superimposition is bound up with stratification and archaeology, and consequently with the notion of
different levels. A good way to show the history of this garden
would be to construct it in successive steps, from the deepest
and oldest to the most elevated and recent.

The very nature of our knowledge concerning the various
periods of the garden will imply, however, different attitudes as
regards the treatment of different levels. Thus if we wished to reconstruct the axis according to its original conception, it would
be because we had available to us precise information as to how
it would have been. It is the same for the two rows of groves that
run along the axis, for they form the very setting for this axis.

On the other hand, there is only a general plan of the paths
and the disposition of the beds from the period preceding Le
Nôtre. To give a record of that period we propose to dig down
30 cm in the area between the northern limit and the Le Nôtre
beds (in our project) and the Terrasse des Feuillants. This excavation parallel to the axis of the garden has as its aim to perpetuate and confirm the presence of the axis, and to show that
before Le Nôtre, there was a different garden there.

At the same time this excavation will help to reduce slightly
the traffic noise coming from the Rue de Rivoli. However, the
lack of detailed knowledge of the garden that is only sketched
in Androuet du Cerceau's plan suggests that this area should remain as flat as possible, the soil being meticulously covered by
terracotta and decorated with glazed ornaments, thereby accentuating clearly the difference of the levels. This surface, carefully
laid out, will enclose grass surfaces, except near the Place des
Pyramides, where the reestablishment of a boxwood knotwork
interspersed with flowers will be offered to the public.

The various lawns sketched out on the previous historic parterres that come together in a line will be punctuated at all four
angles by groups of trees. They will either be put at the disposal
of contemporary creative artists or be put to temporary use, as
well as providing a playground for children. The puppet theater, in a new form and on a new base, could stay in its existing

position. We would also like to give opportunities for installations such as a traveling theater, installations that have not so far benefited from permanent fixtures in the area.

This whole area, now in a simplified form, having rid itself of too imposing a precedent, and having lent itself to what is most contemporary, would therefore be devoted to the possibilities of freedom of invention.

Beside the flowered parterre of boxwoods already mentioned, the transition between du Cerceau's area and Le Nôtre's will be made possible at the north end of the round pool by means of a parterre, whose path design comes from the time of André Mollet and was repeated in a reinvented form by his direct successor, André le Nôtre.

Symmetrically disposed between the round pool and the terrace by the water's edge, the parterre of the *jardin réservé* would remain as it is with its sculptures, but it would be restored. It would extend toward the east as far as the southerly opening of the underpass. This area would remain slightly raised in relation to Le Nôtre's level which would revert to the original plan.

The section of the garden that is currently the most deprived is undoubtedly the area planted with chestnuts that runs along the terrace by the water's edge. Too shady, it is practically never frequented by the public in its present state. On this surface we suggest, 1.7 m above Le Nôtre's surface, and by getting rid of the present chestnut trees, establishing a larger water terrace, thus making another feature parallel to the axis (reminding one of the close proximity of the Seine). This surface is meant to be looked at by those coming to lean on the guard rail of the terrace, situated 2.5 m above this new surface.

The person strolling would be able to look, from there, at the interior of the garden and contemplate the calm stretches of water beneath, which to those below appear as springs and cascades. The water, like the meadow and the terracotta ground cover, is unavailable to the public: this interior body of water would link the three pools of the Louvre and the octagonal pool.

This garden, in which different moments in the history of garden art would be evoked, allows the visitor to suppose that each level continues below the surface it actually occupies: is that not the dream of the archaeologist, the emotion that one experiences at an excavation site? The design of these different surfaces will allow one to suppose that each one continues in and underneath the other. The public will also be able to read, in the garden, engraved in glass, the general plans and elevations from every period, in order to reconstruct them in the imagination, with the help of present and tangible elements. Inscriptions carved in stone and dispersed throughout the garden will show the public that here or there such and such an important historical event took place.

One will also be able to visit the underground parts, built beneath the water-garden at the site of Bernard Palissy's cave, where all that we know about his time and his work, as well as the garden architecture in France of the sixteenth century, will be evoked in a small museum (conservatory).

If, up to this point, we have shown that the organization of the site has tended to confirm both the Pyramide–Défense axis and the built garden, it must also allow perpendicular and diagonal circulation. Because of this we especially single out the entry extending the pathway coming from the Place Vendôme and leading through the Pont de Solferino toward the Musée d'Orsay.

A meticulously executed ground cover and the inclusion of a

slope as far as the Seine will allow the visitor first to pass by the cascades of the water garden, and then to discover the entries to the Bernard Palissy conservatory on the edge of the Seine, and eventually other features such as a bookshop specializing in the art of gardens.

The waterside terrace will become continuous again while introducing a pathway permitting access to the Pont de Solferino and to the Seine.

Even if the embankment traffic remains as it is, the water garden, with its flowing water, its murmuring sounds, would nullify the traffic noise and, on the other hand, produce its own music.

A vast underpass starting at the Place de la Concorde and extending to the Louvre would absorb the flow of cars so as to allow the transformation of the surface above into an esplanade serving Orsay and the river-side facilities. This esplanade would constitute one of the garden's main entries.

For the unity of the garden, the ground covers have been conceived according to stratification, the principle of which is essential to the scheme. Each level will be joined to its neighbouring level by slopes and stairs.

The ground cover of pathways parallel to the axis will remain continuous throughout the garden. On the other hand in the transverse direction, the pathway surfaces will change as the visitor moves from one garden area to another.

In the Medici area, large grassed surfaces, hedged by smooth terracotta pathways, will give the public the opportunity to relax in the sun. In the Le Nôtre section the surface will be of compacted sand.

The ground will be granular and made of different gravel types for the *jardin réservé* from the nineteenth century.

This differentiated organization of circulation should create a rhythm for the visitor/user and allow discovery, on the other hand, of the stratifications, which are being put on display.

The Park of Duisburg-Nord / 1991

Relationships Between the Park of Duisburg-Nord and Its Surroundings

The creation of a park like that of Duisburg-Nord puts into play a number of different levels, which depend on one another and involve different scales.

In the first place, there is the neighborhood scale. This is the most local, affecting the districts that surround the park and, at the same time, the immediate vicinity of the park, which is an industrial area. On this scale, the problem is one of the relationships between the park, the industry on its perimeter, and the residential districts.

This scale is significant not only in relation to the surface extent of the park, but also in relation to the fact that there is a historical and industrial patrimony involved, symbolizing the Ruhr as a whole and expressed by the presence of blast furnaces and areas overcome by pollution.

A second scale in terms of which the park would be perceived is that of the town of Duisburg itself. Besides being a district and neighborhood park, it would be a park for the whole town, by virtue of its size and its means of communication.

The third scale is different in character. It is that provided by the River Emscher, which is at present canalized throughout and heavily polluted. On this scale, the park aims to reevaluate the role of the Emscher, and change the nature of the region: it would be symbolic of the rehabilitation of the Ruhr and of its new image. This scale introduces a most important theme, that of the water being discovered again, and purity being rediscovered through the water.

The conception of the park must take into account these different levels.

Today, or the Park of Duisburg-Nord on the Neighborhood Scale (Zone A)

So it will be those living in the district who will benefit first of all from the park. It is a prolongation of their everyday life. They will get there by automobile, on foot, and by scooter, to visit what is at the moment lacking in their lives and sorely needed: playgrounds, allotments, football pitches, and fishing ponds. These people will make for sections of the park where they will be able to find all they want on the level of leisure, sport, and recreation, as arranged by the representatives of the various associations whom we have met, and by the local government services. The group of required facilities is located in our project within a specific zone (A1), and this zone will be planned in concert with these associations, the elected representatives, the technical services of the town, and their supervisors.

Everyday Life and Leisure of the Neighborhood Prolonged into the Park

Within the A1 zone, we draw distinctions among three categories:

1. parts that have already been fitted up and could be seen as adequate from a landscape point of view;
2. parts already dealt with which we think are in need of improvement;
3. surfaces where we have already foreseen the installation of a certain number of facilities, suggested to us in the way previously mentioned

All the areas within the A1 zone will therefore be planned in concert with all the different partners who wish to take part in the operation, representing numerous different interests.

Everyday Life Brought to the Park by Traffic, the Highway (Zone A2)

Zone A will also comprise a second part (A2), which relates not only to the district, but also to the roads crossing the park. The presence of the two roads will make it easy for all those living in Duisburg and the other Ruhr towns as well as those in the neighborhood to get to the park.

So it is important that there should be no contradiction between the facility offered by the highways and the effect they have in bordering the park, which could affect the particular character of this zone dedicated to the neighborhood. This section will thus have to be in sympathy with the road in its symbolism. Stopping areas and other possibilities (which will be discussed with the inhabitants and with the road authorities of Nord-Westphalia) will be developed on a non-commercial basis: repair shops for various types of vehicle, a track for children and adults to try out their model cars, and a motorbike racing track, which will obviously cause a lot of noise but is very much in demand from all the local motor-racing enthusiasts. A museum of old cars could also be installed there.

All these sections in Zone A are linked to contemporary needs. They have to figure in the park, as the designer cannot act as a judge of people's wishes. He is there to help them to develop and organize their activities without harming others.

So the fishermen must be able to fish, the children to fly their

model planes, and the bikers to rev up their engines . . . But that is not the whole of the park. The next part to be considered is the factory section.

Yesterday: The Blast Furnaces

With the factory, we pass from the life of today to that of yesterday. But if we do so without warning we will have no idea that we have crossed a threshold in time, and this will result in confusion.

To get to this new surface, we therefore need to be shown that we are changing periods and crossing a gap in time. But how can this transition between today—as we have just described it in terms of its installations—and yesterday—as we will find it in the presence of the blast furnaces—be adequately illustrated and symbolized? We must give material form to this difference in period by expressing it in terms of landscape. We suggest that this should be done through a frame of vegetation—just as a stained-glass window is surrounded by lead in order that the colored glass held within it may shine with its own brilliance, or a painting is framed to make it stand out from the wall.

So we need a frame of vegetation to detach the fraction of the park associated with today from that which forms its yesterday, the blast furnaces. But while it was still working, the factory was a closed and forbidden place. Its shadow hung over the town like that of a workers' fortress where metals were fused and forged. The factory must consequently neither be dissolved in the activities of the town nor be lost in the activities of the park. The dignity of the spot—the mystery and sense of fear inspired by it—must be retained (in particular, through appropriate night-lighting), which implies a necessary separation from the rest of the park and the town.

The division between the two periods and the symbolism of the blast furnaces therefore combine to necessitate something in the order of what I would call (invoking a term derived from locks on a canal) a *temporal pen.* This pen would acquire its material presence essentially in the form of rows of trees. Thus it would only be after passing through these distinctive rows that the visitor would come upon the factory and its own surface areas.

As far as the industrial buildings are concerned, we have retained on our plan the buildings that are considered most important by architectural experts who have studied the matter. We will ultimately discuss these choices with the various authorities, but we are already in a position to insist that these buildings will have to be used with great prudence. They are the temples of past industry and should not serve as garages or infant schools. They symbolize the working habits of a great moment in the history of humanity, when iron and steel were used for the benefit of the whole population. We cannot predict at this moment what future generations will make of this legacy. We must therefore conserve the buildings in their potentiality, that is to say, leave open the possibility of what we can hardly imagine today—their restoration to partial working. Visitors must be allowed to exercise their imagination on this possibility, through the very fact that large areas have been left empty. Some of these buildings will nevertheless be offered as a home to societies whose activities have a direct relationship to the place and what it formerly produced.

To give an analogy for this proposal, we should recall that we are engaged on a park at Rochefort-sur-Mer, which surrounds a maritime arsenal of the seventeenth century. Here the local authorities have gradually and very wisely provided space for a conservation agency concerned with shorelines and lakesides, an international center for the sea and the National League for the Protection of Birds. It is obvious that anything relating to the history of metals would have a special place in Zone B; festivals connected with mining and metallurgy would also be social activities of special relevance to the area.

Given that we need to keep a sense of distance—the distance of yesterday—from the factory and to respect its specific qualities, we will have to treat the ground surfaces that offer access to it in the image of the stern workers who used to be employed there. So each of the industrial buildings will rest on its original floor, but the visitor would reach it by crossing smooth white surfaces, of the same composite material as station platforms, etc., which would be raised above the actual ground level by about 40 percent and would allow the visitor to discover the buildings. Between these surfaces and the buildings enclosed by them— which would thus have the appearance of promontories—surfaces of lawn would figure, absolutely smooth and replicating the plane surfaces of the smooth, white "platforms."

These platforms covered with synthetic flooring, which would extend all around the factories, would allow the visiting areas to be defined and grouped together at the same time. To prevent accidents and to preserve the buildings, guard rails could be added.

The Emscher Canal in Zone B

Near the blast furnaces, the Emscher Canal will again be visible in its formal treatment. Two scales of reading will be used. An internal scale will be provided by a series of belvederes, which will punctuate its length in a regular rhythm. These belvederes are designed to offer a closed view onto the water, which will be cleansed from pollution; they will be placed halfway up the slope within the V-section of the canal. Benches placed below the hedges will indicate where stairways are to be found.

On the level of the geometric line that separates the enclosure of the blast furnaces from the canal itself, there will be a whole system of rectilinear hedges giving access in the course of the walk to the entire industrial site and, in particular, featuring the silhouettes of the blast furnaces. Seen from the height of the canal, the geometric rhythm of the white walkways covered in composite materials will also incorporate the perfectly mown, plane surfaces of lawn that separate them from the blast furnaces.

Placing the Park's Yesterday Between Today and the Day Before Yesterday

The theoretical need to delimit today and yesterday has impelled us to think of a principle of separation between these moments in time, which we have called a "temporal pen." But the Park of Duisburg-Nord has need of other distinctions besides the necessary one between yesterday and today, in order for its message to be revealed. To come to terms with this problem, we should go back to the very name of the park. Does it not rely on the term Emscher? Yet what remains today of this former river? It has been diverted from its former course, canalized, polluted, and deprived of its true nature. Yet this very Emscher has supplied the name for the whole operation of replanning the Ruhr area: the Emscherpark. The river thus remains, in spite of everything, the theme and symbol of the park, its guiding thread. Yet how could we establish the difference between the Emscher of today and the Emscher of yesterday (since the canal was dug at that stage) if we did not also bring into play an Emscher of the day before yesterday, an Emscher from before the factory was built, an Emscher associated with the old countryside, with rippling clear water, fish, birds, and fields?

The principle of diversifying the course of the Emscher through the different zones can be explained as follows:

1. It reflects the banks bordering it.
   1.1. In the garden of the day before yesterday, it follows the ancient serpentine course, facilitating the establishment of a rural context (with pasturing on the banks subject to flooding, fields where there is no flooding, etc.)
   1.2. Near the blast furnaces, its course is rectilinear within the V-shaped canal bottom, but it is set up as a walkway with clipped trees and an overall view of the furnaces.
   1.3. It passes in an underground channel under the temporal pens (particularly near the Thyssen steel factory, which is still operating) and the lines of trees that define the pens.
   1.4. Near the small allotments, it acquires its canalized industrial form again for financial reasons, but this time it

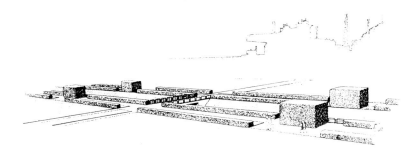

**30a. The time before
yesterday.**

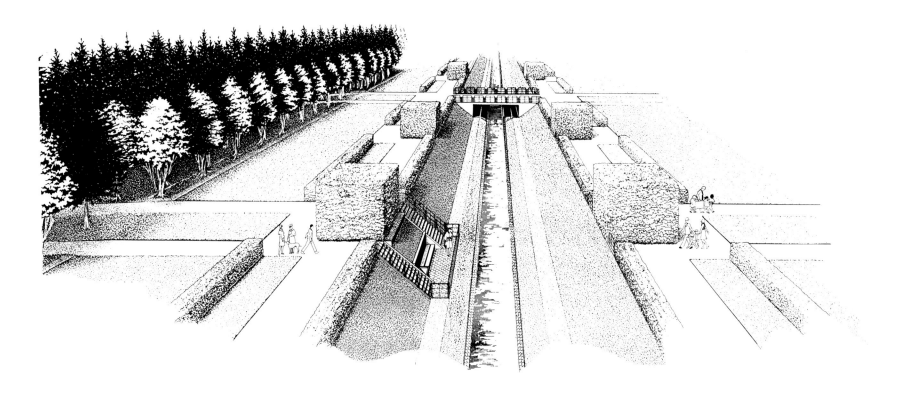

is bordered with free vegetation and it opens onto lakes
and their users.

2. Its actual course is only completely altered in the
   countryside of time past. Elsewhere the banks are only
   modified to make a number of activities possible.
3. The level of the bottom of the canal remains as it is in the
   three last sections of its course. However, the level of the

water surface changes so as to obtain a greater quantity of
water and better access to the fishing areas of the last
section of its course.

It is only through the presence of this idyllic Emscher that we
can appreciate the presence of another Emscher—that which
has been turned into a canal where it interacts directly with the

154   Inflecting the Landscape

factory, in the zone relating specifically to yesterday. The difference in the two treatments, and also of course the difference in the areas which they traverse and symbolize, will serve to bring out their reciprocal qualities.

So there will be a contrast between a landscape of time past—that of the old Emscher with its sinuous curves and banks—and the Emscher of yesterday, straight and canalized, up against a factory with its adjoining land, the very landscape that suits this canal, since it is the product of an inevitable transformation of nature.

Moreover, we must have the day before yesterday in order to understand yesterday. But that involves not simply restoring a river; it is also a matter of context. The fields in the zones liable to flooding will provide feed for cattle, the fields in the zones not liable to flooding will be available for forage, and wind and water-mills (there were about ten of these along this section of the Emscher up to the pre-industrial period). This will be our Zone C.

The Day Before Yesterday: The Countryside of Time Past of Idyllic Nature (Zone C)

In this part of the park, we will thus have the river reconstructed in all its meandering course, with the clean water serving the fish, insects, and aquatic plants. But the river bed will be moved from the place it occupied when it flowed naturally. We will also retain, from the same period, the principle of a distinction between land liable to flooding and not so liable. This distinction will be expressed visually by the differential use of land meadows in the "flooding" areas and fields in the "non-flooding" areas, and consequently by the different forms of vegetation that grow there, though the river will never be in spate. The landscape of time past will also comprise two farms, where it will be possible to observe the rural life of former times in all its aspects. These farms will nourish in their fields the cows and horses that draw the carts used to visit this fraction of the park. It will also be possible to fish in the river, visit the mills, and have their workings explained. So people will be practically qualified to understand the functioning of the ancient rural economy. There will also be reconstituted peasant fêtes with music, banquets, balls, and gaiety as in the old days.

Using Space in the Countryside of Time Past

The two farms foreseen by the project will be devoted essentially, as regards their agricultural practices, to the raising of cattle, horses and sheep, with three central aims:

1. setting up a genuine activity of raising livestock for meat production (veal and lamb) directed toward the regional market;
2. securing the upkeep and raising of horses for leisure activities within the park (horse riding, cart rides, carriages . . .);
3. forming a visible display of farming in the open air over fenced fields, which would be accessible to the public and providing them with a living picture of countryfied, pastoral nature.

30b. Yesterday.

The water mills and the windmill will be able to process in the traditional manner a proportion of the cereals gathered in the adjoining fields.

In order to obtain some diversity, one of the farms will be devoted to raising sheep and cattle. The other will be devoted to horses, but it will also offer a staging of the ancient rural prac-tices of the Ruhr (woodwork by craftsmen, ironwork, leather-work, wool, linen, etc.).

So the surface of the idyllic garden will need to be reconsti-tuted as a semi-woodland, where the space is divided into par-ticular locations defined by hedges and wood undergrowth that favors the wild fauna.

The essential point of orientation will be the river and its mills, with the banks planted with alders, ashes, willows, and poplars. The river will be lined by pathways where it is pleasant

to go on foot or on horseback; other paths will lead to the meadows and the wooded places inside or on the periphery of the
idyllic garden. The stroller will be able to daydream beside the
slow waters and follow the meandering curves of waters made
iridescent by resting dragonflies, into quiet backwaters, over
aquatic plants that quiver in the wind. A little further on, these
wavelets will froth up in the wheels of the mills and form little
rocky waterfalls, which will enable small stretches of water to be
kept for the benefit of fishermen and the observation of king-
fishers.

In the woods, visitors will be able to breathe in the scent of
hawthorn and plum blossom in the springtime, and refresh
themselves later in the cool of the leafy glades, before venturing
into the sunlight of the rich clearings where insects buzz among
the bushes. Along the pathways maintained between the hedges,
the bands of woodland, and the more densely wooded sections,
moreover, they will be able to delight in the birds as they fly
and sing.

Tomorrow (Zone D): Experiments
for the Garden of the Future

Through bringing in Zone C, we have in effect restored the presence of the Emscher in order to give the gardens of today and

yesterday a new meaning by placing them within a logical and
technical sequence. When each of the terms of this sequence
is present, it can be seen that we lack a future term, or at least
a metaphor of the future, without which the sequence will get
fixed in a nostalgic, backward-looking frame of mind. Surely
the art of gardens has in the past opened up the horizons of the
future, as, for example, in the eighteenth century, when monuments were raised, at the edge of parks, to the glory of Captain
Cook. It is not only a question of doing one's best in the realm of
the possible, where gardens are concerned; the garden must be
a mode of exploration, of achieving a new dimension.

In this sense the Emscher cannot be the whole of the Emscherpark. But, if we examine the significance of this river for
the region, we see that water is also life, metamorphosis—and
insofar as the presence of the factory still symbolizes the metamorphosis of mineral matter, a garden for the future of the park
could be based on precisely this theme, which would also allow
a rethinking of some of the technical problems that relate to the
land at present.

Spaces for the future might therefore comprise gardens and
laboratories of specific kinds dealing with different themes.

Gardens and soil laboratories: gardens where there could be experiments involving all the systems for cleansing the soil resulting from the nearby laboratories of pollution. Gardens where these systems would be put into practice would be made visible and explained to the public with, in parallel, the planting programs this process would make possible at each stage in its development.

Gardens and sound laboratories: experimental laboratories concerned with the types of sound associated with the different types of space found elsewhere in the garden. These sounds, produced on the edges of the park as well as within it, would be subject to transformation and would allow all kinds of games with the public. For example, there could be a gradation/transformation of sounds from the "polluted" to the natural, ending up with invented sounds that would imply thinking about a sound aesthetic.

Throughout the garden itself, there would be transformation of intrusive sound, recorded on roads, in surrounding factories, etc.; study of natural sound, birdsong, the whistling of the wind through plants and foliage, noises made by carts, plows, mills, etc.; study of sound and music made possible by the reinvention of the sounds previously mentioned and their mixing with musical sounds, themselves recognizable but opening the door to a whole variety of concerts, etc.

Water gardens: laboratories with experimental pond cultures where different temperatures of water would allow the growth of different forms of water plants, and others where unusual forms of vegetation would be brought together in unusual combinations; water gardens with cascades in which the stones struck by the sheets of water would be in movement, and jets of water in a constant state of transformation would form changing volumes across their full extent.

Gardens of animals: laboratories where garden fauna would be studied in different ways, and spaces where it would be possible to observe and compare hedgehogs, garden tortoises, frogs, etc., as well as common but little-known insects such as the different types of hovering flies, which would be bred together with the flowers that are necessary for their survival.

Gardens of smells: beside the laboratories where new ways of generating smells—by both natural and non-natural means, such as flowers changing scent in the course of their blooming— would be the object of study. The public would be able to visit gardens with scented flowers of new kinds produced by laboratories and experience experimental spaces involving smells in various different ways (organs using keyboards of smells, etc.).

From Ice to Steam

The sequence of gardens and experimental spaces that have just been described would remain on a merely functional level if they were not accompanied by something capable of forming a counter balance to the massive technical presence of the nearby factory. An object is needed that would take up the process of metamorphosis by industrial means and convert it into a process accessible in plastic terms. That is where the notion of the Emscher undergoing metamorphosis for the future, as an aquatic milieu favorable to life, could also be brought out. In fact, the life of our planet takes place in the interval between two extremes, the cold of the polar ice on one hand and the heat of volcanoes on the other. But the activity of life, however much it has to preserve itself by avoiding these two extremes, always seeks at the same time to probe their limits. Surely it is a remarkable thing that humanity, the most unprotected animal there is, manages through ingenuity to bring minerals to temperatures as low as absolute zero and as high as those found in metallurgical furnaces? All this is, of course, in the service of a process of metamorphosis that is beneficial to life.

In just the same way, humanity seeks in its pleasures to develop and combine extremes, the sugary and salty as in *duck à l'orange*, warmth within ice cold as in the sauna, ice within warmth as in *omelette norvégienne*. The object we are suggesting for the heart of Zone D will be composed of a cold part, utilizing ice in its natural and non-natural aspects (colored ice architecture accessible to the visitor): ice that will be transformed into flowing water so that it issues upon a series of swimming pools separated by cascades, with their edges progressing from hard to soft and the water becoming warmer and warmer by graded stages. The installation will end with a lake of tepid water where there will be multicolored natural and non-natural fishes, out of which will emerge an island of red and orange glass that shelters greenhouses in the form of the tormented relief patterns of lava flows. These will contain all kinds of palm trees and tropical plants, distinguished by the fact that they are varieties invented by man, and beaches of colored sand heated to different temperatures, whose quality of grain will move from the finest powder to shingle—all these materials being man-made.

Associated with this whole installation will be services offered by the park. There will be shops providing ice-cream for the public, spaces evoking both the polar ice and the cold surfaces of the planets Jupiter and Neptune. On the other hand, volcanoes and tropical territories will be featured together with Venus and its torrid clouds, as recent explorations have revealed them to us. Between the cascades, the public will be offered a number of water games to play, such as "ballules" sliding on aquatic toboggans. They will also have access to a diving bell, which in its slow descent, will reveal to the visitor, through a vertical basin of water, the depths of the waters of the sea, and the phosphorescent creatures that live there . . .

This "ice to steam" installation will be constructed on a platform passing over the railway track. It will be at its highest point there (the pole of coldness) and will become progressively lower through different levels as the cascades and pools already mentioned follow one another, finally being raised up again to a second level of height (the pole of heat).

This theme will require a number of specific studies, but the dreamlike quality suggested above will remain the dominant perspective. A system of electrical transportation, which causes no pollution, will be used to pass between Zones B and D.

The Temporal Pens

The principle of separation between zones must have a timeless quality, and consequently it must avoid any form of stylistic reference that would connect it with the garden *à la française* or the garden *à l'anglaise*. This implies an uniform overall treatment that would be, on the one hand, applied to vegetation—since the context is that of gardens, parks and landscapes—and, on the other hand, expressed through an unexpected use of form, which is always the same, and extends throughout the whole park, so that it can be easily appreciated as constituting an overall framework. This is the reason for the proposal that the temporal pens should be marked by rows of trees, pointing in the same direction, rows that would alternate between deciduous and evergreen varieties, and different types of coloration.

The systematic oblique orientation of the trees in relation to a north-south axis would form the common denominator of this framing vegetation. When the composition changes, the contrast between their own identity and that of the different gardens defined by them would be at its maximum level.

Two hypotheses are offered for the realization of this scheme, which would be subject to further discussion. The first is already represented on the plan. It involves a row of deciduous trees alternating with a row of conifers for the countryside of time past (Zone C); three rows of deciduous trees and a row of conifers for the area of the blast furnaces and its canal (Zone B); two rows of deciduous trees and a row of conifers for the gardens of the future (Zone D).

The second proposition involves the planting used for forestry schemes. In order to emphasize this demarcation by means of trees, the ground level of the temporal pens would be raised up in relation to the gardens framed by them. Moreover, these pens would include all circulation, in particular the bicycle tracks, the numerous points of entry, and the car-parking facilities.

Last, the treatment of the ground surface in all these internal highways will be carried out with a cement that has been colored deep green in the mixing process, so that it will be clear that the highways are associated with the vegetation and not simply with transport, even though transport must function effectively at the same time.

The Green Belt of Frankfurt / 1992

A Statement by Bernard Lassus Given at the Town Hall in Frankfurt

Résumé:

The constitution of the Grüngurtel, the green belt, of Frankfurt, poses two problems: what are its boundaries and the nature of the places which constitute it? Will the reduction of pollution be sufficient to shape its landscapes?

That belt is revealed as an ensemble of heterogeneous places which do not have to be standardized by a treatment that aims to give them a common unity, but, on the contrary, accentuated in their differences by mutual valorization and set within an explicit limit. The cleansing of the polluted places cannot resolve the landscape problem, environment and landscape being two different notions: one is technical, the other cultural.

John Dixon Hunt, the well-known historian of the art of gardens, thinks that there are two processes used by landscapers: those who plan by subtracting, like Capability Brown in the eighteenth century, and, on the contrary, those who fill up, in reality the most usual type. The latter type of intervention, being more visible, is obviously more recognizable. But the intervention is seen even in the process of subtracting. Thus one recognizes the boundaries of the "natural" parks of Brown, because his hand could be detected in those parks, and not beyond them.

This preamble on boundaries is in order to know how the "Grüngurtel" will be perceived, not when leaving Frankfurt, but when arriving there from another town. Thus one must discover the "green belt" in respect of what precisely will be its difference from another place. If the towns surrounding Frankfurt later develop, not necessarily green belts but parks, how, when coming from these towns, or from the country, will we discover the green belt of Frankfurt? Indeed, it surrounds the city and one goes through it to enter the city, but that statement itself reveals the question of the "in itself" of that belt, which would not need the city to exist. As a matter of fact, can that dissimilar ensemble of orchards, rural exploitation, preindustrial zones, and forests be perceived as an entirety from one of its points of crossing? Not by its road signs, because stripes on a horse do not make a zebra.

To avoid that artifice, I should turn the question upside down: does the Grüngurtel in fact constitute an entirety? In relation to what? To the city? Perhaps it would require, then, many convergent interventions, which will nevertheless not be able to avoid having a connection with the area beyond the belt. Moreover, each of those interventions must not be in destructive contradiction with the rest, if one wants to obtain what I call a mutual valorization, through which each intervention reveals, through its contrasts, its neighbors. But let us go back to the difference between what the green belt would be from one side, *outside* the city, and, from the other side, *in relation* to the city. If the inhabitants, the travelers of today, move around, they no longer explore a fundamental relationship with ancestral space, as if were making a journey from houses where they feel secure, to the wild forest, where they can be devoured by wolves. The classical art of garden, based on the opposition between the discovery of the unknown (the vast and impenetrable forest) and a human known world (the castle)—that art no longer exists and has taken with it the outposts of that exploration: the trimmed trees, the middle terms between forest and constructed forms. One could today even reverse the terms of that old opposition by stating that it is the city that is wild, with unemployment, insecurity . . . while nature, outside the city, seems so harmonious and welcoming!!!

An indication of the loss of the old sensory referent that we used to call wild, the confusion affecting the ordering of our sense experience when going from city to nature, provides the basis on which we have to concentrate our efforts: the old outposts, trimmed trees, become industrial forest or waste land. Today, since those places are no longer given within old polarities, they need to be reinvented. It is not the formal solution of a problem by development that makes a place a landscape. The place as such is anterior to the use made of it. There is no longer today the old movement of meaning-formation that permitted identification of places between two precise poles; we have instead juxtapositions of places identifiable through interactions from place to place. I make a point of the fact that I have not said anything about activities yet, even in a justifiable aside, because, methodologically, a dissociation between place and use appears indispensable in the process of development. That dissociation is in itself a factor enabling the creation of the place by new users, since it will keep in store some surprises that were not directly anticipated for certain activities.

Consequently, what relationship can place the entity Grüngurtel between the places that form it and what exists beyond those places? The ensemble of the analyses and propositions on the Grüngurtel make a reflection on several scales possible now: from place to place within the green belt and other exterior places, and this without and then with the city; from activities to non-hierarchized activities, but specific to the places. After the elaboration of those places, a methodology of inventive analysis, on a wider scale, permits the definition of the concept Grüngurtel.

By forgetting Frankfurt, one notices then that those places are totally *dissimilar*, and that the Grüngurtel remains an entirely only in its opposition to the city, which is not sufficient. Its dissimilar pieces are on a scale of differentiation such that the belt includes all the other country areas that surround the other towns on the outskirts of Frankfurt and finds itself too large to have a constituted Grüngurtel, in relation to the rural areas surrounding the towns next to Frankfurt.

To reason simply in relation to the concept of "going back to nature" would only be to go back to the zero point of efficiency, nothing more, of the environment, for it is not because one re-creates the myth of nature-environment that one has thus created one or some landscapes, or, more precisely, places of nature suggesting specific landscapes. Cleaning up will certainly resolve the problem of the quality of the environment, but not the problem of the Grüngurtel as a landscape in relation to Frankfurt and, above all, in relation to the other town belts or the surrounding ruralities.

Thus, the green belt has to be new, an invented nature. The attitude of adopting a *common denominator* specific to the Grüngurtel, on each of the places that form it, would reduce the differences between those places. We would then have valorization of the concept Grüngurtel in connection with the places and even at their expense. On the contrary, could we not consider a linear common denominator of the limits of those places, one that would make them as floating islands in the green belt? One can consider furthermore a third mode of connection: the transfer of one of the characteristics proper to a place into the place to which it is juxtaposed, on each occasion that the limits may be differentiated, and so on, that is, a series of *delayed contrasts* from place to place.

It is the relevance of the interactions between those places as well as the specificity of the places themselves that will make the Grüngurtel what it has to be: a specific case and a place where the dream becomes concrete and the concrete gives rise to dreams.

A Landscape Slope—The Rest Area of Nîmes-Caissargues / 1992

To show that a Mediterranean ambiance is not simply a matter of vegetation, climate, and so forth but a form of process that can be set into operation, I would like to take a concrete instance: I shall demonstrate here how the plan for a highway linking Arles and Nîmes gave rise to the conception and ultimately the completion of a rest area.

Straightaway I should explain the problem of scale that confronted the person involved with this idea. A local space had to be established in the path of a route linking Italy to Spain. This is the kind of difficulty that cannot be resolved in the abstract, but has to be thought through each time in terms of a specific terrain—in this case Caissargues—which was put forward by the Société des Autoroutes du Sud de la France, as the leader of the project.

The Caissargues-terrain was an enormous one of 35 hectares, close to the town of Nîmes, with a huge quarry of 30 hectares from which the very materials previously used for road-building had been taken. It was on the site of this quarry that it was proposed to place a rest area on each side of the new highway leading from Arles to Nîmes. The programme involved installing parking places for heavy trucks and also for light vehicles, putting in toilets, and establishing a small museum to take account of the discovery in the same area of the so-called remains of the "Lady of Caissargues" as a result of the movements of earth caused by the highways.

What was my judgment on the site? First, there were strong gusts of wind from which the visitors had to be protected; second, before the excavation had been carried out and the quarry created, there had been a plateau extending toward one of the slopes leading down to the valley where the town of Nîmes is situated. From this place it was therefore possible to see the town in its full extent; it was in fact the first place on the route from which it became possible to observe the building façades of Nîmes on the far-off, gentle slope opposite. In the immediate neighborhood of this quarry there was a little scrubland, then, on the outside of the terrain, a few tufts of bushes, also vines, young pines, a farm on the horizon, and, of course, this view over the town. I was aware, by the way, that the rest areas the Société des Autoroutes usually put in were around 16 hectares and on a divided site.

I must now tell a little story to illustrate the more general context of the installation of this rest area. Mr. Vivet, the Director-general of the society, was responsible for coming up with the idea that nowadays, in the circumstances of the new highway plan and the number of rest areas that it involved, highway societies were the most important patrons in the realm of gardening. The areas had to be functional, but there was also the problem of creating gardens. One fundamental issue relating to the art of gardens has to be made clear at this point: it is an art that first of all and essentially implies laying out the ground as architecture, that is to say, choosing its form; the ground can then be planted, that is, decorated. From this perspective, the reconstitution of the initial terrain in this particular place, Caissargues, was bound to be of fundamental importance, as regards the landscape-bearing site and the garden to be placed on it. But was the ground at our disposal, which was already there—the ground at the bottom of the quarry—really the ground for this place and its new garden?

At the outset, it did indeed seem much the most logical solution to make use of the quarry because it was already there (and what is more, could serve as a shelter from the wind). But further reflection along landscape lines produced arguments that

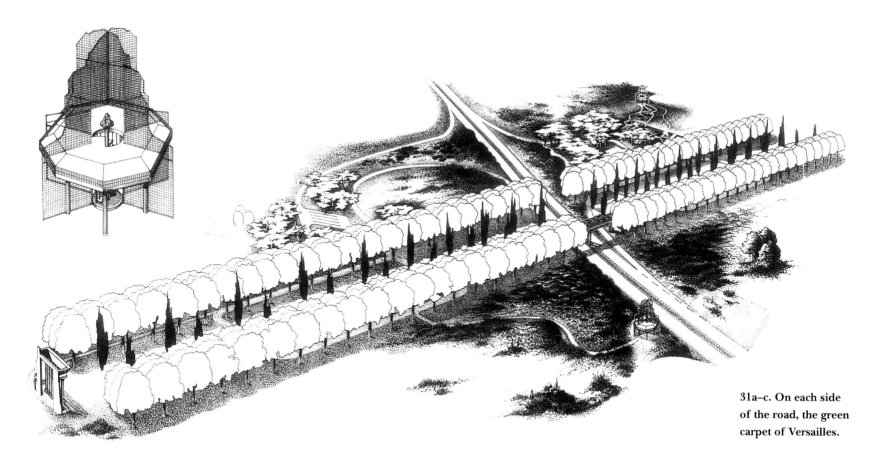

31a–c. On each side
of the road, the green
carpet of Versailles.

were more powerful, as regards the way the place could be envisaged. This place did not need to limit itself to the site where the
intervention took place—the quarry—but stretched far beyond
the quarry and the terrain surrounding it; its distinctive qualities
could be utilized and incorporated in the rest area.

There could be no question of justifying what had been a
recent excavation of the ground, which flagrantly negated the
local element. The terrain was in fact still part of what I would
call a landscape entity: a place essentially characterized by the
slope that led down into Nîmes. In other words, it was not a
slope for the sake of a slope, nor was it the bottom of a quarry,
but it was the slope that led in the direction of Nîmes: between
the plateau and the beginnings of the sloping valley where Nîmes
was to be seen, at the very point where the slope enabled the
town to appear from a specific point of view. There could be no
question, in my view, of burying oneself in the ground. Recon-
stituting the initial slope allowed one to recover the same level
as the scrubland, the farm, and the vines. Nonetheless, the use
of 350,000 square meters of rubble was only enough to fill up

the terrain in a less than satisfactory way: it was only possible to
achieve a level slightly below the initial level specified on the old
plans. But at the same time an important technical problem had
been solved, as we reused the rubble derived from the construction of the new highway.

Now that the slope had been reconstituted, I obtained what
can be called the "degree zero" of place, on which it was possible
to begin again with landscape.

The situation was now easy to analyse: the rebuilt slope facili-
tated a direct view over Nîmes, which was perpendicular to the
autoroute. Via this slope, there could develop an interplay with
the town and a break, from the town's point of view, with the
highway system, at the very point where the slope itself broke
up the terrain. The place could serve both as a stop for travelers
and long-distance truck drivers and as a garden belonging to the
nearby town.

So what form was the slope to take as a rest area and garden?
As indicated in the illustrations, we have here a long ribbon of
grass, emphasized by three rows of African lotuses and punc-

tuated by groups of three cypresses in the middle, divided in two by the highway and so forming two distinct surfaces. When the project was officially presented, Mr. Bousquet, the Mayor of Nîmes, made the comment: "You are bringing me a park for my town." But in spite of appearances, this is not just geometry for the sake of geometry but something closer to irony. Surely a highway is a royal road, a path that sets its mark on sites in contravention of the ancient routes. I felt that the closest parallel to my project was in fact the "green carpet" at Versailles, which is about 300 meters long, on a similarly majestic scale, and gives access to a far-off landscape. By doubling the length of this

well-known feature, I acquired the means at the same time of making a formal connection between the two parts of the area, and of commenting in a light-hearted way on the inadequacy of gardens on the usual scale in responding to the problems of the highways. I also succeeded in posing a question: is the double lawn crossed by the highway, or vice versa? You will understand that it is not up to me to provide the answer.

The game is made more complex if we also take account of the two slopes of the "green carpet." In effect, there is a slight longitudinal slope, which can be perceived along the 700 meters of the rest area divided by the highway through the change in levels; but there is also a transverse slope, which offers access to other parts of the terrain and can only be appreciated by a visit on the spot. Mr. Bousquet has willingly given permission for the highest part of the area to receive the colonnade of the old theater of Nîmes, a nineteenth-century building that burned down and has recently been replaced by the new gallery designed by Norman Foster. As opposed to the inhabitants of Nîmes, general visitors will not be aware that these columns have not always been there, and they will be provided with a viewing facility that will help them replace these remains in their minds, within the precise situation and period to which they belonged before the fire caused them to be transported to their present location. This is the first time a classified historic monument has been moved to form part of a newly installed place, with the specific purpose of stressing its "Nîmesness." This factor again gives point to the question asked above.

From within the garden, it was unsatisfactory to have just a vague view over the town. So I suggested that on each side of the area a belvedere should be built, one of two floors and the other of one, to take account of their different positions on the site. These also function as follies, which form a counterpoint to the double historical presence of the museum of the Lady of Caissargues and the colonnade, and they provide a point of view over the highway. These belvederes have been designed to follow the profile of the Tour Magne, one of the most impressive monuments in Nîmes, and carried out with the aid of grille surfaces and metallic tubes similar to those used by the architect Jean Nouvel in the construction of the Néamausus buildings. But it was not enough to have these constructions alone to guarantee the presence of the town in a sufficiently vivid form, since the silhouettes were not easy to recognize. So two stone maquettes of the Tour Magne were designed to be placed inside each of the two belvederes. This play on scale enables the tactile presence of the maquettes to conjure up the genuine presence of the Tour Magne.

My idea was to place a strong emphasis on the Roman quality of the rest area in order to match the Roman identity of Nîmes, which is situated precisely on the old Heracleian road leading to Spain. In this sense the rest area with its columns, its profiles and maquettes of the Tour Magne (and perhaps, at a later stage, its "nimetta," a brick replica of the town plan of Nîmes) is an attempt to create for our own period a foretaste of this Romanness, from the Spanish direction, while at the same time offering an aftertaste from the Italian direction: a belvedere garden looking in both directions.

It is not my place to say whether the site will in fact work in this way. But it is obvious that the accumulation of different references can be a contributory factor. In any case, it will depend on the use people make of the area, which is already becoming impressive. In other places, there would undoubtedly be quite different realities making themselves felt if we posed the question of the relationship of the site and the objects to be placed there, not in terms of the site being the object, but in terms of the interrelation of a number of sites and a number of objects. Defining this relationship is a matter of artistic ethics, since—as we must never forget—what exists has a habit of carrying all before it.

General Principles of a Kinetic Light Work / 1993

Particular to the A72 Clermont-Ferrand–Saint-Etienne

From the different conversations we have had with motorists using their vehicles at night, it is evident that they want to have visual information on what is "before them" as they progress, what is "before them" corresponding not only to the movement of the road itself, but also to what that movement is inscribed within, that is, the general movement of the terrain.

That request is a response to the wish not to be surprised, most of the drivers with whom we have had a conversation being inclined to prefer illuminated motorways.

That unanimity in response has thus led me to give preference to this way of looking at the route.

In the example we are featuring, the route can be defined and summarized with the following equivalences: straight line equals plain and flat, bend equals relief plus descent or ascent. From that, a first hypothesis emerges and permits finding a visual form for that route. Certainly, the notion of flatness, slope, bend, or ascent gives precise indications, but these are far too general. That is, they do not identify specifically the A72 between Clermont-Ferrand and Saint-Etienne.

Thus, it seems necessary to me to find a better factor for identification. Given the importance of the relief, it seems interesting, in order to discern the specificity of the places, to represent in the form of a relief profile heights regularly spaced at 50 meters (along the heights from 300 to 800 meters), and to place that reading in relation to a lengthwise profile. That permitted me to see that there existed on that route a certain number of, what I called, topographic "thresholds," that is, sections of the route where the altitude changes more rapidly than at other spots on that same route. The route has the look of a sort of curve, in the shape of a flattened hat, at the point where it crosses the stretch of the Monts du Forez.

That the height is thus relative to a minimal distance according to five precise thresholds, defines much more specific new fractions, all the more so because, in daylight, the motorist can easily see that those thresholds are close to Thiers, to Saint-Marcel d'Urfé (where a fortress dominating the whole region was situated long ago); the two lowest thresholds being those of Ravaux and Souternon, announcing on the one hand, the valleys of the Dore and Allier, and on the other, the valley of the Loire; the highest threshold, Cervières, being on the profile, a point of separation between two drainage basins.

Those thresholds introduce a logic at the same time common to the relief, to human establishments, and to the more recent path of the A72. That is not obvious when one moves about on the profile and does not know the places.

In daylight, one of the charms of the A72 is the quality of the landscapes discovered in the course of that journey along the highway. Indeed, a sample survey carried out by the students at the University of Clermont-Ferrand informs us that this section is considered beautiful.

It is clear, bearing in mind the quality of the landscape discovered in daylight, and the relative absence of light-points linked to the presence of the habitat, that the section becomes, at night, only a series of differing movements. What I mean is that it is now knowable by night only by that series of movements. It is equally clear that, by revealing with light some spots significant from a cultural point of view, the lighting would not at all restore the quality particular to the places traversed, for a route

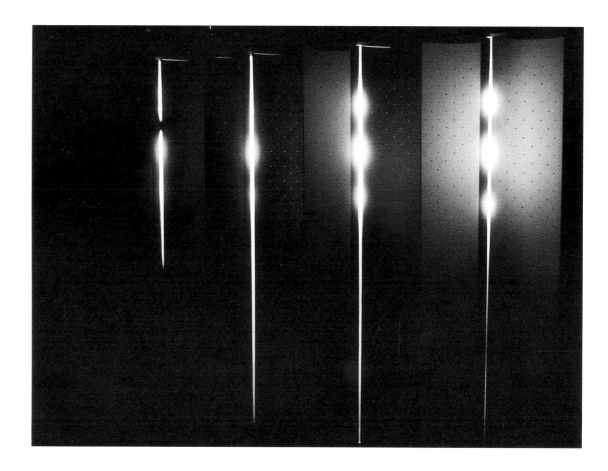

**32. Ambiance 10, 1965.
Red and green tubes
bend before the green,
orange, and red curves.
Height, 2.20m, length
6.00m, depth 0.60m.**

between two towns is, from a global point of view (that is, a land-scape point of view), much richer than the sum of the singular places which comprise it.

In conclusion, the portion of landscape being illuminated would only be slightly representative of the places crossed at night.

Several possible attitudes result from this.

First Hypothesis

The point is to represent the route by distinguishing its two sides by a luminous tube of a different color which would be placed above or in place of the crash barriers.

The linearities put in place would be longer on the external side of the bends. The middle of the bends would be indicated by a transformation of the continuous linearity by a luminous broken line.

In the descents, since those need to be the most marked, there would be a doubling or tripling of the linearities or broken lines.

Thus, if, in a general way, the bends will be marked each time, the straight lines will be particularly marked on the descent.

The permanence of a color along the route will permit the driver to locate far distance by the precise localization of the road and, at the same time, will introduce a luminous effect through a stepping of lines.

Now the question is to take heed of the particular places through which one passes.

Let us not forget that it is in terms of landscape or discovery of landscape that the road is identified. If in certain cases some constructed monuments could be illuminated, like the church of Saint-Rémy, the most specific feature of that road would be that some fractions of landscape, those which are large in surface, would be lit. Thus the question becomes one of choosing some of those places, since it is out of the question, for obvious reasons of cost, that the entirety of the route could be the object of such treatment.

As characteristic places, I retain precisely the thresholds, or the places situated on the edges of the thresholds, that permit at the same time as those few particular landscapes, the general relief of the road to be made manifest.

Each of the light systems would be at the same time a certain color, different in each case, but the same if the threshold corresponds to a passage of road in the same section of altitude.

My first proposition would permit having along the length of the route, by sections, the colored patterns that the tubes create out of their interplay with the landscapes—that is, five thresholds, plus the entry of the section. Hence an aesthetic game between patterns of two colors and a monochrome lit surface of a third color. In other words, a luminous ambiance, a soft, diffused light, on which would be inscribed the colored lines of the route.

I obtain by this means a relationship that is unusual between pattern and surface: the surface here evoking also the volume.

The games would equally create an opposition of significance between highway lines and the biggest possible surfaces, for those surfaces would be of a natural order: meadows, rocks, silhouettes of trees, and hillsides.

The opposition between feature/pattern/inscription and vast surfaces, even in a small number of cases, would create five images or representations of the landscape to discover.

One sees clearly, in this first hypothesis, that one has to choose the thresholds in terms of the quality of the landscape selected.

The Optical Bushes / 1993

Exhibition Fair at Niort: Gardens and Fruits of a Passion

The idea of the garden created for the exhibition was based on the natural spectrum of colors represented by a series of colored bands:
red/orange/oranged yellow/pale yellow/pale blue/blue/ultramarine/violet
They were separated by double lines of colors that opposed their contrasts of color, so that each double term of that discontinuity valorized each term of the continuity. Thus I obtained the series:
red/*yellow + blue*/**orange**/*blue + violet blue*/**orange yellow**/*green + red*/**pale yellow**/*red + violet*/**pale blue**/*ultramarine + green*/**blue**/*orange + pale blue*/**ultramarine**/*yellow + red*/**violet**

It was a way to express, in the field of colors, the theory of faults that I have tried to apply to the art of gardens on several occasions, especially the project of the Garden of Returns at Rochefort sur Mer.

This set of colors, which I first developed in a project dating from October 1962, led me, in 1967, to Ambiance 11, an apparatus using movable painted bands reflecting on distorting mirrors, but I was not at that time able to extend it to flowers. The garden planned for Niort, with a surface area of 126 square meters, thus allowed me to appreciate the relationship between these two works based on the same principle. The flower-bands were intended to display the naturality of the colored spectrum, but the double-painted boards juxtaposed to them were opposed to it in many different ways: contrasts of lines (boards) and bands (flowers), contrasts of colors of flowers in relation to each other, contrast of painted colors in relation to each other, contrast of material (between paint and flowers), contrasts of natural colors with painted colors. All of which allowed me to

verify, for the first time, that the painted boards valorized the colors of the flowers.

It was possible to realize the project in two ways: on the one hand, by using flowers of the same species everywhere, for example, tulips; on the other—and this was the solution chosen—by using flowers of different species for each color. It had been impossible to find enough flowers of the same species to compose all the bands of colors planned.

The new variation of the species of different flowers added another contrast, the shapes of the flowers—the patterns of the corollae—to the contrasts initially sought for: of microvariations of the same shape for the same floral species, the microvariations of shades of color, and sizes for the same color in each band of flowers. However, that bending of the initial constraint still did not permit the realization of certain colors with appropriate flowers, especially in the blue range, so that, finally, the bands of painted colors had to play that role. Taking that defect into account has revealed, in the end, a supplementary contrast.

The initial organization was imaginable more appropriately on a surface plane thanks to which everyone could observe at leisure the contrasts produced. To introduce two planes of reading, of different heights, within that organization, incorporated the question of discontinuity introduced between the two planes. I had thus to ensure a passage from one to the other.

Gardens normally use bushes for such passages. Could we imagine that, at infinity, horizontality could transform into verticality by a sort of turning over, since, perspectively, the parallel horizontal lines not only join once more in the horizontal but rise there too? I have thus used an oblique mirror that carries the horizontal foreground to the middle ground through the

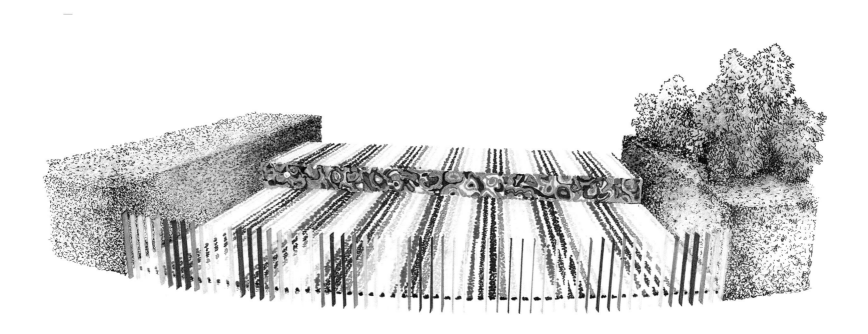

continuity of geometric lines. That obliquity of reflected flowers, very striking when one observes the garden without moving, I called the *optical bush* in order to draw attention to its natural side.

The continuity of the three planes was so effective that visitors did not notice the difference between the flowers and their reflections, except when they moved around and bent down to try to understand what they were seeing, destroying the logic of that visual continuity by their action. In that way, the same principle, initially static in 1962, then explored in 1967 through the concrete mobility of the colored bands reflecting on distorting mirrors, found here a new expression with the mobility of the visitors.

The ambiguity of real flowers, real colors, reflections of flowers, and reflections of colors really created a continuity between natural elements and painting, and what is more, through the contrast of painted lines (indicated by the barrier) the naturality of the colored spectrum realized with flowers, which stood in opposition to the naturality of the flowers, in fact enhanced the colors and the patterns of the corollae. They became still more flowers, and still more colors.

The Gardens of Peace at Verdun / 1993

The Main Terrace

The ground of the terrace would be treated with gray paving stones in order to give an impression of depth, for this surface does not have to give the impression that it reflects the light, but that it is a firm tactile reference. The long walkway would also be dotted with other paving stones, larger, of a slightly warmer color. Those, engraved with sentences, would be placed facing different moments offering possible views, and readable only with that in mind. Giving consideration to the significance of the Centre Mondial de la Paix, those sentences would be taken from different Nobel Peace Prize winners, who would be asked to write them. In connection with that, one can envisage diverse types of public manifestations as an accompaniment. The constant rhythm of those paving stones and of their corresponding sentences would give an impression of infinity since that walkway would not have either a beginning or an end; that is, no particular development would clearly resolve it in such terms.

Finally, along the length of the terrace would be placed big containers in which would grow bushes and plants with white flowers. Replacement of those flowers would be ensured all through the summer, so that there would be a continuous flowering on the terrace. That implies the building of a greenhouse to permit a constant supply of flowers. Concerning their shape, the containers will subsequently be the subject of a special study that will have to specify their sizes, shapes, and colors, which I already see in a range of solid greens. They would be crowned with a sculpted toric motif representing a kind of vegetable braid composed of an interlacing of olive leaves. A second crown can be envisaged whose motif would be one of an interlacing of palms. These two types of vegetation are the explicit symbols of

Peace. It is essential that those different-sized containers are designed specifically for the Centre Mondial. Copies could also be offered for sale with white flowering plants.

The section of the terrace that is considered as a moat and situated between the palace and the episcopal garden could be developed accordingly: first, to use paving stones identical to those of the terrace, but with a greater density of flower containers; and second, to affirm a meaning for the moat by installing white water-lilies in the basin. That seems to me to correspond better to the passage from the notion of terrace to that of moat. A stabilized ground would cover the lower terrace and its access. There one could find plants in the open ground and, along the walls, climbing plants with white flowers. In the largest places, a few trees would be planted.

The Actual Garden of Plants of Peace

Located at the highest level of the spaces given over to the gardens; the nearest part of the construction that surrounds these places is also the one farthest from view. It is there that a greenhouse with two spaces would be erected. The deepest space would be large enough for palm trees. The second space, semicylindrical and of a lower height, would be for a very old olive tree transferred from the south. It would be placed on a pedestal covered with sand. The greenhouse is necessary because these different plants cannot withstand the heavy cold of the local climate and will need an artificial atmosphere. From the greenhouse, and moving down toward the episcopal garden, will stretch in succession a turfed lawn, a path on stabilized ground, then a white square garden, slightly sunken, with a surface area

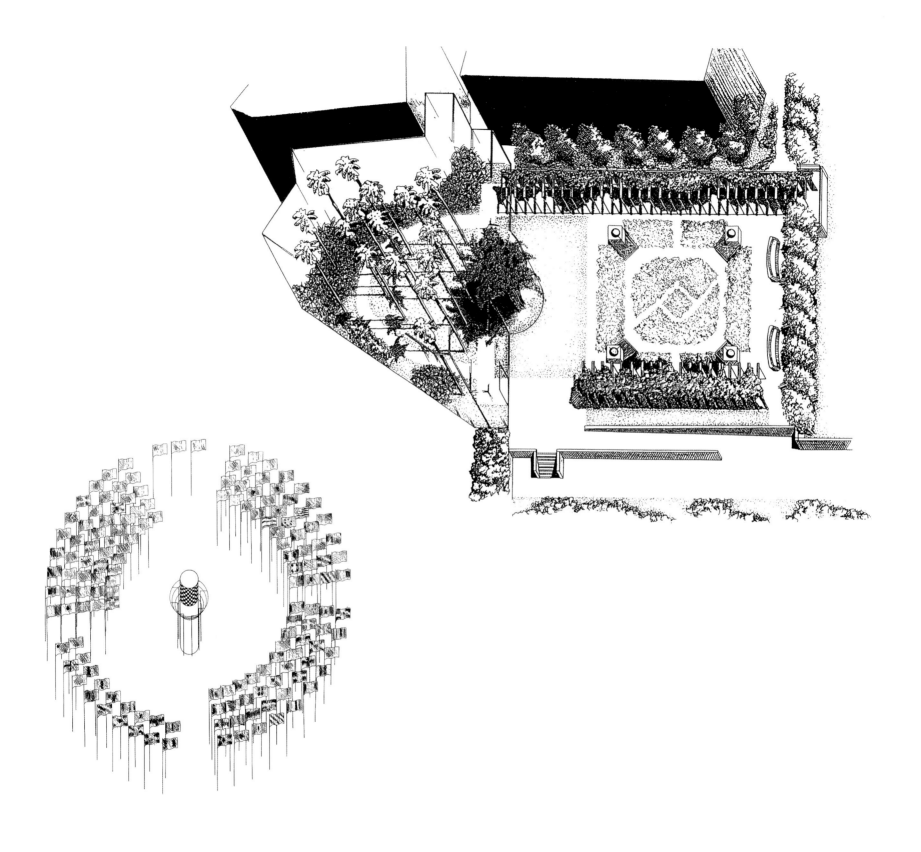

The dovecote.

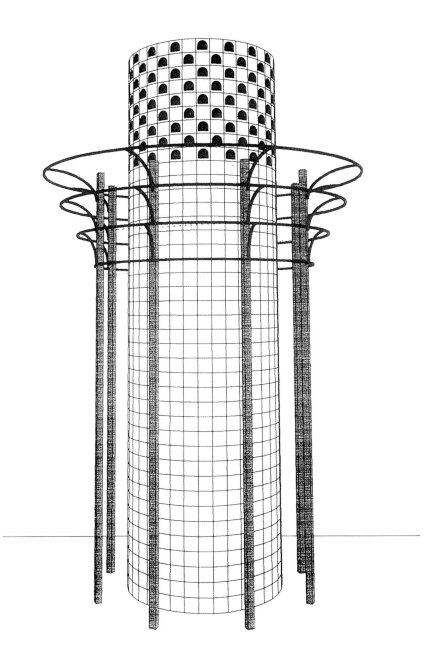

of 484 square meters, in which will be gathered several dozen white flowering plants of various species and different heights. Very narrow paths will permit walking in the sunken garden. At its four outer corners will be placed fountains. They will consist of two parts: a high level formed by a sphere activated by the pressure of water, from which the water will pour to a second level, a basin with an aquatic surface similarly animated.

On each of those spheres will be engraved a representation of a quarter of the globe. From both sides of that garden and perpendicular to the episcopal garden will be built pergolas covered with climbing plants, still with white flowers. One of the pergolas, the longest, will end in a belvedere on the episcopal garden. To enjoy the view, on that last garden forming a terrace, next to the belvedere, several benches especially designed for the place will be installed.

The Large Platform Between the Fort and the Episcopal Garden

This space we wish to develop in the future could already carry, at its center, a white dovecote more than 12 meters high, housing a flock of doves. The dovecote would be surrounded by a set of poles, bearing all the flags of the world grouped by continents. The ensemble would stand resplendent on a vast well-kept meadow, which would await later development related to the animals of Peace.

The ensemble of all these spaces brought together would form the Gardens of Peace at Verdun.

The Walk in the Quarries at Crazannes / 1995

Prelude

The quality of the places on the site of the quarries at Crazannes derives from the relationship between the perceived danger of spaces cleared by the extraction of stones and the artificial development of the places, as a result of the transport of unused waste onto the high parts, which is associated with a strong vegetable growth. That vegetable growth is particularly distinguished by the magnificent outgrowth of the scolopendrium ferns, which reach a quite exceptional density there.

The Circuit

The difficulties of the circuit are linked to the need for ensuring security. A study of the dangerous features of the site has been made by Antéa and has shown that one can devise a safe circuit, the one presented here. Besides the security of the visitors, there is the necessity for protecting the plants, especially the scolopendrium ferns that grow on the circuit.

Following the work carried out by Antéa, I propose that the visitors move along the length of the circuit on a footbridge roughly raised in relation to the levels of the ground. The visitors would be asked not to climb down from the footbridge, so that they may feel that, outside of that path, they would no longer be safe. That is obviously not the case within the limits of the envisaged route, but such a safety device has, as its main objective, the aim of discouraging visitors from damaging the vegetation.

To confirm that impression, a guard-rail would enclose

1. the belvederes as priority;
2. what we call the "gathering places," which will be dotted here and there along the circuit;
3. the footbridge itself, at certain points in the visual field.

The extent of the frequentation in relation to the fragility of the vegetation, which necessarily implies the adherence of visitors to the footbridges on the circuit, led me to plan three types of places: spots where one passes—the footbridge and the gathering places; spots where looking is the essential fact—the belvederes; and, finally, spots to admire, but where the circuit and the pedestrians do not enter.

The Spots Where One Passes

The spots where one passes are formed by two types of surfaces, the footbridges as such and the gathering places.

The footbridges are slightly raised so that it is not necessary to install guard rails along their whole length. However, guard rails will be installed at certain points of the route so that there is no need in those spots to signify to the visitors that they must not step down. That safety device of avoidance is also, let us recall, the most effective for the protection of the vegetation.

Specific planting will be carried out along the length of those footbridges. However, the point is not to bring the presence of the scolopendrium ferns closer to the circuit, but simply to dissuade the visitor from going on to the terrain by using thick bushes, impenetrable ones, that stand in the way. If it is possible,

35a. The "land art" installation along the highway toward Saintes.

35b. Preliminary study of real to fake rocks.

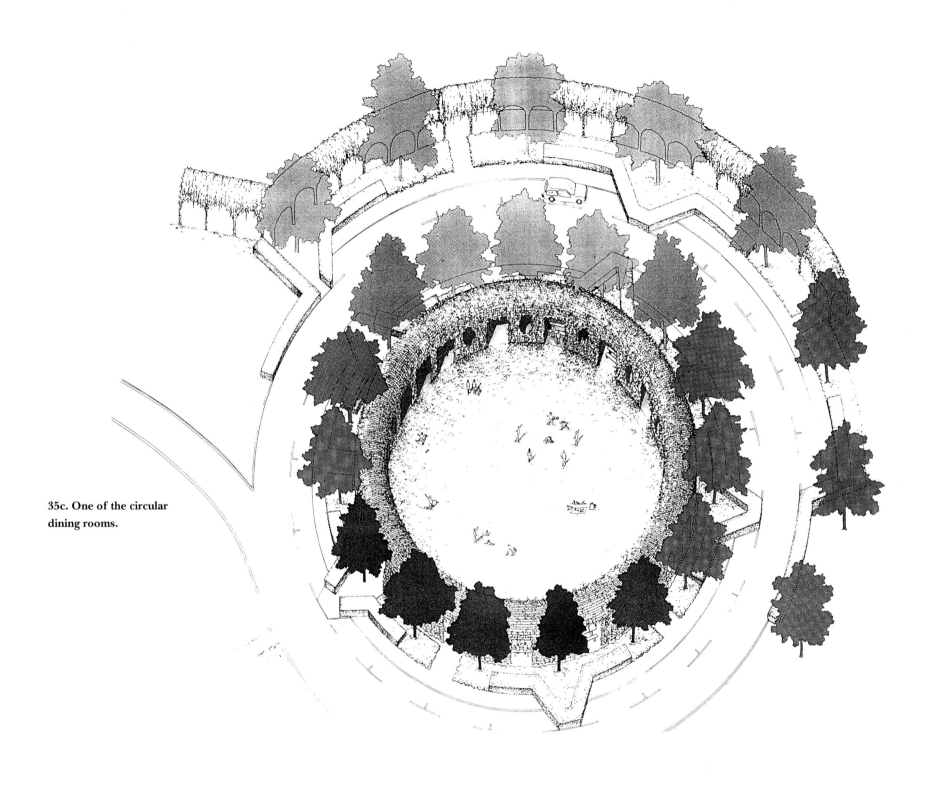

35c. One of the circular dining rooms.

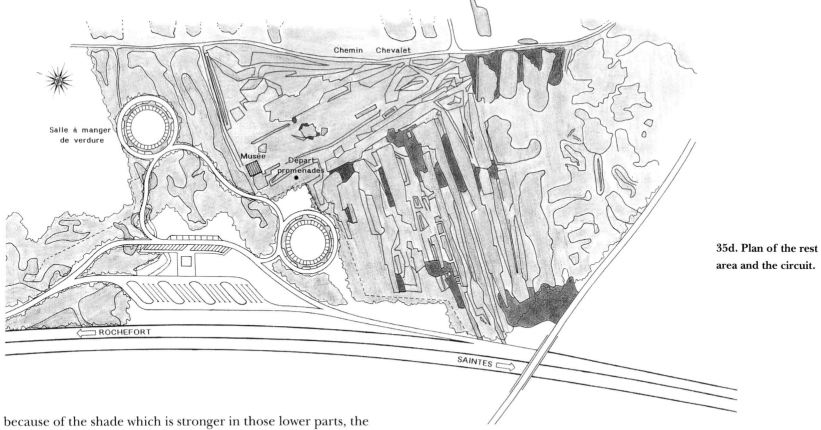

Salle à manger
de verdure

Chemin   Chevalet

Musée
Départ
promenades

ROCHEFORT
←ROCHEFORT

SAINTES ⇨

35d. Plan of the rest area and the circuit.

because of the shade which is stronger in those lower parts, the species of bushes will be chosen from among those that one can already see in similar situations on the quarries. The platforms for the gathering of visitors will be totally enclosed by guard rails allowing the public to look and chat while leaning on their elbows.

The Spots for Looking From

These are the belvederes from which one will be able to view long perspectives without entering them. These belvederes, also in wood, will be totally enclosed by guard rails, to prevent the public from stepping down into the places themselves. Taking into consideration the configuration of the terrain, two of them will be higher than the ground. In those cases, of course, the presence of guard rails is obligatory according to regulations.

On the ground of the successive "quarries for looking at," the old paths will be destroyed by digging them over, then plant-

ing scolopendrium ferns there to signify clearly, in yet another way, that those places are inaccessible. That will likewise increase their mysterious side. In the experience of some local groups it has been shown that these ferns can easily be transplanted and will take root again without difficulty. In the high parts of those "quarries for looking at," plantings would be carried out locally in a way that either improves the romantic aspect, or repairs the destruction brought about by the former workings.

From one of the belvederes, one could even catch sight of a newly installed pond in which would be reflected the entrance of one of the subterranean rooms. That pool would be in a way the symbol of the newly established places.

To sum up, I would say that the belvederes are treated in the same way as the gathering places, but that they have a different and raised geometric form.

_179_ The Walk in the Quarries at Crazannes
179 The Walk in the Quarries at Crazannes

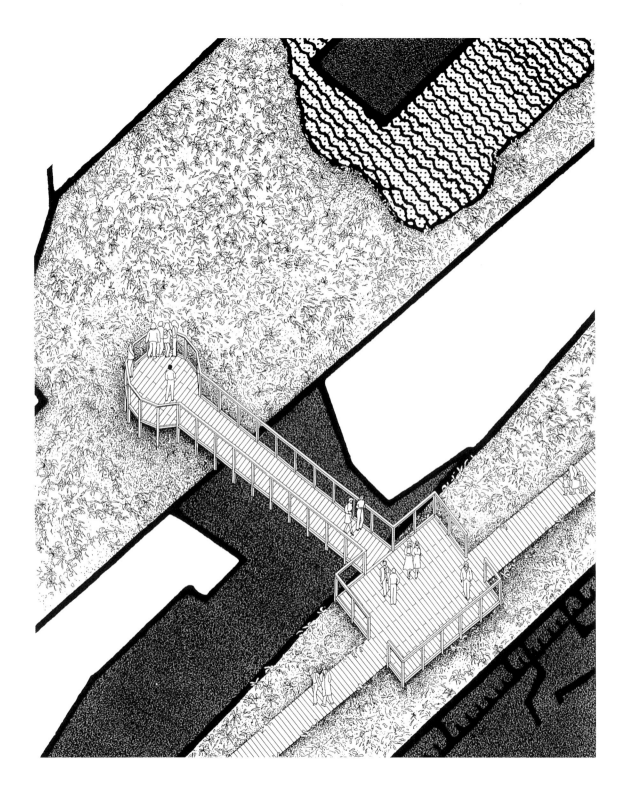

35e. One of the belvederes on the quarries walkway.

The Visit of the Circuit

As an initial rule, the proposed circuit could be visited in a tour lasting 20 to 30 minutes, under the direction of a guide in charge of a group of 15 to 20 people. That number is only an indication, for the gathering places can receive a greater number of visitors.

The groups could follow each other every 10 minutes at busy periods, but always under the direction of a guide. In the periods of low frequentation, a single guide will probably be sufficient, but during the summer months, when the crowds will be greater, one can easily imagine that 3 or 4 guides will be needed so as not to keep the visitors waiting.

Thus, it is more or less 90 people per hour who would pass through the place, which indicates that a coach tour will be able to visit in 2 or 3 groups. That leads me to envisage the installation of wooden benches to keep the visitors waiting at the entrance to the circuit. Other benches will also be planned at a third and two-thirds of the way along the route in order to relieve sudden tiredness. Concerning the preservation of the safety of the place in the absence of a guide, it will be necessary to consider that question at a certain point. As an example, in periods of low frequentation, the single guide working would open and close the gate of the circuit himself. In the periods of greater frequentation, one person would always act as supervisor at the entrance.

35f. One of the views of the quarries with their numerous ferns. The circuit is organized so that visitors cannot damage the ferns by stepping on them.

Afterword

Stephen Bann

Note by the Series Editor

These two commentaries by Stephen Bann appeared as prefaces to the only attempts to present Bernard Lassus's work that have so far appeared in English, in the Journal of Garden History *3 (1983) and 15 (1995) respectively. They are reprinted here as a third commentary on Lassus's work (in addition to the two Introductions by Peter Jacobs and Robert B. Riley) and as a historical record of the English reception of the work of this important French landscape architect.*

(1983)

At a 1981 conference devoted to "The Minimal Intervention" in landscape,[1] Bernard Lassus accompanied both his opening and his closing remarks with a brief illustration. In the first case, he projected a color slide of his "Ambiance 6," a work dating back to 1965.[2] A close-up picture of vivid red tulips is invaded from the right-hand side by a human thumb, which holds a small strip of white card: the card is thus irradiated with the reflection of the tulip, and we learn, in Lassus's words, that "the tulip is also a volume of light" colored differently from its surroundings. In the second case, at the end of the conference, Lassus did not present an image, but recounted a brief story. When a particular African tribe was brought out of the dense forest in which its life had been spent and introduced to the clearing, individual members of the tribe tried vainly to shake hands with people who were many yards away. Accustomed as they were to seeing their fellow human-beings at very short distances, they concluded that the figures they saw in the clearing were doll-sized beings who were nonetheless very close to them.

These two points of reference could be taken as a paradigm for the development of Bernard Lassus's work over two decades, since they demonstrate at the same time the considerable shift in emphasis his studies have undergone and the basic unity between the different stages of his career. In 1965 Lassus was completing a long series of experiments on the variable relationships between color, surface, movement, and ambient light which he identified with the title "Ambiance." To a certain extent these works fitted into the contemporary category of "kinetic art," and they had been included in exhibitions which bore that rubric. But it is important to recognize that they had at the same time a directly utilitarian function. Lassus had begun to experiment with the possibilities of artificial light as a result of a commission from a commercial company in 1957, and his foundation of the Centre de Recherche d'Ambiances in 1962 was an attempt to bring together specialists from different domains—architecture, psychology, sociology, poetics—in order to permit more far-reaching projects than were open to the individual artist.

---

[1] "L'Intervento minimo," 3 convegno Internazionale sui Parchi, organized on behalf of the Centro Studi Belice and the Deutscher Werkbund by Lucius Burkhardt and Bernard Lassus at Gibellina, Sicily, 10–12 September 1981.

[2] A limited edition of the work was published by Coracle Press in London in 1980. Lassus has exhibited prints and publications at the Coracle Press Gallery, e.g., the photographic series "The Pines," January/February 1981.

The tulip of "Ambiance 6" was, then, in 1965, a demonstration of the possibilities of reflected light: it fitted within the series of "Brise-lumières" constructions that Lassus had exhibited widely in the 1960s, and ran parallel to the schemes of interior coloration he was carrying out at the same time in various sites throughout France. By 1981, however, it had acquired a new significance, directly in keeping with the theme of "Minimal Intervention." Lassus repeats the gesture of inserting the white card into the cup of the red tulip. The glow of red light extends over the lower surface of the card. Then it is withdrawn. But, suggests Lassus, a new significance has been created. We may no longer see the physical effect of the reflection, but we *know* that the tulip is also "a volume of light"—*un air rosé*. In a sense, this illustration becomes the pendant to the story about the African tribe. If the hapless tribesman shows how our reading of space is directly related to our expectations, and that we will establish a wildly improbable field of relationships rather than forgo the perceptual set of prior experience, then the tulip is an indication that leads in the contrary direction. The tulip is changed by the experiment. We see it differently. But this is because we are able to retain at once the physical presence of the unaltered tulip, and the "poetic" transformation it has undergone.

If I choose to begin this brief essay on the work of Bernard Lassus with these two complementary parables, it is with the aim of establishing from the first a particular style, both of thought and of presentation, which is his most original contribution to the contemporary debate about landscape. It would not have been difficult to provide him with a conventional biography, marked in particular by his appointment as Professor of Architecture at the Ecole des Beaux-Arts, Paris, in 1969, and a conventional series of practical achievements, ranging from dining rooms to ocean liners, from the façades of blocks of apartments to prize-winning garden designs such as the "Garden of the Anterior," which is republished here. But this would be to falsify the issue from the start, since Lassus's originality lies precisely in the way he supersedes the distinctions between the "practical" and the "poetic," between the architect and the poet or artist, which weigh so inflexibly upon contemporary planning. If Lassus has chosen to concern himself with "Landscape" rather than the experimental art-works of his earlier career, this is not because of any shift in emphasis from the visionary to the practical. Quite the opposite, he maintains that the formulation and solution of the problems of "Landscape" can only be attempted from the widest possible cultural basis. Confronted with the obtuseness of modern architects, whose only solution to the accusation of inadequate planning is reduction to a *tabula rasa* and reconstruction *ex nihilo*, Lassus insists on the extraordinarily complex character of the landscape experience and its irreducibility to formalist dogma. Landscape and the garden are for him the Achilles' heel of the architecture of the Modern Movement. Having been largely disregarded in the assumptions of modernist architects and planners, the landscape dimension reasserts itself as a paradigm of the multiple relations that bind us to the visible, and tangible, world. If we are to understand this complex affiliation, how can we possibly dispense with the aid of the painter, the poet, and the historian?

Another way of putting the matter would be to say that Lassus's work has developed in direct conjunction with the extraordinary recent expansion of interest in landscape and the garden. But its purpose has been precisely to avoid the temptation of archaism and nostalgia that inevitably accompanies such a rediscovery. For Lassus, the more we know about the gardens of the past, the more we recognize their intimate binding within the poetic and cognitive concerns of their own day. To the extent that we also recognize how different our own concerns are bound to be, we will never make the mistake of supposing a particular pattern or mode to be absolute. As Lassus puts it in his project for the Parc de la Villette: "The cultural prolongation of the symmetrical garden, which is such an attractive form despite its hierarchical quality, should not blind us to the fact that gardens have almost always foretold in advance the relationships between man and nature, and between society and nature." In other words, the painstaking recreation of the "jardin à la française" can only be an archaeological exercise. But if we understand how fully such a garden pattern corresponded to the assumptions and preconceptions of its period we can also take a chance on predicting the likely relationships that will emerge between man and nature in our own times.

This point requires a certain emphasis because it is, in a sense, a piece of self-criticism Lassus has made of his own earlier projects. In the late 1960s, he was commissioned to provide a work for a new school at Guénange, in Lorraine. His solution to the brief—which deliberately avoided the temptation of creating an isolated "mural" or sculpture—was a descending structure of balls of enameled metal, mounted on steel stalks, which simulated the effect of a topiary garden. Where the topiary hedge mediated between the constructed form of the house and the luxuriance of natural vegetation, the "artificial bush" sought

to fulfill the same mediating function between the aggressive, metal-framed building and the surrounding trees. But Lassus's concern to insert transitions within the continuum from the wild to the domestic—from nature to culture—becomes the object of a rhetorical question in the study, "Depth: A Vertical Beyond Measurement," which is republished here. "Can we any longer attempt the traditional ways of progressively conquering wildness with constructed forms in the horizontal dimension?" he asks. His series of studies and projects are an attempt to answer this question. They form a unified sequence precisely because they are all concerned with the fascinating possibilities which open up once the "classic" solution is left in suspense.

The brief text on "The Well," dating from 1972, indicates very economically the resources Lassus felt compelled to draw upon in order to galvanize the imagination of his client, and his readers. The perpetually falling pebble is a physical impossibility—but it is also an imaginative possibility. Lassus uses the collective memory of the child's game in order to show how conventional expectations can be dislocated and new meanings substituted: in the working model of the Well which was exhibited at the Musée des Arts Décoratifs in 1975, the falling pebble was shown to trigger off not merely the imaginative stimulus of the absence of sound, but the bizarre effect of quite unrelated sounds and commotions. The close connection between this project and the "Garden of the Anterior" is therefore evident. Where the Well invites the reader, or visitor, to convert the spatial dimension of depth into the poetic reading of an "impossible" space, the Garden of the Anterior makes use of a real depth (the pond of Saint-Bonnet) to conjure up the local myth of the "drowned village" (*village englouti*). The entire planning of the Garden of the Anterior presupposes indeed a repudiation of the horizontal dimension—clear visibility, easy paths, and wide vistas of vegetation—in favor of the rediscovery of the "vertical" dimension in which time and space are conjoined. It is a rejection of the "measurable" in favor of what Lassus calls the "demeasurable"—or "the immeasurable of the imagination."

At this point the reader may well ask what significance Lassus intends to give to the superseding of the "horizontal" by a "vertical" or "demeasurable" scale. In what context does he place the suggestion that the traditional way of passing from "wildness" to the "constructed form" is no longer applicable? What kind of evidence can he adduce to demonstrate the claim, which the project for the Garden of the Anterior to a certain extent takes for granted? The answer is to be found in three further writings in this collection: the first in the form of a story, the second in the form of a theoretical and didactic essay, the third in the form of a garden design for the museum site at the Parc de la Villette in Paris.

"The Monument" answers the question posed here by the slightly surprising device of venturing into science fiction. But the waywardness of this sortie is subsumed in a more serious purpose. A clue lies in the two sets of quotations Lassus appends to the text—as if they too existed as "monuments" to a particular way of seeing man's relationship to Nature. In the first quotation, from William Chambers, there is an extraordinary evocation of the wildness of a particular habitat, presumably that of a part of China. Pierre Boitard goes even further in conjuring up an overwhelming impression of "Distopia," with a description that spares nothing of a sensational or terrifying impact, even invoking "the horrible story of the innumerable cruelties committed in these very places by the outlaws and brigands of ancient times." The purpose of introducing these citations is, of course, to convey the particular kind of equilibrium in which the eighteenth-century architect, Chambers, and the early nineteenth-century gardener, Boitard, situate themselves and their garden schemes. For Boitard to be able to teach "the art of composing and decorating gardens," there must exist—as a kind of monstrous *double face*—the entirely wild side of Nature. Somewhere on the surface of the globe—perhaps in China for Chambers—there must be, if not a totally undiscovered "virgin" wildness, at least a potent and coherent image of Nature's beneficence turned to malevolent frenzy. We are reminded of the text which accompanies one of Goya's finest etchings: "The Sleep of Reason engenders monsters."

If Bernard Lassus sites his story of "The Monument" on the Moon, this is first of all to point out that such an economy of the imagination is no longer possible. Or rather, it has in a certain measure submitted to redistribution. As the last white patches have vanished from the map of the world—as China has finally lost its monstrous otherness and become a mecca for tourists—the new wildness has been discovered. The Moon takes over the missing place in the equation, and by contrast with the rocky landscape of the Moon, the whole Earth "should have been transformed into a Garden of Eden or a Garden of Delights." Lassus's second interpolated section contains Milton's description of the Garden of Eden, as powerful a representation of the Garden as Utopia as the "Distopian" models of Chambers and Boitard. We have, in other words, two sides of the same coin. And just as Chambers and Boitard define the order of their garden "composition" with reference to the disorder of Distopian landscape, so the Abbé de Lille appends Milton's vision as a model of order and harmony in a treatise that is itself devoted to "the art of embellishing landscapes."

Yet the idea that the Earth might have become, in relation to the Moon, a "Garden of Eden" is raised only to accentuate the irony of such a suggestion. Lassus's main purpose in celebrating "Man's first step on the Moon" is to point to the possibility of the new "vertical" or "demeasurable" dimension that can be imaginatively identified with this prodigious extension of Man's exploratory field. Just as the tulip was changed by being perceived as a volume of colored light, so the Earth has been changed by being viewed from the Moon. And we, as inhabitants of the Earth, have begun to learn to look for new landscapes, or to read old landscapes in a different way. The next step in the argument that follows the story of "The Monument" is the sustained discussion of "Depth" in which Lassus recapitulates some of the most central themes of his work on landscape, at both the practical and the theoretical level. In particular, he devotes some attention to his work on the "habitants-paysagistes," or dweller-landscapers,[3] whose example was one of the first indications that he should look for the new landscape approach in the achievements of poetic transformation—the "demeasurable" effects—which such "naïve" practitioners were creating in the modest areas available to them. But this powerful corroboration of his approach from such an unexpected quarter is not left to make the case on its own. If Lassus mentions the Abbé de Lille as evidence of the close connection between poetics, global

exploration, and garden design in the eighteenth century, he is no less willing to give credit to a poet of the present century who has returned to the issues of landscape again and again, and with deepening insight. Francis Ponge's remarkable meditation on propinquity and distance in landscape corresponds exactly to Lassus's long-standing and fundamental distinction between the visual and the tactile scale.[4]

In spite of the interest of such a didactic formulation, it is appropriate that I should conclude this survey with a further complete garden scheme—a successor to the "Garden of the Anterior." In conjunction with the established plan to build a science museum on an important and newly available site, Lassus has drawn up a scheme originally named the "Garden of Dreams," but now retitled the "Garden of the Planets" after its most ambitious feature. The underground planetarium, with its homage to Neil Armstrong and its separate chambers devoted to the different planets, is indeed an appropriate summation of the course of studies traced in this series of texts. With its "bottomless pit," recalling Jules Verne's *Journey to the Centre of the Earth*, it reinterprets the original concept of the Well, while drawing upon the kind of mythic material that was put to use in the "Garden of the Anterior." It establishes on a literal level—which is of course the level of the designer's brief—the connection of the garden scheme with the achievements of modern science and discovery. But in doing so it reinforces Lassus's commitment to a new view of Nature: "a third form of nature, a nature we have chosen and intended." It is as if we had left the forest and

[3] Lassus, *Les Jardins imaginaires* (Paris: Presses de la Connaissance/Weber, 1977); reviewed in *Journal of Garden History* 1, 1 (1981): 108–10.

[4] See Francis Ponge, "Le Carnet du bois de pins" and other texts in *La Rage de l'expression* (Paris: Mermod, 1952).

entered the clearing, and were looking around ourselves in some bewilderment. What, asks Lassus, do we intend to do with our liberty?

(1995)

The great interest of the early schemes of Lassus lay in the fact that they implied nothing less than a new poetics of landscape. Concepts like the *démesurable*, or "demeasurable," were invoked to emphasize the supreme importance of the imagination in formulating new ideas of space. Contemporary reference points, like the landing of *Apollo* on the Moon, were adduced to prove the point that garden design was bound to follow the radical revision of our notions of distance and "wildness" that had accompanied the arrival of an age of mass tourism and global travel.

All these projects had their roots in Lassus's earlier training, first as a painter in Fernand Léger's studio and second as a kinetic artist participating in group exhibitions at the same time as he developed the applications of his ideas to environmental design through the Centre de Recherche d'Ambiances. In the period between 1975 and 1980, covered in the previous section, Lassus convincingly showed that the scope of his work was not confined to local and specific interventions (as with the sculptural and environmental achievements of the previous decade), but required the challenge of a very substantial project to bring it to fulfillment. Unfortunately, this challenge never materialized. "The Garden of the Anterior" won a competition for a park in the new town of L'Isle d'Abeau, but the design was never carried out. The competition for the Parc de la Villette, having run its course once and then been restarted with an even louder fanfare of publicity, resulted in a short-listing for "The Garden of the Planets" and a final victory for the post-modern confection of Bernard Tschumi, over whose subsequent development it is best to draw a veil.

Yet by the early 1980s Lassus had already embarked on a more concrete and promising scheme. In the summer of 1982, his "Garden of Returns" for the Corderie Royale at Rochefort, in the Charente, won first prize in a competition dedicated to retrieving this historic site from decay and neglect. In this case, a more favorable wind was behind the project from the start, which became an irresistible momentum when the originally local initiative was adopted as one of the President of the Republic's *grands projets*. The text published here, which dates from 1987, testifies to the fact that the new garden was, by that date, well and truly launched. Its official opening, by the Secrétaire d'État aux Grands Projets, Emile Biasini, was on 21 June 1991. Its success was further ratified when, at the end of 1993, the town of Rochefort received the Grand Prix National in the area of *patrimoine* for the achievement of rescuing the Corderie and its surroundings from their becalmed condition.

It would be factitious to claim that there is a radical break between the texts published in 1983 and the subsequent texts illustrative of Bernard Lassus's "Landscape Approach." And it would be misleading to argue for such a break simply on the grounds that now he has evidently overcome the barriers initially provoked by his originality, and has moved from projects to concrete realizations. For one thing, he has been concerned over a very long period—beginning in 1973 and finally concluded only in 1989—with the exceptionally large-scale and concrete realization: the creation of *Ville-paysages*, or urban landscapes obtained from the systematic painting of building façades in the former mining towns between Metz and Thionville.[5] For another, he has continued to draw on the color studies of his kinetic period, often with surprising and delightful results: in May 1993, his *buissons optiques* exhibited at Niort involved the translation of abstract color studies with intense optical effects into the hardly less dazzling array of juxtaposed flowering plants.

Nor has Lassus in any way abandoned the phase of his career that aroused particular interest among anthropological circles in France and forms a unique contribution to contemporary garden history. At the Dumbarton Oaks colloquium on "The Vernacular Garden," held in 1990, he presented a dazzling paper on "The Garden Landscape: A Popular Aesthetic."[6] The data he and his students had collected in the 1960s relating to the activity of what he termed *habitants-paysagistes* were clearly still relevant to his practice (particularly so as regards the urban renewal mentioned in the previous paragraph). The extraordinary garden designs of M. Pecqueur, at one time mayor of a small commune not far from the town of Béthune, have continued to provide him with fresh insights, ripe for incorporation in his later practice as opportunities have taken concrete form.

So what are the new themes and possibilities implicit in these new texts? "The Fountain Way" (1983), is an excellent example of a transitional project, similar in its poetic form to the projects of the 1970s, yet gaining an additional dimension from the fact that it was indeed carried out. In "The Well" (1972), Lassus experimented with the notion of the imaginative perception of depth: exhibition visitors were invited to participate in a model situation, where stones thrown into a well provoked not the expected splash, but a sonic reaction quite disproportionate to their expectations.

"The Fountain Way" also springs from the desire to manipulate popular reactions through a poetic disruption of expectations; in this case, however, it is time, rather than depth, that provides the empathetic dimension. The "Provençal fountain," being perceived as old, lends to the whole footbridge a character of being antecedent to the modern highway. The effect is not without its purely functional justification. If the footbridge is to be attractive to its potential users, and prevent them from endangering their lives in crossing the highway, it has to acquire other characteristics over and beyond that of merely offering a safe passage. Poetics supplement function. But, on the other hand, function becomes dysfunctional without poetics.[7]

At one stage, Lassus was anxious to obtain a genuine Roman mosaic to place in the bowl of the (newly constructed) fountain. Such mosaics were not in short supply in the Marseilles area. Surely there could be no more economical way of stressing the point that this hollowed-out rock, with its traditional fountain,

[5] The whole scheme is exhaustively documented in Lassus, *Villes-paysages: Couleurs en Lorraine* (Metz: Batigère, 1989).

[6] Lassus, "The Garden Landscape: A Popular Aesthetic," in *The Vernacular Garden*, ed. John Dixon Hunt and Joachim Wolschke-Bulmahn (Washington, D.C.: Dumbarton Oaks, 1993), pp. 137–59.

[7] In the footbridge designed for the Marseilles area, the "Passerelle du Parc des Salles" at Istres, Lassus accentuated the attraction of the bridge by incorporating a fable into the design of the ornamental ironwork; see "The Snake and the Butterflies" in this volume.

did indeed antedate the frantic carriageways of the Marseilles conurbation? Here is a good example of how Lassus has begun increasingly to exploit the possibilities of "historical depth" as an integral part of the poetics of depth that he began to develop in such projects as the Well and the Garden of the Planets. From that perspective, the "authentic" historical insert is simply one element—though potentially a decisive one—in a programme that must necessarily imply the "reinvention" of a particular site's historic potential, through all the means at the garden designer's disposal.

Lassus must have been agreeably surprised when, almost ten years after he failed to secure this final piece in the jigsaw for "The Fountain Way," an authentic historical fragment of grandiose proportions fell into his lap, so to speak, for the design of the highway rest area of Nîmes-Caissargues. The original colonnade of the nineteenth-century theater of Nîmes, displaced by Norman Foster's new *Carré pour l'art*, has been relocated (though a *monument classé*) on this entirely new site.

In fact, the connecting thread through virtually all the schemes from 1983 to 1993 is the recuperation and reinvention of the historic past. In this connection, Lassus's position is luminously clear, and can serve as a powerful rejoinder to so many of the confused and nostalgic arguments used in defense of "conservation" and "heritage" in the contemporary world. The authenticity of the historical object does not reside simply in its identity with itself: as a museum piece ratified by scholarly consensus and detached from the everyday milieu. On the contrary, it becomes authentic to the extent that it communicates within a wider context: it must be made accessible to the senses, and this inevitably implies that it should take its place within a continuum of sensory impressions for which the designer assumes responsibility.

This process of development can often take the form of what the rhetorical critic identifies as metonymy: a process of displacement and substitution is employed to stress the presence of the real, which cannot be evoked directly. In the case of Nîmes-Caissargues, the whole purpose of Lassus's complex and remarkable scheme is to evoke the adjacent presence of the city, and so to make it imaginatively present. This involves not only opening up the lines of sight, to a certain extent, but also reconstructing, in a deliberately schematic form, the impressive silhouette of the Tour Magne, and even projecting a reduced model of the whole city for the new site. The classical colonnade fits exactly into this overall scheme: it is both Nîmes and not Nîmes, displaced from its urban situation (where it was in effect a relatively modern interloper) and forms a historical reference point in the area, which has already been pre-constrained to historical readings through the formal treatment of the garden itself.

Lassus is especially enthusiastic about the present opportunities being offered by the French sociétés des autoroutes.[8] Here is a form of patronage for the garden designer that can encourage particularly ambitious and sophisticated schemes (the likelihood

[8] He is also working on a project for a rest area at Crazannes that would utilize the remains of extensive quarry workings. The intention is to place miniature stone carvings of buildings throughout Europe, which were constructed with Crazannes stone, in the artificial caves there. See also the volume of essays edited by Lassus and Christian Leyrit, *Autoroutes et paysages* (Paris: Editions du Demi-Cercle, 1995) and "The Walk in the Quarries at Crazannes" in this volume.

of this enlightened approach catching on outside France appears, at the moment, almost non-existent). But a different sort of challenge is posed by the projects that involve a historical reconstruction of some kind on a site that is already saturated with historical objects and meanings. Lassus's design for the Tuileries, "a reinvented garden," envisages the existing space as a kind of historical palimpsest. We can never in fact "restore" the gardens to their pristine state, because such a site bears the successive traces of a whole succession of different designs, some of them only accessible at an archaeological level. And yet, to think of redesigning this important area of central Paris, adjacent to the newly fitted-out "Grand Louvre," without taking into account its prestigious past is a patent absurdity.

Lassus's plan for the Tuileries takes into account the most important of the successive designs for the gardens, and exposes them to view, using a variation in heights to make the point that they can only coexist in terms of a layering of different temporal strata. It also takes careful account of the vistas intended to open up (though progressively obscured) between the Arc de Triomphe of the Carrousel and its grandiose successor, at the Etoile. One can safely assert that the design chosen by the French government, which is now undergoing extensive modification, did not even approach the subtlety and suggestiveness of Lassus's proposal.

There is certainly no lack of interest among post-modern architects and designers of the present day in the historical and indeed "archaeological" development of contemporary sites. Peter Eisenman's work over the decade 1978–88, recently collected together in a fine exhibition, goes under the title of "Cités

de l'archéologie fictive."[8] A good deal of fiction does indeed have to underscore Eisenman's archaeology when the site envisaged happens to be Long Beach, California—or, at the opposite end of the scale, when it involves the *embarras de richesses* of Venice or Siena.

In relation to this highly intellectualized approach, Lassus remains devoted to the principle that the historical or archaeological trait must be reinvented in its sensory plenitude and in such a way that it can form part of a sequence of differences that are instantly accessible to the spectator. In his design for the park of Duisburg-Nord, in the Ruhr, the polluted River Emscher must be allowed to resume its winding, pastoral identity in at least one section of the site: this is not to annihilate the industrial past of the river, but precisely to emphasize it, through bringing into juxtaposition two stages of its former history. In connection with this extensive and fascinating project, Lassus develops the concept of the "temporal pen": just as a canal needs locks in order to pass from one level to another, so the reconstitution of history depends essentially on the possibility of marking a temporal shift through a discontinuity of sense perceptions. Mere continuity allows meaning to ebb away.

This is a point of central importance in Lassus's treatment of the contemporary industrial landscape. Admittedly he has envisaged the Emscher restored to its "idyllic," pre-industrial state, and a superficial reading of the project would conclude that this is a symptom of regression and nostalgia. But the precise point

[9] *Cités de l'archéologie fictive: Oeuvres de Peter Eisenman, 1978–1988*, catalog (Montréal: Canadian Centre for Architecture, 1994).

of the river's restoration is to enable us to perceive the blast furnaces of the industrial Ruhr—the landscape of yesterday—in all their "dignity" and "mystery." Hence there is need for a strong contrast: hence also there is need for a transition to make the passage from one landscape to another. Lassus calls this transitional element a "frame of vegetation," and it is significant that he should use a metaphor drawn from the realm of the plastic arts. Unlike the majority of contemporary landscape gardeners, whose training is essentially in architecture, he indicates his allegiance to the perceptual systems traditionally used in Western painting and its antecedents: the blast furnaces should be "framed" by vegetation, "just as a stained-glass window is surrounded by lead in order that the colored glass held within it may shine with its own brilliance, or a painting is framed to make it stand out from the wall."

The project for Duisburg-Nord is certainly Lassus's most ambitious to date, and the one that envisages the maximum number of diverse types of use in its vast site. However, it has to take second place, in any account of Lassus's work over the past decade, to the practical achievement of the Garden of Returns. Here is a scheme accepted in principle in 1982, sketched out in detail five years later, and finally inaugurated, with its second stage ready, in 1991. It is still by no means complete, and the garden amateur may indeed wonder whether the concept of "completion" is in any event applicable to gardening. But there can be no doubt that it already justifies the high expectations Lassus and his collaborators originally placed in it. Here is a garden that at the same time rearticulates the entire spatial location of a historic building, in its relationship to a town, and achieves a symbolic identity based upon the profound links between a former port and the far distant corners of the world.

It is indeed tempting—since it has now been possible to observe the development of the Garden of Returns in all seasons—to seize upon specific details of its appearance over the past few years. It is rarely bustling with visitors, though the museums and services now magnificently installed in the Corderie attract a continuous flow of people and the inhabitants of Rochefort have been quick to take advantage of the leisurely river walk, which is always accessible. Even in the exceptional flood conditions of winter 1993/94, when the Charente had inundated a large area of the neighboring countryside, this river walk remained fully accessible, and the planting of alders and other suitable shrubs to reinforce the bank proved its utility. Indeed, the main decisions about the site have already proved their worth with such incontrovertible success that it becomes difficult to envisage the site as it was before 1982, or to conceive of the genuine radicalism of the strategy that Lassus adopted.

The first aspect of this strategy was to dismiss any idea of treating the seventeenth-century Corderie as a "château" flanked with symmetrical beds and connected by a "royal" alley to the adjoining town. Lassus not only saw the anomaly of fetishizing the (albeit spectacular) stone building in this way, but he also made a courageous decision that would not in any way fudge the issue. From the side of the town the ramparts were to be built up, with the effect that the Corderie could be viewed from a height; access would be mainly from a vast stone ramp descending in parallel to the axis of the building. (Lassus's 1975 scheme for the Garden of the Anterior had already provided as a central feature a "rampart" separating the "visual" and the "tactile" scales of participation.) From the side of the River Charente, the façade of the Corderie was to be viewed through a screen of shrubs and small trees, which would allow the boat passenger and the riverside walker to discover it intermittently, and from different angles. Although the site is totally different, the system used by Lassus recalls nothing so much as the successive views of the ruins of Rievaulx Abbey in Yorkshire, viewed through "cuts" in the trees from the upper terrace. In each case, the planting helps to focalize a series of views obtained in a specific walk (or boat trip) from one point to another. In the case of the Corderie, the strategy has the effect of splitting up an inordinately long façade, whose proportions did not derive from aesthetic considerations but from the practical necessities of the cordage industry.

The planting of the garden followed the logic of this initial decision not only in helping to determine the way in which the building was to be viewed, but also in utilizing the different spaces for very distinct purposes. Whereas the area between the Corderie and the river contains the expected riverside plants alone, the more formal space created by the reinstated rampart and the ramp leading down from it has been tenanted with exotic trees, whose striking effect is accentuated by their placing. A phalanx of Virginian tulip trees occupies the ramp itself, like an invading army, while the splendid sequence of palm trees—outlined against the seventeenth-century building—leaves us in no doubt that the exotic connections of Rochefort are being revalued, and re-presented, in the garden scheme. Yet this is not simply an attempt to strike a note of tropical splendor in an otherwise conventional range. Lassus wishes to bring out the

fact that Rochefort was one of the prime places through which the new, exotic varieties passed into Europe, before becoming naturalized and planted on a wider and wider scale. Hence, he draws up, by the side of the river, rows of "tontines" designed for the transport of such varieties. (These concrete moulds are themselves planted with suitable species, according to the time of year.)

The ultimate ambition to make the Garden of Returns a place famous for the cultivation of begonias—and thus to commemorate in Rochefort the name of the naval commander who gave his name to the species—derives clearly from the principle that Lassus keeps in mind throughout his landscape planning. To commemorate, or mark a place symbolically, is not simply to strike a note of nostalgia and regret for the historic past: it is to reincorporate a dimension of richness that would otherwise be lost and, in so doing, to reinvest the present with fresh perceptions and new opportunities.

This is the fundamental ambition that underlies all of Lassus's current work and gives it exceptional interest and urgency. It is noteworthy that he is not only engaged with the specific challenges offered by different locations, with their widely disparate histories; he is also engaged with the more basic issues, which structure the entire debate about the identity of places in the contemporary world. The art of landscape has always been conceived, in its most vital moments, as a means of conjuring up "the spirit of the place." It is fitting that one of the most recent texts published here should be a searching investigation of the conditions under which the "new spirit of the place" can be revived, in the inevitable circumstances of a post-industrial society.

Index